Perl Programming
Scripting and Automation

Contents

Introduction

Perl, Practical Extraction and Report Language, is a highly versatile and dynamic programming language with a rich history dating back to its creation in 1987 by Larry Wall. Originally designed as a text-processing language, Perl has evolved over the years to become a robust and versatile tool suitable for a variety of tasks ranging from web development to system administration, and from data manipulation to network programming.

The purpose of this book, "Perl Programming: Scripting and Automation," is to provide a comprehensive introduction to Perl for beginners. Through detailed explanations, practical examples, and logical progression of topics, this book aims to make learning Perl accessible and engaging to those new to programming and scripting.

This book begins with the foundational aspects of Perl, focusing initially on understanding what Perl is and its historical context. Following this, the book proceeds to guide readers through installing Perl on various platforms and running their first Perl scripts, thus establishing the basic structure of a Perl program. Thereafter, readers will become acquainted with the Perl interpreter and the extensive documentation available, equipping them with the necessary resources to seek help and expand their knowledge independently.

As the chapters advance, the book delves into core Perl concepts such as basic syntax, variables, data types, and control structures. Through clearly defined sections, readers will gain a solid understanding of Perl statements, operators, input and output operations, and string manipulations. Special emphasis is placed on debugging techniques, ensuring that readers can efficiently troubleshoot and refine their scripts.

In the following chapters, the book covers the essential topics of subroutines and functions, illustrating the significance of modular and reusable code. Regular expressions, a powerful feature of Perl, are explored in detail, providing readers with the skills to perform complex text-processing tasks efficiently. Practical examples demonstrate how to apply these concepts effectively in real-world scenarios.

A key component of Perl programming is file handling, and this book provides an in-depth exploration of various file operations, including reading from and writing to files, managing file handles, and handling errors. The book further extends this knowledge by introducing Perl modules, offering insights into using built-in and CPAN modules, and guiding readers on creating their own modules for enhanced functionality and organized code.

The introduction to object-oriented Perl marks the transition from fundamental to advanced programming techniques. Concepts such as classes, objects, inheritance, and encapsulation are thoroughly explained, enabling readers to build robust, scalable, and maintainable applications.

To conclude the journey, the book delves into advanced Perl programming topics such as complex data structures, advanced regular expressions, and memory management. Readers will also explore interfacing Perl with other languages, concurrency, and parallel processing techniques, thus preparing them to tackle sophisticated programming challenges.

The structured layout of this book ensures a smooth learning curve, allowing readers to build on their knowledge as they progress through the chapters. Each topic is presented in a clear, concise manner, supplemented with examples and exercises that reinforce the concepts discussed.

By the end of this book, readers will have acquired a well-rounded understanding of Perl programming and scripting. Equipped with this knowledge, they will be capable of developing effective and efficient scripts to automate tasks, process data, and build powerful applications.

Chapter 1

Introduction to Perl

This chapter provides an overview of Perl, detailing its definition, historical development, and primary uses. Readers will learn how to install Perl on different systems and run Perl scripts. The chapter also covers the basic structure of a Perl program, familiarizing readers with the Perl interpreter and available documentation. Practical information on seeking help with Perl and creating a first program is included, along with common use cases of the language.

1.1 What is Perl?

Perl, which stands for Practical Extraction and Report Language, is a high-level, general-purpose, interpreted, and dynamic programming language well known for its powerful text processing capabilities. It was developed by Larry Wall in 1987 as a highly flexible and capable language for handling text manipulation tasks in Unix scripting. Over the years, Perl has evolved substantially, integrating features from other programming languages such as C, awk, sed, and shell scripting, thereby establishing itself as a versatile tool for both task automation and complex programming challenges.

At its core, Perl excels in text processing, including tasks that involve pattern matching with regular expressions, extracting and formatting text, and converting data formats. The language syntax is designed to be straightforward and expressive, catering to a wide range of programming activities — from quick script writing to full-fledged application development.

Perl's syntax facilitates these text-centric tasks exceptionally well. Consider the example of matching and replacing text within a string. Perl makes use of its powerful regular expression engine to perform such operations succinctly and efficiently. Here is an example of a Perl script designed to replace the word Perl with Perl Programming Language:

```
#!/usr/bin/perl
use strict;
use warnings;

my $text = "Welcome to Perl!";
$text =~ s/Perl/Perl Programming Language/;
print "$text\n";
```

In this example, the substitution operator s/// is used to find the word Perl in the variable $text and replace it with Perl Programming Language. The regular expression capability, symbolized by = , is a hallmark of Perl's text processing strength.

A key attribute of Perl is the type system, which is context-sensitive rather than strictly typed as found in many other programming languages. Variables in Perl are prefixed with symbols that denote their type: $ for scalars (single values), @ for arrays (ordered lists), and % for hashes (key-value pairs). The following illustration highlights the use of different Perl data types:

```
#!/usr/bin/perl
use strict;
use warnings;

# Scalar example
my $scalar = 42;
print "Scalar: $scalar\n";

# Array example
my @array = (1, 2, 3);
print "Array: @array\n";

# Hash example
my %hash = ('key1' => 'value1', 'key2' => 'value2');
print "Hash: key1 = $hash{'key1'}, key2 = $hash{'key2'}\n";
```

Perl is designed to be pragmatic, which is reflected in its "There's more than one way to do it" philosophy. This flexibility allows developers to solve problems in multiple ways, capitalizing on their personal experience and coding preferences. As a result, Perl code can be both concise and highly expressive, facilitating rapid development and debugging.

Furthermore, the Comprehensive Perl Archive Network (CPAN) plays an instrumental role in Perl's ecosystem. CPAN is a vast repository containing over 185,000 open-source Perl modules that can be leveraged to extend Perl's functionality without having to write code from scratch. These modules cover a wide range of applications including web development (with frameworks like Catalyst and Dancer), database interaction (DBI), network programming, and more. To illustrate, installing a CPAN module can be done as follows:

```
cpan install JSON
```

Once installed, the module can be used within a Perl script:

```
#!/usr/bin/perl
use strict;
use warnings;
use JSON;

my $json_text = '{"name": "Alice", "age": 30}';
my $data = decode_json($json_text);

print "Name: $data->{'name'}, Age: $data->{'age'}\n";
```

Given Perl's combination of simplicity, flexibility, and power, it remains a valuable language in many fields, notably in system administration, web development, network programming, and bioinformatics. Its capacity to handle complex text manipulation and data extraction tasks efficiently makes it a go-to choice for many programmers worldwide. Through its continuous evolution, Perl retains its standing as a robust scripting language with a loyal and active community.

1.2 History of Perl

Perl, an acronym for Practical Extraction and Report Language, was created by Larry Wall in 1987. Wall, a linguist turned programmer, designed Perl as a Unix scripting language to make report processing easier.

The inception of Perl was driven by Wall's necessity to produce numerous reports from various text files and searching through large log files. During this period, existing Unix tools such as 'awk' and 'sed' were somewhat limited in their capabilities. Wall sought a more powerful language that amalgamated the features of these tools while adding enhanced data manipulation abilities and greater flexibility.

Larry Wall first released Perl on 18 December 1987.

```
print "Perl 1.0 was introduced on December 18, 1987.\n";
```

Perl underwent substantial evolution through multiple versions since its original release. The initial release, Perl 1.0, encapsulated all the fundamental features that Larry Wall originally conceptualized. Over the next several years, the language would continually expand, both in terms of syntax and functionality.

The second major milestone was the release of Perl 2.0 in 1988, which included a variety of bug fixes and increased functionality. However, it was the release of Perl 3.0 in 1989 that marked a significant advancement, integrating regular expressions which are now integral to Perl's identity. Perl's capabilities with text processing firmly established it as a powerful scripting language.

```
Regular expressions were integrated into Perl with version 3.0.
print "Perl 3.0 introduced regular expressions in 1989.\n";
```

Perl 4.0, released in 1991, continued the trend of adding valuable features and improvements. This version improved the language's stability and performance, as well as enhanced its documentation. Considered a significant evolution, Perl 4.0 became widely adopted and supported by a robust community of developers.

The most groundbreaking change came with Perl 5.0, released in 1994. This version brought about extensive enhancements which fundamentally altered the language. Some key features of Perl 5.0 included the introduction of references, modules (packages of reusable code), and an enhanced object-oriented programming model. These changes made the language vastly more powerful and versatile.

```
Perl 5.0 introduced references and support for objects.
print "Perl 5.0 was released in 1994 with major enhancements.\n";
```

Continuing from Perl 5, subsequent releases have brought incremental but significant improvements. Perl 5.8, released in 2002, introduced Unicode string representation, threading, and improvements in support for object-oriented programming.

In 2003, Perl 6 was announced as a major redesign of the language. However, it became clear that Perl 6 would diverge significantly from the principal development path of Perl. This led to two distinct languages: Perl 5 and Raku (formerly Perl 6), with Raku being officially renamed in 2019.

```
Perl 6 was later renamed to Raku.
print "Raku (formerly Perl 6) diverged from Perl 5 development.\n";
```

The persistence and adaptability of Perl underscored its continued relevance. Perl 5 maintained a steady release cycle, incorporating updates that ensured it adapted well to modern computing paradigms. This evolution maintained its compatibility with earlier scripts while enhancing performance and expanding capabilities.

Understanding the history of Perl provides important context about its development and adoption. This insight allows a deeper appreciation of its syntax and functionality, emphasizing the deliberate design decisions that informed its creation and evolution.

1.3 Installing Perl

Installing Perl on your system is a pivotal first step for leveraging its scripting and automation capabilities. Perl is versatile and can be installed on various operating systems such as Windows, macOS, and Linux. This section provides detailed instructions for installing Perl on each of these platforms.

Windows Installation

1. Navigate to the Strawberry Perl website (https://strawberryperl.com/) to download the latest version of Strawberry Perl. Strawberry Perl includes a compiler and make tools, which are essential for running and building some Perl modules.

2. Select the appropriate version for your system architecture (32-bit or 64-bit) and download the installer.

3. Once the download is complete, run the installer. You will be prompted through a series of installation steps.

- Accept the license agreement. - Choose the installation directory. The default is usually `C:\Strawberry`. - Proceed with the installation by clicking `Next` through the remaining prompts until the installation is complete.

4. After installation, verify that Perl is correctly installed by opening the Command Prompt and typing the following command:

```
perl -v
```

This command should output the version of Perl that has been installed.

```
This is perl 5, version 32, subversion 1 (v5.32.1) built for MSWin32-x64-multi-thread
```

macOS Installation

Perl comes pre-installed on macOS. However, to ensure that you have the latest version of Perl, you might want to use a package manager such as Homebrew.

1. If you do not already have Homebrew installed, you can install it by running the following command in the Terminal:

```
/bin/bash -c "$(curl -fsSL https://raw.githubusercontent.com/Homebrew/install/
    HEAD/install.sh)"
```

2. Once Homebrew is installed, install Perl by typing the following command in the Terminal:

```
brew install perl
```

3. After installation, verify that Perl is correctly installed by typing:

```
perl -v
```

The expected output should confirm the Perl version installed through Homebrew.

```
This is perl 5, version 34, subversion 0 (v5.34.0) built for darwin-thread-multi-2level
```

Linux Installation

Most Linux distributions come with Perl pre-installed. The instructions below provide steps to ensure you have the latest version or to install it if it is not already present.

1. For Debian-based distributions (e.g., Ubuntu), you can update or install Perl using the following commands:

```
sudo apt update
sudo apt install perl
```

2. For Red Hat-based distributions (e.g., Fedora), use the following commands:

```
sudo dnf install perl
```

3. After installation, verify that Perl is correctly installed by typing:

```
perl -v
```

The version information should be displayed as:

```
This is perl 5, version 30, subversion 3 (v5.30.3) built for x86_64-linux-gnu-thread-multi
```

Ensuring No Conflicts

After installation on any operating system, it is essential to ensure that there are no conflicting versions of Perl present, especially if multiple Perl versions were installed from different sources. Confirm the location of the Perl binary being used by executing:

```
which perl
```

This command should output the path to the Perl interpreter, generally one of the following:

```
/usr/bin/perl
/usr/local/bin/perl
/opt/local/bin/perl
```

By following these detailed installation steps, you can successfully set up Perl on your system, ready to start scripting and automating tasks.

1.4 Running a Perl Script

Perl scripts can be executed in multiple environments, providing versatility in the development and deployment of code. This section covers the process of running a Perl script from different interfaces, including command-lines and Integrated Development Environments (IDEs). It also addresses execution permissions and essential troubleshooting steps.

To run a Perl script from the command line, first ensure that Perl is installed on your system. If Perl is correctly installed, verify its presence by executing the following command:

```
perl -v
```

This command will display the installed Perl version, confirming the installation. Next, navigate to the directory containing your Perl script using the cd command. Suppose the script is named example.pl; you can execute it by entering:

```
perl example.pl
```

The system will process the script and return any output to the terminal. Consider the following simple script example.pl containing one line:

```
print "Hello, World!\n";
```

Executing perl example.pl will produce:

```
Hello, World!
```

In some environments, it may be desirable to make the script directly executable, bypassing the need to invoke the Perl interpreter explicitly. To accomplish this on Unix-like systems, start the script with a shebang line:

```
#!/usr/bin/perl
print "Hello, World!\n";
```

The shebang (#!) indicates the path to the Perl interpreter. After ensuring this line is at the top of the script, set the appropriate execute permissions using the chmod command:

```
chmod +x example.pl
```

Now, the script can be run directly:

```
./example.pl
```

The output remains:

```
Hello, World!
```

To streamline the execution process, consider configuring your environment's PATH variable to include the directory containing your scripts. This allows execution without navigating to the exact script location each time.

Running a Perl script in Integrated Development Environments (IDEs) can further enhance productivity by offering a graphical interface and numerous development tools. Popular Perl-compatible IDEs include Padre, Eclipse with EPIC plugin, and Visual Studio Code with Perl extensions. While each IDE has unique features, most require configuring project settings to specify the location of the Perl interpreter. Once configured, running the script typically involves a few clicks, providing an integrated approach to coding, testing, and debugging.

Troubleshooting common errors when running Perl scripts involves examining error messages returned by the interpreter. Syntax errors, for example, often yield messages specifying the erroneous line number:

```
syntax error at example.pl line 1, near ","
Execution of example.pl aborted due to compilation errors.
```

This output suggests an issue on line 1, guiding the user to investigate the script for misplaced commas or other syntactic mistakes. Other common issues include missing modules or incorrect shebang lines—

each prominently indicated in the error messages.

Attention to detail when setting permissions and using accurate paths ensures a smooth experience running Perl scripts across various platforms and environments.

1.5 Basic Structure of a Perl Program

A Perl program typically begins with the declaration of the interpreter, known as the shebang line, at the top of the script file. This line tells the operating system which interpreter to use to execute the script. The shebang line is written as:

```
#!/usr/bin/perl
```

The #!/usr/bin/perl line specifies the path to the Perl interpreter on a Unix-like system. On Windows, this line is not strictly necessary, as the association of .pl files with the Perl interpreter is handled differently.

Immediately following the shebang line, it is common practice to use strict and warnings directives to enforce good coding practices. These pragmas, when enabled, help catch common errors and enforce a cleaner and more maintainable coding style. This is done with the following lines:

```
use strict;
use warnings;
```

The use of strict ensures that all variables must be declared either via my, our, or local before they are used, thus preventing accidental creation of global variables due to typos. The warnings pragma provides helpful warnings about dubious constructs, which can aid in debugging and improving code quality.

Next, the actual code of the Perl script follows. Perl scripts are essentially a sequence of statements, each ending with a semicolon (;). Variables in Perl are prefixed with special characters ($, @, %), which denote scalar, array, and hash variables respectively.

The standard variable types and a few typical operations are as follows:

```
# Scalar variable
my $name = "John";
print "Hello, $name\n";

# Array variable
my @numbers = (1, 2, 3, 4, 5);
```

```
print "First number is $numbers[0]\n";

# Hash variable
my %ages = ("John" => 30, "Lisa" => 28);
print "John's age is $ages{\"John\"}\n";
```

In the above example:

- A scalar variable $name holds a string value.
- An array variable @numbers holds a list of numeric values.
- A hash variable %ages holds key-value pairs.

Control structures in Perl, such as conditional statements and loops, are similar to those in C-like languages. Below are examples of an if conditional and a for loop:

```
# Conditional statement
if ($name eq "John") {
    print "It's John.\n";
}

# Loop
for my $num (@numbers) {
    print "Number: $num\n";
}
```

In the first block, the if statement checks if the scalar variable $name contains the string "John". The eq operator is used for string comparison. In the second block, a for loop iterates over the array @numbers, printing each number.

Perl subroutines (functions) encapsulate reusable code and are defined using the sub keyword:

```
sub greet {
    my ($person) = @_;
    print "Hello, $person!\n";
}

greet("Alice");
```

In this example, the greet subroutine takes one argument $person and prints a greeting. The subroutine is then called with the argument "Alice".

While this covers only the most basic elements, the structure and syntax presented here form the foundation of Perl programming. Despite its simplicity, Perl's flexibility allows for a wide range of programming styles and paradigms.

1.6 The Perl Interpreter

The Perl interpreter is the essential component that executes Perl scripts. Understanding its operation and features is crucial for efficient Perl programming. Perl is both a language and an interpreter. The interpreter reads Perl code, compiles it into bytecode, and then executes it. This section will delve into various aspects of the Perl interpreter, showcasing how to start it, use command-line options, and understand its execution process.

To begin using the Perl interpreter, it is typically invoked from the command line or terminal with the perl command followed by the script name. For example, to run a script named example.pl, one would use:

```
$ perl example.pl
```

Command-line Options

The Perl interpreter supports numerous command-line options that allow for flexible script execution. Some of the most commonly used options include:

- **-e**: Execute code provided directly on the command line.

  ```
  $ perl -e 'print "Hello, World!\n";'
  ```

  This option is useful for executing short scripts or testing small pieces of code without creating a file.

- **-w**: Enable warnings.

  ```
  $ perl -w script.pl
  ```

  Enabling warnings is highly recommended as it helps identify potential issues and deprecated features in the code.

- **-c**: Check syntax without executing.

  ```
  $ perl -c script.pl
  ```

  This option is valuable for verifying the correctness of code without running it, ensuring there are no syntax errors.

- **-d**: Run the script under the Perl debugger.

  ```
  $ perl -d script.pl
  ```

The debugger is a powerful tool for tracing through scripts and identifying logic errors.

- **-T**: Enable taint checking.

```
$ perl -T script.pl
```

Taint checking is crucial for security, especially in scripts that interact with external data, ensuring that potentially unsafe data does not compromise system integrity.

- **-I**: Specify directories to include in the search path for libraries.

```
$ perl -I /path/to/library script.pl
```

This option is used to include additional directories where Perl should look for modules and libraries.

Execution Process

When a Perl script is run, the Perl interpreter performs a series of steps to execute the script:

- **Compilation Phase**: The script is read and compiled into an internal bytecode representation. During this phase, the interpreter checks for syntax errors and translates the code into an executable format.
- **Execution Phase**: Once the code is compiled, the interpreter executes the bytecode. The execution might involve multiple stages such as variable initialization, subroutine calls, and handling of control structures.

Both phases occur in-depth and encompass various sub-steps. It's essential to understand some of the key internal mechanisms:

Contexts

Perl uses different contexts to evaluate expressions, primarily scalar and list contexts. The context determines how expressions are parsed and evaluated.

```
my @array = (1, 2, 3);
my $count = @array; # Scalar context: $count gets the number of elements in @array
my @copy = @array; # List context: @copy gets a copy of @array
```

Environment Variables

The behavior of the Perl interpreter can be influenced by environment variables. Some of the most significant ones are:

- PERL5LIB: Specifies additional directories to search for modules.
- PERL5OPT: Provides default command-line options to the Perl interpreter for every execution.
- PERLLIB: Similar to PERL5LIB, used primarily for backward compatibility.

Embedding Perl

Perl can also be embedded into other applications using the perlxs and perlembed interfaces. This allows for extending applications with Perl's scripting capabilities or writing Perl scripts that interface directly with C code.

Example Execution

To illustrate a typical execution, consider the following simple script example.pl:

```
#!/usr/bin/perl

use strict;
use warnings;

print "Enter your name: ";
my $name = <STDIN>;
chomp($name);
print "Hello, $name!\n";
```

Running this script with the Perl interpreter:

```
$ perl example.pl
```

Results in:

```
Enter your name: John
Hello, John!
```

This example demonstrates the basic flow of reading input from the user and printing output, managed by the Perl interpreter.

Understanding these aspects of the Perl interpreter provides a solid foundation for script execution and development, harnessing the full potential of Perl's versatility and flexibility.

1.7 Using the Perl Documentation

Effective use of Perl documentation is integral for efficient coding and mastering the language. Perl provides extensive documentation via its ‘perldoc‘ utility, which enables users to access vast resources on Perl modules, functions, and various language constructs. Understanding how to navigate and utilize this documentation is a valuable skill.

The ‘perldoc‘ command is a powerful tool available in Perl’s default installation. To access the documentation, open a terminal or command prompt and use the following syntax:

```
perldoc [option] [topic]
```

Where [option] allows for specifying various modes of operation, and [topic] is the subject you are seeking information about, such as a module name, function, or specific Perl script feature.

To get started, you can access the general Perl documentation by executing:

```
perldoc perl
```

This command provides an introductory overview and a list of documents included in the Perl distribution. These documents are often categorized into several sections such as tutorials, reference manuals, and FAQs dedicated to different aspects of Perl programming.

For module-specific documentation, use:

```
perldoc Module::Name
```

Replace Module::Name with the name of the module you wish to explore. For instance, to find documentation on the ‘strict‘ module, which is commonly used to enforce good coding practices by restricting unsafe constructs, run:

```
perldoc strict
```

The output will outline the functionalities of the module, providing detailed information about its usage and examples.

Additionally, you can retrieve documentation on Perl functions. For instance, to get detailed information on the ‘print‘ function, use:

```
perldoc -f print
```

The -f option specifies that the topic is a function, ensuring the correct documentation is retrieved.

Moreover, the Perl documentation includes comprehensive tutorials which can be particularly beneficial for beginners. For a structured tutorial on Perl, access:

```
perldoc perlintro
```

This tutorial introduces Perl's syntax and essential concepts, guiding readers through writing and understanding basic scripts.

The 'perldoc' utility also offers FAQs addressing common questions and issues encountered by Perl users. For insights into frequently asked questions specific to various Perl versions and modules, run:

```
perldoc perlfaq
```

To delve deeper, you can access more specific FAQs, such as 'perlfaq1' through 'perlfaq9', each covering different topics ranging from general language usage to system-related queries.

Occasionally, you might need to refer to the documentation of an installed CPAN module. In such cases, the command is analogous; simply provide the module's name:

```
perldoc Module::InstalledFromCPAN
```

Some command options enhance readability and accessibility. For example, to view the documentation with enhanced syntax highlighting and pagination, consider using:

```
perldoc -o term -u
```

Here, the -o term option formats the output for terminal viewing, and -u forces the output to be in unformatted (plain) text.

Readers are encouraged to explore the 'perldoc' manual page itself for a full list of options and capabilities offered by this utility:

```
perldoc perldoc
```

In summary, proficient use of Perl documentation via the 'perldoc' utility not only aids in answering specific questions but also significantly enriches the learning process by providing structured and comprehensive references. Engaging with the documentation regularly promotes better understanding and more effective use of Perl's robust capabilities.

1.8 Getting Help with Perl

Obtaining assistance with Perl is essential for both novice and experienced programmers. There are multiple resources available, including online documentation, community forums, and integrated command-line help features. Understanding how to utilize these resources efficiently can significantly enhance your proficiency in Perl programming.

One of the primary means of obtaining help is through the comprehensive Perl documentation, which is bundled with the language upon installation. To access the documentation, use the 'perldoc' command. This command-line tool provides extensive information on Perl modules, syntax, functions, and much more.

```
$ perldoc perl # Provides an overview of commonly used documentation sections
$ perldoc perlsyn # Detailed documentation on Perl syntax
$ perldoc perlfunc # Documentation on Perl built-in functions
$ perldoc perlvar # Documentation about special variables in Perl
$ perldoc perlop # Information about Perl operators and precedence
```

When you need in-depth details about Perl functions or modules, perldoc is invaluable. For instance, to gain insight into the 'print' function or to explore a specific module such as 'DBI', the following commands can be used:

```
$ perldoc -f print # Detailed information on the print function
$ perldoc DBI # Information about the DBI module for database interaction
```

Another critical resource is the Perl community itself. Websites such as Stack Overflow, PerlMonks, and CPAN (Comprehensive Perl Archive Network) host vast quantities of searchable knowledge. These platforms allow you to ask questions, share code snippets, and engage in discussions with other Perl developers.

When seeking help on forums, it is essential to provide clear and concise descriptions of your issue, including any error messages and relevant code snippets. This specificity increases the likelihood of receiving accurate and timely assistance. Below is an example of a well-formulated question on a typical forum:

```
Title: How to Sort a Hash by Its Values in Perl?

Question:
I have a hash in Perl where the keys are student names and the values are their scores. I would like to sort this hash by the scores in descending order. Here is my code so far:

my %students = ('Alice' => 90, 'Bob' => 85, 'Charlie' => 92);

foreach my $student (sort { $students{$b} <=> $students{$a} } keys %students) {
    print "$student: $students{$student}\n";
}

Is this the correct approach, or is there a more efficient way to achieve this?
```

The Perl interactive shell, also known as Perl Debugger, can be another resource for immediate help and testing. Invoke it using the 'perl -d' command. This shell supports execution line by line, breaking, and inspecting variables, aiding significantly in debugging and understanding code behavior.

```
$ perl -d -e 42
```

Within the Perl Debugger, commands like 'h' for help, 'p' for printing expressions, and 'x' for examining variables are particularly useful.

```
h # Help - list available commands
p $variable # Print the value of a variable
x @array # Examine the contents of an array
b 10 # Set a breakpoint at line 10
c # Continue execution until you hit a breakpoint
n # Step to the next line (excluding subroutine calls)
s # Step to the next line (including subroutine calls)
```

Finally, the 'perldiag' documentation provides a detailed explanation of Perl's diagnostics and error messages. This resource is integral when debugging code that produces unfamiliar warnings or errors:

```
$ perldoc perldiag
```

Acquiring help with Perl involves leveraging documentation, engaging with the community, and utilizing integrated tools like Perl Debugger and 'perldoc'. These resources collectively form a robust support system that enhances the productivity and capability of Perl developers at any level.

1.9 First Perl Program

The objective of this section is to guide you through the creation and execution of your first Perl script. We will cover each step in a methodical manner to ensure a comprehensive understanding.

To begin, open your preferred text editor and create a new file. This file will contain your Perl script. Save the file with a .pl extension, which is standard for Perl scripts. For the purposes of this demonstration, let's name the file first_program.pl.

Below is a simple Perl script that prints "Hello, World!" to the screen. Enter the following code into your file:

```
#!/usr/bin/perl
use strict;
use warnings;

print "Hello, World!\n";
```

Let's break down this script into its constituent parts for a clearer understanding.

Shebang Line:

```
#!/usr/bin/perl
```

The first line is known as the shebang line. The shebang (#/) tells the operating system that this file should be executed using the Perl interpreter located at /usr/bin/perl. The location of the Perl interpreter can vary depending on your system configuration. In Unix-like systems, this line is crucial for the script to execute correctly when run as an executable file.

use strict;

```
use strict;
```

The use strict; pragma forces you to declare variables before using them. This reduces the likelihood of programming errors by catching common mistakes, such as typographical errors in variable names.

use warnings;

```
use warnings;
```

The use warnings; pragma enables helpful warnings during compilation and execution, assisting in identifying potential issues within your code without halting the execution.

print **statement:**

```
print "Hello, World!\n";
```

The print function outputs the string "Hello, World!" followed by a newline character (\n), which moves the cursor to the next line after printing.

To execute this script, save the file and open a terminal. Navigate to the directory containing your first_program.pl file. On a Unix-like system, you can execute your script in two ways:

- **Direct Execution**
  - First, make the script executable by altering its file permissions. Use the chmod command:

    ```
    chmod +x first_program.pl
    ```

  - Then, run the script by typing:

```
./first_program.pl
```

- **Using the Perl Interpreter**
  - Alternatively, you can execute the script by explicitly invoking the Perl interpreter:

```
perl first_program.pl
```

For users on Windows systems, you can open Command Prompt or PowerShell and navigate to the directory containing your Perl script. Run the script using Perl interpreter:

```
perl first_program.pl
```

Upon execution, you should see the following output:

```
Hello, World!
```

Running this simple script serves as an introduction to the Perl execution environment and familiarizes you with basic Perl syntax. It is essential to understand that Perl is an interpreted language, meaning the interpreter reads and executes the code directly without prior compilation into machine code.

By adopting the practice of using `use strict;` and `use warnings;`, you ensure that your code follows good programming conventions, helps catch errors early, and adheres to a structured coding standard that is beneficial in complex and collaborative projects.

This foundational Perl program opens the gateway to more complex scripts and automation tasks. Emphasizing clarity, proper syntax usage, and understanding the functionalities of included code lines are crucial in progressing toward more advanced Perl programming techniques.

1.10 Common Use Cases of Perl

Perl, short for Practical Extraction and Report Language, is renowned for its text processing capabilities, strong script execution, and the versatility it brings to both small scripting tasks and large-scale automation projects. This section details the predominant applications of the language, providing a deeper understanding of Perl's functional breadth.

1. Text Manipulation and Parsing

One of Perl's most celebrated use cases is its ability to process and manipulate text files. By leveraging regular expressions, Perl excels in operations such as search and replace, data extraction, and text generation.

```
#!/usr/bin/perl
use strict;
use warnings;

my $text = "The quick brown fox jumps over the lazy dog.";
$text =~ s/fox/cat/; # Replaces 'fox' with 'cat'

print "$text\n"; # Outputs: The quick brown cat jumps over the lazy dog.
```

In this example, Perl uses the substitution operator 's///' to replace occurrences of 'fox' with 'cat' within the string. This demonstrates how Perl processes text in an efficient and succinct manner.

2. Web Scraping and Data Extraction

Perl is frequently employed in web scraping tasks, where it automates the extraction of data from web pages. The CPAN (Comprehensive Perl Archive Network) repository provides modules such as 'LWP::Simple' and 'HTML::Parser' to facilitate such tasks.

```
#!/usr/bin/perl
use strict;
use warnings;
use LWP::Simple;

my $url = 'http://www.example.com';
my $content = get($url);

if (defined $content) {
    print "Successfully retrieved content:\n";
    print "$content\n";
} else {
    die "Failed to retrieve content from $url";
}
```

The snippet above demonstrates fetching a web page's content by using the 'LWP::Simple' module. The 'get' function retrieves the page content, and subsequent error handling ensures the presence of valid data.

3. System Administration

Perl is instrumental in automating system administration tasks. It streamlines file management, process handling, and system monitoring by allowing administrators to script routine operations efficiently.

```
#!/usr/bin/perl
```

```
use strict;
use warnings;

opendir(my $dh, '.') || die "Can't open directory: $!";
while (readdir $dh) {
    print "$_\n";
}
closedir $dh;
```

This script utilizes the 'opendir' and 'readdir' functions to list all the files in the current directory. Such simplicity and power make Perl an indispensable tool for administrators.

4. Bioinformatics

Perl's text processing strength extends into bioinformatics, where it is widely used for DNA sequencing, data analysis, and biological data manipulation. BioPerl, a collection of Perl modules, provides essential tools for the bioinformatics community.

```
#!/usr/bin/perl
use strict;
use warnings;
use Bio::SeqIO;

my $file = "sample.fasta";
my $seqio = Bio::SeqIO->new(-file => $file, -format => 'Fasta');

while (my $seq = $seqio->next_seq) {
    print "Sequence ID: ", $seq->id, "\n";
    print "Sequence: ", $seq->seq, "\n";
}
```

Here, the 'Bio::SeqIO' module parses a FASTA file, a common format for DNA sequences, exemplifying Perl's adeptness in handling bioinformatics data.

5. Automation and Task Scripting

Perl is tailor-made for scripting various automation tasks. From automating backups to generating reports, Perl scripts save time and reduce human error.

```
#!/usr/bin/perl
use strict;
use warnings;
use File::Copy;

my $source_dir = '/source_directory';
my $destination_dir = '/backup_directory';

opendir(my $dh, $source_dir) || die "Can't open $source_dir: $!";
while (readdir $dh) {
    next if /^\.\.?$/; # Skip . and .. special files
    copy("$source_dir/$_", "$destination_dir/$_") or warn "Failed to copy $_: $!";
}
```

```
closedir $dh;
```

This script demonstrates copying files from a source directory to a backup directory by employing the ‘File::Copy‘ module, thereby automating the backup process.

6. CGI Scripting

Perl's flexibility also extends to web development via the Common Gateway Interface (CGI). With modules like ‘CGI.pm‘, Perl facilitates dynamic web content creation.

```
#!/usr/bin/perl
use strict;
use warnings;
use CGI qw(:standard);

print header('text/html');
print start_html('Hello World');
print h1('Hello, World!');
print end_html;
```

This script, a basic CGI script, generates an HTML page saying “Hello, World!” Utilizing ‘CGI.pm‘, Perl allows interactive web experiences and handles form data, session management, and other web functionalities.

The multitude of Perl's applications, from text manipulation to web scraping, system administration, bioinformatics, automation, and web development, underscores the language's robustness and adaptability. The described use cases illustrate Perl's role as a versatile and powerful tool in modern computing environments.

Chapter 2

Basic Perl Syntax

This chapter focuses on the fundamental syntax of Perl, covering statements, comments, and formatting. It explains the various data types and operators used in Perl, as well as basic input and output operations. The chapter also delves into string interpolation, escape sequences, Perl contexts, and basic debugging techniques, providing a comprehensive foundation for writing and understanding Perl code.

2.1 Perl Statements

In Perl, a statement is an instruction for the Perl interpreter to perform a specific action, such as fetching the value of a variable, calling a function, or performing an arithmetic operation. Each statement concludes with a semicolon ;, which signifies the end of the instruction. This section covers the syntax and structure of Perl statements, emphasizing the correct formation and understanding of various types of statements, including simple, compound, and complex statements involving conditional and looping constructs.

At the core, a simple Perl statement might involve an assignment operation or a function call. Consider the following example where a scalar variable is assigned a value:

```
my $variable = 42;
```

In this code, my declares a new lexical scoped variable, $variable refers to a scalar variable, and 42 is the value assigned to this variable. The assignment operator = is used to assign the value on the right-hand side to the variable on the left-hand side.

Perl also supports compound statements, which are composed of two or more simple statements. Here, a function is called to print a string and then an arithmetic operation is performed:

```
print "Hello, world!";
my $sum = 21 + 21;
```

print is a built-in function used to output a string. Once the string "Hello, world!" is printed, the next statement calculates the sum of 21 and 21, storing the result in the scalar variable $sum.

Conditional statements in Perl determine the execution flow based on boolean conditions. The primary conditional constructs are if, elsif, else, and unless. Here's an example of a basic if-else statement:

```
my $number = 10;

if ($number > 5) {
    print "The number is greater than 5";
} else {
    print "The number is 5 or less";
}
```

In this example, if the condition $number > 5 evaluates to true, the string "The number is greater than 5" is printed. Otherwise, the else block executes, printing "The number is 5 or less". Curly braces {} are used to indicate the code blocks that belong to each conditional branch.

Looping statements are crucial for executing repetitive tasks. Perl's primary looping constructs include while, for, foreach, and do-while. Consider this while loop example:

```
my $count = 0;

while ($count < 5) {
    print "Count is $count\n";
    $count++;
}
```

Here, the while loop checks the condition $count < 5. As long as this condition is true, the loop body executes, printing the current value of $count and then incrementing $count by 1 using the increment operator ++.

Combining conditions and loops can lead to more sophisticated constructs. For instance, nested loops enable the repetition of tasks within another loop. This next example demonstrates nested for loops:

```
for (my $i = 0; $i < 3; $i++) {
    for (my $j = 0; $j < 3; $j++) {
        print "i = $i, j = $j\n";
    }
}
```

The outer loop runs with $i varying from 0 to 2. For each iteration of the outer loop, the inner loop runs with $j also varying from 0 to 2, leading to a combined output of all pairs of (i, j) values.

Perl statements can also involve logical and list operations. Logical operations use operators such as and, or, and not to combine and invert conditions:

```
if ($a > 0 and $b < 0) {
    print "a is positive and b is negative";
}
```

In list operations, like the foreach loop, you can iterate over a list of values:

```
my @array = (1, 2, 3, 4);

foreach my $element (@array) {
    print "Element: $element\n";
}
```

This example declares an array @array and iterates over each element using the foreach loop, printing each element in turn.

By understanding these fundamental statement constructs, you can build robust and complex Perl scripts. Each type of statement serves a specific purpose, allowing for clear, expressive, and efficient code. This foundational knowledge is critical as you delve deeper into Perl programming, enabling more advanced techniques and applications.

2.2 Comments in Perl

Within Perl scripts, comments serve as an essential tool for enhancing code readability, providing explanations, and facilitating collaboration among developers. Comments are ignored by the Perl interpreter, thus they do not impact the execution of the script. In Perl, there are two main ways to include comments: single-line comments and block comments.

Single-line comments are preceded by the # character. Anything following this character on the same line is considered a comment and will be ignored by the interpreter. Here is an example demonstrating the use of single-line comments:

```
# This is a single-line comment
print "Hello, World!\n"; # This comment explains the following print statement
```

In the above code, # This is a single-line comment and # This comment explains the following print statement are both comments. The Perl interpreter will process the print statement and ignore the commented text.

Block comments are not natively supported in Perl with a specific syntax, unlike some other programming languages. However, a common practice to simulate block comments is to use multiple single-line comments consecutively. This ensures that larger sections of text can be commented out effectively. Consider the following example:

```
# This is the start of a block comment
# This block comment explains the logic
# behind the following block of code.
# Each line starts with a single-line comment.

print "Block comments are useful for detailed explanations.\n";

# This is the end of the block comment
```

For more extensive block commenting, another technique involves using POD (Plain Old Documentation). POD provides a way to include multi-line comments and documentation directly within the Perl script. POD sections start with =pod and end with =cut. The content between these markers is treated as documentation and ignored by the interpreter.

```
=pod
This is a POD block comment.

This comment can span multiple lines and include detailed explanations
or documentation for the script. POD is also useful for generating
documentation using Perl utilities such as perldoc.

=cut

print "POD comments are useful for extensive documentation.\n";
```

Using POD for block comments has the added advantage of compatibility with Perl documentation tools, enabling the extraction of comments into external documentation files.

Special characters such as $, #, and % in comments do not need to be escaped, unlike their usage in strings or other contexts where they have special meanings. This makes it easy to include such characters in comments without additional syntax considerations. For instance:

```
# The special characters $var, @array, and %hash are included in this comment
    without escaping them.
```

While comments are very powerful for documentation and explanation, it is crucial to use them judiciously. Over-commenting, where every single line of code is explained, can lead to clutter and decrease readability. Conversely, under-commenting can make code maintenance and understanding difficult, especially for others who may work on the same codebase later. Striking a balance is key.

Proper use of comments, both single-line and block (via multiple single-lines or POD), significantly contributes to writing maintainable and understandable Perl scripts, fostering better communication and collaboration among developers.

2.3 Whitespace and Formatting

In Perl programming, whitespace and formatting play a crucial role in enhancing the readability and maintainability of the code. While Perl is relatively flexible with regard to whitespace, adhering to conventional formatting practices helps in producing clean and understandable code.

Perl ignores whitespace characters such as spaces, newlines, and tabs for the most part. These characters can be used freely to format the code. However, whitespace cannot be inserted within tokens (e.g., within variable names or function names). Consider the following example:

```
my $variable = 10;
print $variable;
```

Both of these statements are properly formatted and the whitespace between my, $variable, =, and 10; is optional after each token. Whitespace is used here to enhance readability.

It is important to note that while Perl generally ignores whitespace, there are specific contexts, such as within strings or regex patterns, where whitespace may be taken literally. Therefore, careful attention is necessary when dealing with these contexts.

Indentation is another key aspect of Perl formatting. Perl does not enforce any specific rules for indentation, but it is highly recommended to follow a consistent style throughout the codebase. Indentation typically employs spaces or tabs to delineate blocks of code within constructs such as loops and conditionals. For example:

```
foreach my $i (1..10) {
    if ($i % 2 == 0) {
        print "$i is even\n";
    } else {
        print "$i is odd\n";
    }
}
```

Here, the foreach loop and the if-else statements are indented to show their hierarchical relationship, which aids in understanding the code flow.

Proper use of blank lines can also improve code readability by logically separating different sections or groups of statements within the script. For example:

```
my $name = "Alice";
print "Hello $name\n";

my $age = 30;
print "$name is $age years old\n";
```

The blank line between the two logical blocks of code enhances readability.

Comments often play a vital role in explaining the code. Proper formatting ensures comments are easy to spot and understand. Perl comments begin with the # character and extend to the end of the line:

```
# This is a comment
print "Hello, World!\n"; # This comment is inline
```

Though Perl does not ignore whitespace in comments, consistently spacing comments helps maintain their readability.

Additionally, Perl allows for the use of here-documents to handle multi-line strings, which can also be formatted for better clarity. Here-documents start with « followed by an identifier and end with the same identifier:

```
my $text = <<EOF;
This is a multi-line
string using here-document
EOF

print $text;
```

Whitespace within here-documents is preserved, making it crucial to keep it clean and readable.

In more complex scripts, code layout becomes exceedingly important. Long lines of code should be broken into several shorter lines for better readability. For example, consider the case of a complex data structure initialization:

```
my %hash = (
    'name' => 'Alice',
    'age' => 30,
    'address' => {
        'street' => '123 Maple Street',
        'city' => 'Wonderland',
        'zip' => '12345'
    }
);
```

Here, breaking the hash declaration over multiple lines aligns with good formatting practices, making individual data elements easier to locate and modify.

Adherence to a consistent coding style, leveraging whitespace and proper formatting, facilitates collaboration and maintenance within a team environment. Therefore, it is beneficial to follow community-accepted best practices and guidelines, which often include:

- Using four spaces or a tab per indentation level consistently throughout the script.
- Limiting line length to a maximum number of characters, often 80 or 100, depending on team guidelines.
- Documenting code functionality and purpose through well-placed comments.

In-depth attention to whitespace and formatting ensures that Perl scripts are not only functional but also maintainable and easily understandable, thus fostering a more productive development environment.

2.4 Data Types

Perl, being a dynamically typed language, infers the data type of a variable from its context rather than explicitly enforcing static types. The principal data types in Perl are scalars, arrays, and hashes.

Scalars: Scalars hold single values, which can be either a number, a string, or a reference. Numbers in Perl can be integers or floating-point values. Strings can consist of sequences of characters. Scalars are prefixed with a dollar sign ($).

```
# Assigning an integer to a scalar
$integer = 42;

# Assigning a floating-point number to a scalar
$floating_point = 3.14159;

# Assigning a string to a scalar
$string = "Hello, World!";
```

A scalar can also store references, which are essentially memory addresses of other data structures. This allows complex data structures like arrays of arrays, hashes of hashes, etc.

```
# Reference to an array
$array_ref = [1, 2, 3];

# Reference to a hash
$hash_ref = { 'key1' => 'value1', 'key2' => 'value2' };
```

Arrays: Arrays in Perl are ordered lists of scalars and are prefixed with the at symbol (). Arrays can be manipulated using various functions and operators.

```
# Defining an array
@colors = ('red', 'green', 'blue');

# Accessing array elements
$first_color = $colors[0]; # 'red'
$second_color = $colors[1]; # 'green'

# Adding elements to an array
push(@colors, 'orange'); # @colors now contains 'red', 'green', 'blue', 'orange'

# Removing elements from an array
$last_color = pop(@colors); # 'orange'; @colors now contains 'red', 'green', 'blue'
```

Perl provides a wealth of array functions, allowing complex operations with concise code. Functions such as ‘push‘, ‘pop‘, ‘shift‘, and ‘unshift‘ are essential for manipulating array content dynamically.

```
# Using shift and unshift
unshift(@colors, 'yellow'); # @colors now contains 'yellow', 'red', 'green', 'blue'
$first_color = shift(@colors); # 'yellow'; @colors now contains 'red', 'green', 'blue'
```

Arrays can also be sliced to extract multiple values based on indices.

```
# Slicing an array
@sliced_colors = @colors[0, 2]; # 'red', 'blue'
```

Hashes: Hashes, or associative arrays, are sets of key-value pairs and are prefixed with the percent sign (%). They are useful for representing unordered data and allow quick access to values via their corresponding keys.

```
# Defining a hash
%fruit_colors = ('apple' => 'red', 'banana' => 'yellow', 'grape' => 'purple');

# Accessing hash elements
$apple_color = $fruit_colors{'apple'}; # 'red'

# Adding a new key-value pair
$fruit_colors{'orange'} = 'orange';

# Deleting a key-value pair
delete $fruit_colors{'banana'};
```

Hashes support various operations such as adding, deleting, and checking for the existence of keys.

```
# Check if a key exists
if (exists($fruit_colors{'apple'})) {
    print "Apple color is defined.\n";
}

# Iterating over a hash
while (my ($fruit, $color) = each %fruit_colors) {
    print "$fruit is $color.\n";
}
```

References to hashes enable the creation of complex, nested data structures similar to those possible with arrays.

```
# Nested data structure with hash references
%population = ('USA' => {'California' => 39538223, 'Texas' => 29145505},
               'India' => {'Maharashtra' => 123144223, 'Punjab' => 30141373});

# Accessing nested data
$population{'USA'}{'California'}; # 39538223
```

Scalar, array, and hash data types in Perl provide a robust foundation for building a wide range of applications, accommodating both simple and complex data. Understanding their usage and manipulation is crucial for effective Perl programming.

2.5 Operators

Operators in Perl are essential elements that perform operations on variables and values. Perl supports various types of operators, which can be broadly categorized into arithmetic, string, logical, bitwise, and comparison operators. Understanding these operators is crucial for writing effective and efficient Perl scripts, as they enable complex data manipulations and evaluations.

Arithmetic Operators

Arithmetic operators perform mathematical operations on numeric values. The basic arithmetic operators in Perl are:

```
# Addition
my $sum = 5 + 3; # $sum now holds the value 8

# Subtraction
my $difference = 10 - 4; # $difference now holds the value 6

# Multiplication
my $product = 6 * 7; # $product now holds the value 42

# Division
my $quotient = 10 / 2; # $quotient now holds the value 5

# Modulus
my $remainder = 10 % 3; # $remainder now holds the value 1

# Exponentiation
my $power = 2 ** 3; # $power now holds the value 8
```

String Operators

String operators are used for string concatenation and repetition. The primary string operators in Perl include:

```
# Concatenation
my $greeting = "Hello" . " " . "World!"; # $greeting now holds "Hello World!"

# Repetition
my $repeated = "echo" x 3; # $repeated now holds "echoechoecho"
```

Logical Operators

Logical operators, also known as boolean operators, are used to perform logical operations and return boolean values (true or false). In Perl, the logical operators include:

```
# Logical AND
my $and_result = (5 > 3) && (8 > 6); # $and_result is true

# Logical OR
my $or_result = (5 > 3) || (8 < 6); # $or_result is true
```

```
# Logical NOT
my $not_result = !(5 > 3); # $not_result is false
```

Bitwise Operators

Bitwise operators perform bit-level operations on integer values. The common bitwise operators in Perl include:

```
# Bitwise AND
my $and = 5 & 3; # $and now holds the value 1 (0101 & 0011)

# Bitwise OR
my $or = 5 | 3; # $or now holds the value 7 (0101 | 0011)

# Bitwise XOR
my $xor = 5 ^ 3; # $xor now holds the value 6 (0101 ^ 0011)

# Bitwise NOT
my $not = ~5; # $not now holds the value -6 (bitwise NOT of 0101 is 1010, which is -6
    in signed binary)

# Bitwise shift left
my $shift_left = 5 << 1; # $shift_left now holds the value 10 (0101 << 1 becomes
    1010)

# Bitwise shift right
my $shift_right = 5 >> 1; # $shift_right now holds the value 2 (0101 >> 1 becomes
    0010)
```

Comparison Operators

Comparison operators compare two values and return a boolean value. Perl provides separate operators for numeric and string comparisons.

Numeric Comparison Operators:

```
# Equal to
my $is_equal = (5 == 5); # $is_equal is true

# Not equal to
my $is_not_equal = (5 != 3); # $is_not_equal is true

# Greater than
my $is_greater = (5 > 3); # $is_greater is true

# Less than
my $is_less = (3 < 5); # $is_less is true

# Greater than or equal to
my $is_greater_equal = (5 >= 5); # $is_greater_equal is true

# Less than or equal to
my $is_less_equal = (3 <= 5); # $is_less_equal is true
```

String Comparison Operators:

```
# Equal to
my $str_equal = ("apple" eq "apple"); # $str_equal is true

# Not equal to
my $str_not_equal = ("apple" ne "orange"); # $str_not_equal is true

# Greater than
my $str_greater = ("banana" gt "apple"); # $str_greater is true

# Less than
my $str_less = ("apple" lt "banana"); # $str_less is true

# Greater than or equal to
my $str_greater_equal = ("banana" ge "apple"); # $str_greater_equal is true

# Less than or equal to
my $str_less_equal = ("apple" le "banana"); # $str_less_equal is true
```

Assignment Operators

Assignment operators are used to assign values to variables. They include the basic assignment operator and combined operators that perform an operation and assignment in one step.

```
# Basic assignment
my $var = 5; # $var now holds the value 5

# Add and assign
$var += 3; # $var now holds the value 8

# Subtract and assign
$var -= 2; # $var now holds the value 6

# Multiply and assign
$var *= 4; # $var now holds the value 24

# Divide and assign
$var /= 2; # $var now holds the value 12

# Modulus and assign
$var %= 5; # $var now holds the value 2

# Exponentiate and assign
$var **= 3; # $var now holds the value 8
```

Other Operators

Perl also provides several other operators that are useful in specific contexts:

Range Operator:

The range operator ('..') is used to create lists of sequential numbers or strings.

```
my @numbers = (1..5); # @numbers now holds (1, 2, 3, 4, 5)
my @letters = ('a'..'d'); # @letters now holds ('a', 'b', 'c', 'd')
```

Ternary Operator:

The ternary operator ('? :') is a concise way to perform conditional assignments.

```
my $max = ($a > $b) ? $a : $b; # $max holds the larger of $a and $b
```

Operators are the building blocks for performing computations and data manipulations in Perl, enhancing the functionality and readability of scripts. The appropriate use of these operators enables more efficient and effective coding practices.

2.6 Input and Output

Perl's input and output (I/O) capabilities are robust and flexible, accommodating a range of data handling scenarios from simple interactive commands to complex file manipulations. This section explores the essential functions and syntax required to read from and write to files, as well as handling standard input and output.

Reading from Standard Input is typically achieved using the <STDIN> filehandle. To read a single line from the standard input, use the <STDIN> filehandle as follows:

```
my $input = <STDIN>;
chomp($input);
```

The above code snippet reads a line of input from the user and assigns it to the variable $input. The chomp function is used to remove the trailing newline character that is included when the user presses Enter.

For multiple lines of input, a while loop is commonly used:

```
while (my $line = <STDIN>) {
    chomp($line);
    print "You entered: $line\n";
}
```

This loop continues to read lines from standard input until an end-of-file (EOF) is encountered, processing each line in turn.

Writing to Standard Output is achieved through the print function. Here is an example of printing a string to the console:

```
print "Hello, World!\n";
```

To include variables, make use of double-quoted strings for interpolation:

```
my $name = "Alice";
print "Hello, $name!\n";
```

Reading from Files requires opening the file using the open function. This function takes at least two arguments: a filehandle and the filename. Optionally, a third argument specifies the mode of the file operation. For reading from a file, use the < mode:

```
open(my $fh, '<', 'file.txt') or die "Could not open file: $!";
```

The or die segment is a common Perl idiom for error handling, ensuring the program gracefully terminates if the file cannot be opened.

Once the file is open, read its content line by line using a while loop:

```
while (my $line = <$fh>) {
    chomp($line);
    print "File content: $line\n";
}
close($fh);
```

It is essential to close the filehandle after operations are complete to free up system resources.

Writing to Files involves opening the file in write mode using the > mode:

```
open(my $fh, '>', 'output.txt') or die "Could not open file: $!";
print $fh "This is a test.\n";
close($fh);
```

The above example writes a line to output.txt. If the file does not exist, it will be created. If it does exist, it will be truncated.

Appending to Files uses the » mode, which opens the file without truncating its existing content:

```
open(my $fh, '>>', 'output.txt') or die "Could not open file: $!";
print $fh "Adding another line.\n";
close($fh);
```

Output can also be formatted using various formatting functions. The printf function offers more control over output format:

```
my $number = 42;
my $name = "Alice";
printf("Name: %s, Number: %d\n", $name, $number);
```

The printf function uses format specifiers within the format string, preceded by the percent sign (%). The %s specifier is used for strings, while %d is used for integers. These specifiers are replaced by the subsequent variables passed to printf.

Reading command-line arguments in Perl can be achieved using the @ARGV array. Each element of this array corresponds to a command-line argument supplied to the script:

```
print "First argument: $ARGV[0]\n";
print "Second argument: $ARGV[1]\n";
```

To iterate over all supplied arguments, you can use a foreach loop:

```
foreach my $arg (@ARGV) {
    print "Argument: $arg\n";
}
```

The ARGV array provides a straightforward way to handle input parameters for scripts, enhancing their flexibility and utility.

Advanced file I/O operations can be managed using the built-in Perl functions and modules that support binary data reading/writing, file locking, and more. For instance, the seek function allows for repositioning the file pointer, which can be crucial in certain applications:

```
seek($fh, 0, 0); # Move to the beginning of the file
```

Reading and writing operations become more complex when dealing with binary data, necessitating the use of the binmode function to ensure correct handling of such data:

```
open(my $bin_fh, '<', 'binary_file.bin') or die "Could not open file: $!";
binmode($bin_fh);
```

Understanding these fundamental aspects of Perl's input and output capabilities is critical for effective scripting and automation tasks. Practicing these I/O operations in varied contexts will enhance proficiency in Perl programming.

2.7 String Interpolation

In Perl, string interpolation is a powerful and flexible feature that allows variables and expressions to be embedded directly within double-quoted strings. This capability facilitates the construction of dynamic strings at runtime, maintaining readability and conciseness of the code. Understanding string interpolation is essential for effective Perl programming, particularly in scenarios involving text processing and dynamic content generation.

The syntax for string interpolation in Perl involves embedding variables inside double-quoted strings. For instance, consider the following code snippet, where a variable is interpolated within a string:

```
my $name = "Alice";
print "Hello, $name!\n";
```

When executed, this program produces the output:

```
Hello, Alice!
```

Perl recognizes that $name is a variable within the string and replaces it with its current value. This substitution occurs only within double-quoted strings, as single-quoted strings treat the dollar sign ($) as a literal character:

```
my $name = "Alice";
print 'Hello, $name!\n';
```

The output of this code would be:

```
Hello, $name!\n
```

To enhance clarity and prevent ambiguity during interpolation, it is possible to provide explicit boundaries for variables using curly braces {}. This is particularly useful when concatenating variable names with other characters or variables:

```
my $name = "Alice";
my $occupation = "developer";
print "Hello, ${name} the $occupation!\n";
```

This enforces clear variable boundaries, resulting in:

```
Hello, Alice the developer!
```

For cases where a more complex expression needs to be interpolated, Perl allows the use of expressions within double-quoted strings by enclosing them in curly braces. The expression is evaluated, and its result is inserted into the string:

```
my $a = 5;
my $b = 3;
print "The sum of $a and $b is ${\($a + $b)}.\n";
```

This ensures the expression $a + $b is evaluated correctly, outputting:

The sum of 5 and 3 is 8.

Furthermore, the special variables such as $$, $@, $_, and others are interpolated within double-quoted strings. For example, the Perl process identifier can be included in a string:

```
print "The current process ID is $$.\n";
```

If the process ID were 12345, the output would be:

The current process ID is 12345.

Another powerful feature of Perl's string interpolation is the handling of arrays and hash elements. When interpolating arrays, each element is joined by the default separator, which is a space, unless specified otherwise. Below is an example with an array:

```
my @colors = ("red", "green", "blue");
print "Colors: @colors\n";
```

The output of this code would be:

Colors: red green blue

If the array must be displayed without the default separator, one can use the array within a block and specify a different separator:

```
print "Colors: @{[join(', ', @colors)]}\n";
```

This produces the output:

Colors: red, green, blue

When it comes to hashes, interpolating specific elements is straightforward. Hash keys can be provided in the curly braces to get the desired value:

```
my %points = ("Alice" => 10, "Bob" => 20);
print "Alice has ${points{Alice}} points.\n";
```

This correctly displays:

Alice has 10 points.

It should be noted that in some complex cases where the special meaning of characters results in unexpected behavior, one might need to escape certain characters using the backslash (\). For example, if a variable name immediately follows a dollar sign not intended for interpolation:

```
print "He earned \$500 this week.\n";
```

This ensures the dollar amount is interpreted correctly, resulting in:

```
He earned $500 this week.
```

In Perl, string interpolation extends beyond simple variable and array handling to accommodate more intricate text constructions, benefiting dynamic script creation and seamless text manipulation. The correct application of interpolation techniques can drastically improve code clarity and maintainability.

2.8 Escape Sequences

Escape sequences are special characters within strings that provide additional control over text formatting and output. These sequences begin with a backslash (\) followed by a specific character that signifies a particular function. In Perl, as in many other programming languages, escape sequences are commonly used in string literals to represent non-printable or special characters.

The most frequently used escape sequences in Perl include \\, \n, \t, \r, \f, and \b. Each of these sequences modifies the output in a unique way.

```
print "This is a backslash: \\\n"; # Prints: This is a backslash: \
print "This is a newline character:\n"; # Inserts a new line
print "This is a horizontal tab:\tEnd of tab\n"; # Inserts a tab
```

In the code above:

- \\ prints a single backslash (\).
- \n inserts a newline character, effectively moving the cursor to the beginning of the next line.
- \t inserts a horizontal tab, which typically moves the cursor to the next tab stop.

Other escape sequences, although less frequently used, are equally important:

- \r (carriage return) moves the cursor to the start of the current line without advancing to the next line.
- \f (form feed) advances the cursor to the top of the next page.
- \b (backspace) moves the cursor one position back, effectively allowing you to overwrite the previous character if needed.

Consider the example below to see how each of these escape sequences affects the output:

```
print "Before carriage return...\rAfter carriage return\n";
# Output: After carriage return
# Since \r moved cursor to the line start, "Before carriage return..." is overwritten

print "Page 1\fPage 2\n"; # Prints: Page 1 followed by form feed and then Page 2 on
    new page
print "12345\b6\n"; # Backspace removes 5 and adds 6, resulting in 12346
```

In more advanced scenarios, you may encounter escape sequences for binary data or Unicode characters:

- \x{NN}, where NN represents hexadecimal digits, is used for arbitrary Unicode characters.
- \cX signifies a control character, where X is any character that maps to an ASCII control character.

```
print "Unicode character: \x{263A}\n"; # Prints a smiley face (Unicode U+263A)
print "Control character example: \cC\n"; # Prints the control character equivalent of
    Ctrl+C
```

Escape sequences are particularly powerful when combined with string interpolation, making it possible to programmatically insert special characters into strings. This capability is invaluable for formatting and managing text-based data in scripts.

Additionally, Perl provides mechanisms to avoid processing escape sequences by using single quotes for strings or by escaping the escape sequence itself with a double backslash:

```
print 'This is a newline: \n'; # Prints the literal string: This is a newline: \n
print "This is an escaped backslash: \\\\n"; # Prints: This is an escaped backslash: \
```

Understanding and correctly using escape sequences is crucial for text manipulation tasks, enabling scripts to handle complex text formatting requirements in an automated and efficient manner. This section has introduced essential escape sequences in Perl, illustrated through simple examples to ensure clarity and practical comprehension.

2.9 Perl Contexts

Perl is a context-sensitive language, which means that the interpretation of expressions can change based on their context. Contexts determine how expressions are evaluated and what kind of data types are returned. Two primary contexts in Perl are scalar context and list context. Understanding these contexts is crucial when writing idiomatic and effective Perl code. This section explores scalar context and list context with detailed examples to illustrate how Perl interprets expressions differently under these contexts.

Scalar context refers to situations where an expression is expected to yield a single value. This single value can be a number, a string, or a reference. Many operators and functions behave differently when used in scalar context versus list context. To make this clear, let us consider the behaviour of the localtime function.

```
# Scalar context usage of localtime
my $time_scalar = localtime();
print $time_scalar;
```

When localtime is called in scalar context, it returns a string representation of the current date and time. This can be verified by executing the above code and observing the output.

In contrast, list context refers to situations where an expression is expected to yield a list of values. If localtime is used in list context, it returns a list of time components (second, minute, hour, etc.).

```
# List context usage of localtime
my ($sec, $min, $hour, $mday, $mon, $year, $wday, $yday, $isdst) = localtime();
print "Seconds: $sec, Minutes: $min, Hours: $hour\n";
```

This time, localtime returns a list of nine elements. Each element represents a specific component of the current time. Hence, the way the values are interpreted by Perl depends on the context in which localtime is called.

Another example demonstrating context sensitivity is the wantarray function. The wantarray function allows you to check the context in which a function is called. If called in list context, wantarray returns true. In scalar context, it returns false.

```
# Function to check context
sub check_context {
    return wantarray ? "List context" : "Scalar context";
}
```

```
# Calling the function in scalar context
my $context = check_context();
print "Context is: $context\n";

# Calling the function in list context
my @context_list = check_context();
print "Context is: @context_list\n";
```

In the above example, the check_context function returns different results based on the context in which it is called. This functionality is useful for writing context-sensitive subroutines that can adapt their behavior accordingly.

Array and hash operations also exhibit different behaviors in scalar and list contexts. Consider an array @array and a hash %hash.

```
my @array = (1, 2, 3, 4, 5);
my %hash = (a => 1, b => 2, c => 3);

# Scalar context for array
my $array_size = @array;
print "Array size: $array_size\n";

# List context for array
my @array_elements = @array;
print "Array elements: @array_elements\n";

# Scalar context for hash
my $hash_size = %hash;
print "Hash size (keys and values): $hash_size\n";
```

In scalar context, @array returns the number of elements in the array. In list context, it returns the list of elements themselves. For %hash, scalar context returns a string representing the total number of key-value pairs.

Finally, it is important to understand how certain operators behave differently under different contexts. The <> operator, frequently used for reading lines from a file or standard input, behaves differently depending on the context of its usage.

```
# Reading file in scalar context
open my $fh, '<', 'filename.txt' or die "Cannot open file: $!";
my $line = <$fh>;
print $line;

# Reading file in list context
open my $fh, '<', 'filename.txt' or die "Cannot open file: $!";
my @lines = <$fh>;
print "@lines";
```

In scalar context, the <> operator reads a single line from the filehandle $fh. In list context, it reads all lines at once and returns them as a list.

Understanding Perl contexts and knowing how different functions and operators exhibit context-sensitive behaviors is essential for writing effective Perl scripts. This knowledge allows for the correct interpretation and usage of expressions, leading to more predictable and intended script behaviors.

2.10 Basic Debugging Techniques

Debugging is an essential skill in programming, and Perl provides several tools and techniques to aid developers in detecting and resolving issues within their scripts. Mastery of these techniques is vital for developing efficient and error-free code. This section will cover the usage of the 'use warnings' and 'use strict' pragmas, the built-in Perl debugger, and selective printing for manual inspection.

UseWarningsPragma

The 'use warnings' pragma helps identify potential issues in your code by generating warnings. To enable warnings, include the following line at the beginning of your Perl script:

```
use warnings;
```

Common warnings include the use of uninitialized variables, deprecated features, and syntax issues. Consider the following example:

```
my $x = 10;
print $y; # $y is not initialized
```

Executing this script with 'use warnings' will generate a warning:

```
Use of uninitialized value $y in print at script.pl line X.
```

UseStrictPragma

The 'use strict' pragma forces the programmer to declare variables before using them, thus helping to catch spelling mistakes and scoping issues. Enable strict mode by adding:

```
use strict;
```

Consider the following example without strict mode:

```
$x = 10;
print "$x\n"; # $x is implicitly declared
```

This code will run without errors, but may lead to unintended behavior.

With strict mode enabled:

```
use strict;
my $x = 10;
print "$x\n"; # $x must be explicitly declared with my
```

Running this version without proper variable declaration will result in an error:

```
Global symbol "$x" requires explicit package name at script.pl line X.
```

Perl Built-in Debugger

Perl includes a robust built-in debugger. To invoke the debugger, use the '-d' flag when executing the script:

```
perl -d script.pl
```

This will present the debugger prompt:

```
Loading DB routines from perl5db.pl version X.XX
Enter h or 'h h' for help, or 'man perldebug' for more help.

main::(script.pl:3):    print "Debugging Perl!\n";
  DB<1>
```

Some commonly used debugger commands include:

- 'n' - Execute the next statement without stepping into subroutines.
- 's' - Step into subroutines.
- 'p' - Print the value of an expression.
- 'b' - Set a breakpoint at a specific line or subroutine.
- 'c' - Continue execution until the next breakpoint or program end.

To set a breakpoint at line 10, use:

```
DB<2> b 10
```

Selective Printing for Manual Inspection

Another straightforward debugging technique involves inserting print statements to monitor variable values and program flow. For example:

```
my $a = 5;
my $b = 0;
print "Before division: a=$a, b=$b\n";
my $c = $a / $b;
print "After division: c=$c\n"; # This line will not execute due to division by zero
```

Running this script identifies where the issue occurs due to the output:

```
Before division: a=5, b=0
Illegal division by zero at script.pl line X.
```

By strategically placing print

statements, one can trace the code execution path and inspect variable states at different stages.

Applying these basic debugging techniques makes it possible to detect and resolve common errors effectively, thereby enhancing the reliability and maintainability of Perl scripts. Integrating ‘use warnings‘ and ‘use strict‘ helps enforce good coding practices. The Perl debugger and selective printing provide powerful tools for manual inspection and interactive debugging.

Chapter 3

Variables and Data Types

This chapter covers the different types of variables in Perl, including scalars, arrays, and hashes. It explains variable interpolation, context, and scope, along with special variables and typeglobs. The chapter also introduces constant variables and provides a detailed examination of how data types are utilized and manipulated within Perl programs.

3.1 Introduction to Variables

In Perl, variables are used to store data that can be manipulated and retrieved throughout the execution of a program. They provide a means to label and access memory locations where different types of data are held. Understanding the fundamentals of variables is crucial for efficient Perl programming. This section will address the primary types of variables, their syntax, and basic operations.

Perl supports three primary types of variables: scalars, arrays, and hashes. Each type serves a unique purpose and is denoted by a specific symbol.

- Scalars are prefixed with the $ symbol and hold a single value, which can be either a string, number, or a reference.
- Arrays are prefixed with the @ symbol and contain ordered lists of scalars.

- Hashes are prefixed with the % symbol and store data in key-value pairs.

Example of Scalar Variable:

```
my $scalar_variable = 42;
my $scalar_string = "Hello, World!";
```

Example of Array Variable:

```
my @array_variable = (1, 2, 3, 4, 5);
```

Example of Hash Variable:

```
my %hash_variable = (
    'name' => 'John Doe',
    'age' => 30
);
```

Variables are declared using the my keyword, which limits their scope to the enclosing block, file, or eval. The scope and lifecycle of variables are critical in preventing unintended side effects in code.

Data can be assigned to variables directly or through expressions. Perl provides both numeric and string operations. Scalar variables automatically interpret and store data according to the context.

Example of Contextual Interpretation:

```
my $number = "1234"; # Interpreted as a string.
my $sum = $number + 10; # Interpreted as a number in arithmetic operation.
print $sum; # Outputs: 1244
```

Variable naming in Perl must follow specific rules:

- Names must begin with a letter or underscore, followed by more letters, numbers, or underscores.
- Special characters, such as $, , and %, cannot be used within variable names.

Perl supports both global and lexical variables. A global variable is accessible from anywhere in the program. In contrast, a lexical variable is accessible only within the block, file, or eval where it is declared. Lexical variables are preferred as they help avoid unintended interactions between different parts of the code.

Example of Variable Scope:

```
# Global variable
our $global_var = "I am accessible everywhere";

# Lexical variable
{
    my $lexical_var = "I am accessible only within this block";
    print $lexical_var; # Accessible here
}
# print $lexical_var; # This would cause an error
```

Perl's special variables facilitate various tasks, such as holding predefined values and enabling direct interactions with the Perl interpreter. For instance, the $_ variable holds the default input and pattern-searching space, $ contains the error message from the last eval block, and $$_ represents the process ID of the Perl interpreter.

Example of Special Variables:

```
my $file_contents = <STDIN>; # $_ is used implicitly
if (/pattern/) {
    print "Pattern found in $_\n"; # $_ refers to the default scalar in pattern
          matching
}

eval { die "An error occurred" };
if ($@) {
    print "Eval error: $@"; # $@ captures the error message
}
```

Beyond these foundational concepts, understanding the distinction between different variable contexts—scalar and list—is essential. A scalar context expects a single value, while a list context expects a list of values. The context can change the behavior of operations and functions.

Example of Context Sensitivity:

```
my @values = (1, 2, 3);
my $count = @values; # Scalar context, $count gets the number of elements in @values
    , which is 3
my @new_values = @values; # List context, @new_values gets the elements of
    @values
```

This foundational understanding of variables is essential. Variable declaration, scope, context, and basic operations are cornerstones upon which more complex Perl programming constructs and techniques will be built throughout this text.

3.2 Scalar Variables

Scalar variables in Perl are used to store single values, which can be a number, a string, or a reference. A scalar is denoted by the $ sign followed by the variable name. Scalar variables are versatile and can automatically adjust their type based on the context of their usage. This dynamic typing mechanism simplifies data handling, allowing the programmer to focus on the logic rather than the intricacies of type management.

A scalar variable can be declared and initialized as shown in the following example:

```
# Declaring and initializing scalar variables
my $number = 42;
my $string = "Hello, Perl!";
my $reference = \$number;
```

In the above code, $number is an integer, $string is a string, and $reference stores a reference to the scalar variable $number.

Numerical Scalars

Perl supports various numerical formats, including integers, floating-point numbers, and scientific notation. Internally, Perl uses double-precision floating-point numbers, which provide ample precision for most applications.

Some examples of numerical scalar declarations are:

```
my $integer = 10;
my $float = 3.14;
my $scientific = 1.2e3; # Scientific notation
```

String Scalars

Strings in Perl can be defined using either single quotes (') or double quotes ("). The choice of quotes affects how the string is processed. Single-quoted strings are taken literally, while double-quoted strings allow for variable interpolation and escape sequences.

```
my $single_quoted = 'This is a single-quoted string';
my $double_quoted = "This is a double-quoted string with a variable: $number";
```

In the above example, $single_quoted will remain exactly as it is, whereas $double_quoted will incorporate the value of the variable $number.

Variable Interpolation

Variable interpolation occurs when scalar variables are embedded within double-quoted strings. Perl automatically replaces the variable name with its value, which simplifies string formatting.

```
my $name = "Alice";
my $greeting = "Hello, $name!";
print $greeting; # Output: Hello, Alice!
```

It is possible to escape certain special characters within double-quoted strings. Some common escape sequences include
for a backslash, \n for a newline, and \t for a tab.

Special Literals

Perl provides several special literals like undef, which denotes an undefined value. Variables assigned undef produce errors in strict contexts until they are assigned a defined value.

```
my $undefined_var = undef;
if (!defined($undefined_var)) {
    print "The variable is undefined.\n";
}
```

Type Contexts

Scalars in Perl benefit from context-sensitive behavior. Contexts can be either scalar or list, affecting how expressions are evaluated. In a scalar context, only a single value is expected, influencing functions and operators accordingly.

Consider the following example where the context influences the return value of an array assignment:

```
my @array = (1, 2, 3);
my $scalar_context = @array; # Array in scalar context returns the number of
    elements
print $scalar_context; # Output: 3
```

Operators and Scalar Variables

Perl supports a wide range of operators that work seamlessly with scalar variables. Arithmetic operators (+, -, *, /, %) handle numerical scalars, while string operators (., x) handle string concatenation and repetition.

Examples include:

```
# Arithmetic operations
my $sum = 5 + 10;
my $product = 4 * 3;

# String operations
my $text1 = "Hello, ";
```

```
my $text2 = "world!";
my $combined = $text1 . $text2; # Concatenation: "Hello, world!"
my $repeated = $text1 x 3; # Repetition: "Hello, Hello, Hello, "
```

Scalar Functions

Perl provides various built-in functions to manipulate scalar values. Common scalar functions include length for measuring string lengths, chomp for removing trailing newlines, and lc/uc to convert case.

```
my $msg = "Hello, World!\n";

# Removing newline
chomp($msg);

# Measuring length
my $len = length($msg);

# Changing case
my $lower = lc($msg);
my $upper = uc($msg);
```

3.3 Array Variables

Array variables in Perl are used to store ordered lists of scalar values. The elements of an array can be accessed using their index, which starts from 0. Array variables are denoted by the at sign (@) followed by the variable name. This section provides an in-depth analysis of array variables, ranging from declaration to manipulation, along with syntactical and operational aspects crucial for effective Perl programming.

Declaring and Initializing Arrays

An array can be declared and initialized with a list of values as shown below:

```
# Declaring an array
my @numbers = (1, 2, 3, 4, 5);

# Initializing an array containing strings
my @names = ('Alice', 'Bob', 'Charlie');
```

Accessing Array Elements

Elements of an array are accessed by replacing the at sign (@) with a dollar sign ($) and providing the index of the element within square brackets:

```
# Accessing first element
```

```
print $names[0]; # Outputs: Alice

# Accessing third element
print $numbers[2]; # Outputs: 3
```

Indices can be negative for accessing elements from the end of the array:

```
# Accessing last element
print $names[-1]; # Outputs: Charlie

# Accessing second to last element
print $numbers[-2]; # Outputs: 4
```

Modifying Array Elements

The array elements can be modified by directly assigning new values to specific indices:

```
# Changing the second element
$names[1] = 'David';

# Modifying an element
$numbers[3] = 10;
```

Adding and Removing Elements

Elements can be added to or removed from the array using various built-in functions:

```
# Adding elements to the end of the array
push(@names, 'Eve');

# Adding elements to the beginning of the array
unshift(@numbers, 0);

# Removing the last element
my $last_name = pop(@names);

# Removing the first element
my $first_number = shift(@numbers);
```

Array Slicing

Array slicing allows for extracting multiple elements simultaneously using a list of indices:

```
# Slicing elements from an array
my @partial_names = @names[0, 2]; # ('Alice', 'Charlie')

# Slicing with a range
my @subset_numbers = @numbers[1..3]; # (1, 2, 10)
```

Array Operations

Perl provides various functions to manipulate arrays such as sorting and reversing:

```
# Sorting an array
@sorted_names = sort(@names);

# Reversing an array
@reversed_numbers = reverse(@numbers);
```

Context and Arrays

Arrays behave differently in scalar and list context. In scalar context, an array returns its size:

```
my $size = @numbers; # Size of @numbers array
print $size; # Outputs the number of elements in @numbers
```

In list context, the array returns its elements:

```
my @array_copy = @numbers; # All elements of @numbers are copied to @array_copy
```

Special Array Variables

Some special array variables have predefined meanings, such as @ARGV, which stores command-line arguments passed to the script:

```
# Accessing command-line arguments
my $first_arg = $ARGV[0];
my $second_arg = $ARGV[1];
```

Multi-dimensional Arrays

Although Perl does not have built-in multi-dimensional arrays, it supports arrays of arrays, which can be employed to achieve similar structures:

```
# Initializing a multi-dimensional array
my @matrix = (
    [1, 2, 3],
    [4, 5, 6],
    [7, 8, 9]
);
# Accessing elements
print $matrix[1][2]; # Outputs: 6
```

Array variables offer a versatile way to handle collections of scalar data. Whether for sequencing data, transforming it, or efficiently managing homogeneous or heterogeneous datasets, array operations are fundamental in Perl programming. Proper understanding and manipulation of arrays can greatly enhance the scripting and automation capabilities of Perl developers.

3.4 Hash Variables

In Perl, a hash is a set of key-value pairs where each key is unique. Hash variables are prefixed with the percentage symbol (%). Hashes provide an efficient way to create mappings and are extensively used for look-ups and data associations.

Consider the following example that demonstrates hash variable creation and basic operations:

```
%fruit_colors = (
    apple => 'red',
    banana => 'yellow',
    grape => 'purple',
);
```

Here, a hash named %fruit_colors is created. It maps fruit names to their respective colors. The symbol => used between keys and values is known as the fat arrow and is a visual aid synonymous with the comma operator.

To access an element in a hash, use the key inside curly braces, preceded by a dollar sign ($) when referencing a scalar value:

```
print $fruit_colors{'apple'}; # Outputs 'red'
```

Modifying the values in a hash involves reassigning the value associated with a specific key:

```
$fruit_colors{'apple'} = 'green';
print $fruit_colors{'apple'}; # Outputs 'green'
```

Keys and values can be added dynamically:

```
$fruit_colors{'orange'} = 'orange';
```

To delete a key-value pair, use the delete function:

```
delete $fruit_colors{'banana'};
```

To iterate over all key-value pairs in a hash, the each function provides a convenient method. Iteration is typically handled within a while loop:

```
while (my ($key, $value) = each %fruit_colors) {
    print "$key: $value\n"; # Outputs each key-value pair on a new line
}
```

For specific operations requiring just keys or just values, the keys and values functions are used, respectively. These functions return arrays:

```
@fruit_names = keys %fruit_colors;
@fruit_hues = values %fruit_colors;
```

The exists function checks for the presence of a key in the hash:

```
if (exists $fruit_colors{'grape'}) {
    print "Grape is present\n";
} else {
    print "Grape is not present\n";
}
```

Initialization of hashes using other structures can involve arrays for rapid and sometimes more readable construction of hashes, especially useful for larger datasets:

```
@food_to_price = ('apple', 3, 'bread', 2, 'milk', 1.5);
%grocery_prices = @food_to_price;
```

In situations where order matters, hashes can be problematic since they do not maintain order of insertion. As of Perl 5.18, hashes preserve insertion order but that stability should not be relied upon for algorithms that require consistently ordered elements.

The following code illustrates reading from a hash when dependent on textual or numeric sorting of keys:

```
foreach my $fruit (sort keys %fruit_colors) {
    print "$fruit: $fruit_colors{$fruit}\n"; # Outputs sorted by fruit names
}
```

Error or exceptional condition handling in hash operations should always consider cases of undefined keys, providing robustness to the program code. For instance:

```
my $color = $fruit_colors{'kiwi'} // 'not found';
print "Kiwi color: $color\n";
```

Here, the defined-or operator // ensures a default output if the key 'kiwi' is not in the hash.

Advanced usage of hashes often requires nested structures for representing more complex data schemas. Nested hashes (hashes of hashes) are commonplace:

```
%countries = (
    'USA' => { 'currency' => 'USD', 'capital' => 'Washington, D.C.' },
    'France' => { 'currency' => 'EUR', 'capital' => 'Paris' },
);
print $countries{'USA'}{'capital'}; # Outputs 'Washington, D.C.'
```

Such structures extend to arbitrarily deep levels and require careful dereferencing to avoid mistakes and manage performance. Hashes in Perl also interact seamlessly with JSON and other serialization techniques, facilitating easy exchange of data with web services and storage systems. Efficient use and understanding of hash variables enriches Perl scripting, enabling scalable and maintainable code.

3.5 Variable Interpolation

Variable interpolation in Perl allows for the seamless integration of variable values into strings. This process of interpolation, also known as string expansion, involves the replacement of variables within strings with their corresponding values.

In Perl, double-quoted strings (""string"") support variable interpolation, whereas single-quoted strings ("'string'") do not. This distinction is critical when deciding which type of quotes to use based on the need for interpolation.

Consider the following example to illustrate basic scalar variable interpolation:

```
my $name = "Alice";
my $greeting = "Hello, $name!";
print $greeting;
```

In this example, the scalar variable $name is interpolated within the double-quoted string. The output of this code is:

```
Hello, Alice!
```

Variable interpolation also works with array variables. Let's examine an example involving an array:

```
my @colors = ("red", "green", "blue");
print "The first color is $colors[0].\n";
```

Here, $colors[0] is interpolated within the string to output the first element of the array:

```
The first color is red.
```

Similarly, hash variables can be interpolated within double-quoted strings. Consider the following:

```
my %fruit_colors = (
    apple => "red",
    banana => "yellow",
```

```
    grape => "purple"
);
print "An apple is $fruit_colors{apple}.\n";
```

The output for this interpolation is:

```
An apple is red.
```

Interpolation isn't limited to simple access; it can also handle more complex expressions within curly braces. This can be particularly useful when interpolating hash keys or array indices that are themselves expressions. For example:

```
my $index = 1;
my @numbers = (10, 20, 30);
print "The number at index $index is ${numbers[$index]}.\n";
```

Here, `${numbers[$index]}` ensures that the variable `$index` is correctly interpreted within the context of the array `@numbers`, resulting in the output:

```
The number at index 1 is 20.
```

In the context of hash keys:

```
my %data = (
    'first_name' => 'John',
    'last_name' => 'Doe'
);
my $key = 'first_name';
print "The first name is ${data{$key}}.\n";
```

This script outputs:

```
The first name is John.
```

Perl also allows for complex interpolation using anonymous subscripts and indirect array or hash references. For instance:

```
my @cities = ('New York', 'Los Angeles', 'Chicago');
print "I want to visit ${\$cities[2]} next summer.\n";
```

The use of `\$cities[2]` ensures the correct interpolation of the array element, leading to:

```
I want to visit Chicago next summer.
```

It is essential to be cautious with special characters in variable names during interpolation. For instance, if a variable name follows by a character that could be part of its name, curly braces must be used to delimit the variable. An example scenario might be:

```
my $name = "Alice";
print "This is ${name}'s book.\n";
```

This avoids confusion with 's and outputs:

This is Alice's book.

The use of curly brackets is also necessary when dealing with compound variable names that might collide with surrounding text:

```
my %ages = (Alice => 30, Bob => 25);
print "Alice is ${ages{Alice}} years old.\n";
```

Correct interpolation avoids any ambiguity and produces:

Alice is 30 years old.

Understanding and mastering variable interpolation in Perl is essential for robust and efficient script development, ensuring strings are dynamically and appropriately constructed as per the intended logic of the program.

3.6 Context and Data Types

Perl's rich contextual sensitivity is pivotal in understanding how different data types are manipulated and interpreted in various scenarios. Context plays a critical role in determining the behavior of expressions and variables. Perl primarily differentiates between two contexts: scalar context and list context. Additionally, a special context called void context exists but is of lesser relevance to data manipulation compared to scalar and list contexts.

Scalar Context Scalar context is applicable when a single value is expected. Scalar variables, strings, numbers, and references are typically interpreted within this context. Perl operations return values sensitive to scalar context demands. Consider the behavior of different functions in scalar context:

```
my @array = (1, 2, 3, 4);
my $count = @array;
print $count; # Output: 4
```

In the example above, the assignment @array provides a list, but the scalar $count requires a single value. Hence, the array's length, 4, is assigned to $count.

Moreover, scalar context affects how operations like regular expressions and functions like localtime behave:

```
my $date_time = localtime();
print $date_time; # Output: Mon Nov 14 13:27:33 2022 (example output)
```

The localtime() function behaves differently in scalar and list contexts, returning a formatted string in the scalar context which represents the current date and time.

List Context List context expects a list of values rather than a single value. Arrays and hashes naturally exist within a list context where each element is processed. Evaluations in list context yield multiple values, as shown below:

```
my @time_details = localtime();
print "@time_details"; # Output: 33 27 13 14 10 122 1 317 0 (example output)
```

Here, localtime() returns a list of values representing the second, minute, hour, day, month, year, and other date-time components.

Functions and operators adapt their return values according to the context they are evaluated in. The context can also influence standard operations:

```
my @words = split(" ", "Perl is powerful");
print scalar @words; # Scalar context - Outputs: 3
print "@words"; # List context - Outputs: Perl is powerful
```

The split function divides a string based on a delimiter and returns a list of substrings. When @words is evaluated in scalar context, the array's length (3) is returned. In list context, all elements are returned.

Context Propagation Context can propagate through program constructs and affect nested expressions. Consider the following:

```
my @array = (1, 2, 3);
my ($size) = @array;
print $size; # Outputs: 1
```

Here, ($size) forces a list context for the assignment. The scalar variable $size gets the first element of @array due to this propagation.

Void Context Void context arises when an expression's value is not used. It is often encountered with standalone expressions:

```
my $temp = 42;
$temp + 1; # Expression in void context, effectively ignored
```

In the above code, the expression $temp + 1 is evaluated but not utilized in any assignments or prints, rendering the context void and the result discarded.

Type Coercion Perl's flexible handling of data types includes automatic type coercion where variables can switch types based on context. Scalars holding numerical strings or vice versa automatically adjust:

```
my $number = "42";
my $result = $number + 5;
print $result; # Outputs: 47
```

Here, "42" is a string but is treated as a number in the arithmetic operation, demonstrating Perl's type coercion.

Context and Built-in Functions Several built-in functions exhibit different behaviors based on context. For instance, the wantarray function can be utilized to determine the context within a subroutine:

```
sub context_sensitive {
    return wantarray ? (1, 2, 3) : "single value";
}

my @list = context_sensitive(); # List context
my $scalar = context_sensitive(); # Scalar context
```

In the above subroutine, wantarray returns true if the context is a list, impacting the function's return values accordingly.

Understanding and leveraging context is essential for accurate and efficient Perl programming. Recognizing how contexts influence data types and operations empowers developers to write more predictable and optimized code.

3.7 Variable Scope

In Perl, the scope of a variable refers to the context within which the variable is accessible. There are two primary types of variable scope in Perl: *global* and *lexical*. Understanding these scopes is essential for effective variable management and avoiding unintended side effects in scripts.

Global variables are accessible throughout the entire program, including within subroutines, unless overshadowed by a local declaration.

These variables are declared using our and use vars. Lexical variables, on the other hand, are restricted to the block in which they are declared, including nested blocks, and are defined using the my keyword.

Global Scope

Global variables are declared outside any block and their scope extends to the entire program. They are accessible from any location within the program. Consider the following example:

```
our $global_var = 10;

sub print_global {
    print "Global variable inside subroutine: $global_var\n";
}

print_global();
print "Global variable outside subroutine: $global_var\n";
```

Output:

```
Global variable inside subroutine: 10
Global variable outside subroutine: 10
```

In this example, $global_var is accessible both inside and outside the print_global subroutine because it has a global scope.

Lexical Scope

Lexical variables are declared with the my keyword and are only accessible within the block where they are declared. This type of scope is also known as block-level scope. Here is an example:

```
sub lexical_demo {
    my $lexical_var = 20;
    print "Lexical variable inside subroutine: $lexical_var\n";
}

lexical_demo();
# Attempting to print $lexical_var outside its block will cause an error
# print "Lexical variable outside subroutine: $lexical_var\n";
```

Attempting to access $lexical_var outside the lexical_demo subroutine will result in an error because the variable is not visible outside that block.

Dynamic Scope

Perl also supports dynamic scoping with the local keyword. This is different from lexical scoping and is based on runtime call stack, affecting the global variable temporarily within the dynamic scope of the code execution. Consider the following example:

```
our $dynamic_var = 30;

sub outer_sub {
```

```
    local $dynamic_var = 40;
    inner_sub();
}

sub inner_sub {
    print "Dynamic variable inside inner_sub: $dynamic_var\n";
}

outer_sub();
print "Dynamic variable outside subroutine: $dynamic_var\n";
```

Output:

```
Dynamic variable inside inner_sub: 40
Dynamic variable outside subroutine: 30
```

In this example, `$dynamic_var` temporarily holds the value `40` within the `outer_sub` subroutine and its inner calls. After `outer_sub` execution, `$dynamic_var` reverts to its original value of `30`.

Best Practices for Variable Scope

Using lexical variables by default is generally considered good practice, as it reduces the risk of unintended side effects by limiting variable accessibility. When working within larger scripts or applications, adopting the following practices can further improve variable management:

Algorithm 1: Best Practices for Variable Scope

Input: defined variables in appropriate scopes
Output: optimized variable management and avoidance of conflicts

begin
- Use `my` to declare variables within a limited scope;
- Avoid global variables unless absolutely necessary;
- Use `our` only when variable sharing across multiple blocks or modules is required;
- Localize dynamic scope alterations using `local`;
- Consider readability and maintainability when choosing variable scope.

Incorporating these practices into your Perl programming will facilitate more efficient and error-free code development. Proper scope management ensures that variables are used judiciously, improving both the clarity and performance of your scripts.

3.8 Special Variables

In Perl, special variables have predefined meanings and serve specific functions that assist in various programming tasks. These variables are often marked by punctuation characters to differentiate them from user-defined variables. Understanding and leveraging these special variables can significantly enhance script efficiency and functionality.

$_ **(Default Variable)**: The $_ variable is the default input and pattern-searching space. It is implicitly used in many functions and operators if no other variable is specified.

```
foreach (1..5) {
    print; # prints values 1 to 5
}
```

$. **(Input Line Number)**: The $. variable contains the current line number for the last filehandle accessed, which is useful when processing input line by line.

```
open my $file, '<', 'sample.txt' or die \$!;
while (<$file>) {
    print $. . ": $_"; # prints line number followed by the line content
}
close $file;
```

$/ **(Input Record Separator)**: The $/ variable defines the character sequence that separates records for input operations. By default, it is set to the newline character.

```
{
    local $/ = "\n\n"; # change input record separator to read paragraphs
    open my $file, '<', 'sample.txt' or die \$!;
    while (<$file>) {
        print "Paragraph:\n$_";
    }
    close $file;
}
```

$! **(OS Error Variable)**: The $! variable stores the error message associated with the most recent system call failure, providing useful diagnostic information.

```
open my $file, '<', 'non_existent_file.txt' or die "Error: \$!";
```

$@ **(Eval Error)**: The $@ variable holds the error message, if any, resulting from the last eval command, facilitating error handling in eval blocks.

```
eval {
```

```
    die "An intentional error";
};
if ($@) {
    print "Caught error: $@";
}
```

$? **(Status of Last System Call)**: The $? variable contains the status returned by the last wait or system call, encoded in a manner that provides information about the exit status and signal received by the child process.

```
system("ls");
print "Exit status: $? >> 8\n"; # extracts the exit status
```

$$ **(Process ID)**: The $$ variable holds the process ID (PID) of the current Perl script, useful in multi-process environments.

```
print "Current process ID: $$\n";
```

$< **and** $> **(User IDs)**: These variables store the real (user ID) and effective user ID of the current process, respectively, while $(and $) store the real and effective group IDs.

```
print "User ID: $<\n";
print "Effective User ID: $>\n";
print "Group ID: $(\n";
print "Effective Group ID: $)\n";
```

` **(Quote-like Operators)**: The backticks ` allow for the execution of external commands, capturing their output for further processing.

```
my $date = 'date';
print "Current date: $date";
```

$0: This special variable contains the name of the script being executed, useful for logging and diagnostics.

```
print "Script name: \$0\n";
```

Mastering these special variables enables you to write more concise and powerful Perl scripts, leveraging built-in functionalities effectively. These special variables often serve in implicit contexts, reducing the need for explicit code and improving readability.

3.9 Typeglobs

Typeglobs play a critical role in Perl's flexible and dynamic symbol table implementation. They serve as a means to represent various types of symbols in Perl, including scalars, arrays, hashes, filehandles, and subroutines. A typeglob is denoted by the asterisk (*) symbol followed by a name, such as *symbol. The complete symbol table entry for 'symbol' can be accessed and manipulated using typeglobs.

Typeglobs facilitate aliasing and the manipulation of different types of data by allowing one name to reference multiple types simultaneously. Understanding typeglobs is essential for leveraging Perl's powerful features in advanced scripting and automation.

To exemplify the usage of typeglobs, consider the following code snippet:

```
# Assigning a scalar and a filehandle to the same name using a typeglob
*example = *STDOUT;
$example = "Hello, World!\n";
print $example; # This prints to standard output due to the assignment
```

In this example, *example references both the scalar $example and the filehandle *STDOUT. Consequently, assigning a string to $example and then printing it results in the string being sent to standard output.

Typeglobs can also be used for aliasing arrays, hashes, and subroutines:

```
# Aliasing an array and a hash
*array_alias = \@original_array;
%hash_alias = %original_hash;

# Modifying the original array and hash via aliases
push(@array_alias, "new_element");
$hash_alias{"new_key"} = "new_value";
```

Here, *array_alias is an alias for original_array and %hash_alias for %original_hash. Modifying these aliases directly impacts the original array and hash.

Beyond simple aliasing, typeglobs can be leveraged to manipulate Perl's symbol table directly. This can be particularly useful in dynamic programming, where the structure of the code can change at runtime. For example, dynamically creating subroutines using typeglobs:

```
# Defining a subroutine dynamically
*dynamic_sub = sub {
    my $arg = shift;
    return "Dynamic argument received: $arg";
```

```
};
print dynamic_sub("example"); # Output: Dynamic argument received: example
```

In this code, *dynamic_sub creates a new subroutine reference. This showcases Perl's ability to dynamically define and invoke code structures during runtime execution.

Another powerful feature of typeglobs is their role in the implementation of symbolic references in Perl. This, however, requires careful handling to avoid undesirable side effects:

```
# Using symbolic references
$name = 'foo';
$$name = "This is a symbolic reference.";
print $foo; # Output: This is a symbolic reference.
```

Here, $$name creates a symbolic reference to $foo. This indirect assignment speaks to Perl's flexibility but is generally discouraged, except in controlled scenarios where dynamic referencing is essential.

Typeglobs also provide mechanisms for localizing symbol table entries. This is critical in large scripts or modules where variable namespace pollution can be problematic. By localizing typeglobs, one ensures that changes are confined to a particular scope:

```
# Localizing typeglobs
{
    local *foo = \$bar;
    $foo = "Temporarily reassigned";
    print $bar; # Output: Temporarily reassigned
}
print $bar; # Output: Original value of bar, outside of the scope
```

Within the localized block, *foo temporarily points to $bar, showcasing typeglobs' scope controlling capabilities. The original value of $bar is restored after the block's conclusion.

Given the potential complexity and risk involved in handling typeglobs erroneously, developers should approach their usage carefully, ensuring clarity and intentionality in their code logic. Proper understanding and utilization of typeglobs allow for sophisticated symbol manipulation and advanced dynamic scripting capabilities in Perl programming.

3.10 Constant Variables

In Perl, the concept of constant variables is utilized to define values that remain immutable throughout the execution of a program. Constant variables are particularly beneficial in scenarios where certain values are known in advance and must not be allowed to change, ensuring consistency and aiding in the prevention of inadvertent errors.

Perl provides several ways to define constants, with the most common methods being the use of the constant pragma and the Readonly module. Each method has its own syntax and specific use cases.

Defining Constants with the constant Pragma

The constant pragma allows you to create constant variables by simply importing the pragma and defining constants using the syntax:

```
use constant CONSTANT_NAME => value;
```

For example, to define a constant variable for the value of pi, you would write:

```
use constant PI => 3.14159;
```

This allows you to use PI throughout your program without the risk of it being altered. Attempting to modify PI will result in an error. Here's an example illustrating the usage:

```
use constant PI => 3.14159;

print "The value of PI is ", PI, "\n";

# Attempt to modify the constant
PI = 3.14; # This will cause an error
```

When attempting to modify PI, Perl will produce an error indicating the attempt to change a read-only value.

```
Global symbol "$PI" requires explicit package name (did you forget to declare "my $PI"?) at script.pl line X.
```

Defining Constants with the Readonly Module

The Readonly module offers a more flexible approach to defining constant variables, including scalars, arrays, and hashes. This module not only provides the same immutability guarantees as the constant pragma but also handles complex data structures more efficiently.

First, ensure the Readonly module is installed. If it is not, you can install it using CPAN:

```
cpan Readonly
```

To use the Readonly module, begin by importing it and then utilizing the Readonly keyword to define your constants:

```
use Readonly;

Readonly my $PI => 3.14159;
Readonly my @WEEKDAYS => qw(Monday Tuesday Wednesday Thursday Friday);
Readonly my %MONTH_DAYS => (
    January => 31,
    February => 28,
    March => 31,
    # ... other months
);
```

In this example, $PI is a constant scalar, @WEEKDAYS is a constant array, and %MONTH_DAYS is a constant hash. Attempting to modify any of these constants will result in an error.

Here is an example of accessing these constants:

```
use Readonly;

Readonly my $PI => 3.14159;
Readonly my @WEEKDAYS => qw(Monday Tuesday Wednesday Thursday Friday);
Readonly my %MONTH_DAYS => (
    January => 31,
    February => 28,
    March => 31,
);

print "The value of PI is $PI\n";
print "The weekdays are: @WEEKDAYS\n";
print "January has $MONTH_DAYS{January} days\n";
```

If you attempt to alter any of these constants, such as:

```
$PI = 3.14; # This will cause an error
```

Perl will produce an error indicating the constant's immutable nature.

```
Modification of a read-only value attempted at script.pl line X.
```

Constants and Context

It is important to understand how constants behave in different contexts. When a constant is used in a scalar context, it will behave just like any other scalar. Similarly, constants defined as arrays or hashes retain their contextual properties. For instance, an array constant used in a list context will expand into its constituent elements.

```
use constant FRUITS => qw(Apple Banana Cherry);
```

```
my @fruits = FRUITS; # List context
print "Fruits: @fruits\n";

my $fruit_count = scalar FRUITS; # Scalar context
print "Number of fruits: $fruit_count\n";
```

The output will be:

```
Fruits: Apple Banana Cherry
Number of fruits: 3
```

Constant variables in Perl are indispensable for defining values that must remain unchanged. By leveraging the constant pragma or the Readonly module, you can enhance the reliability and maintainability of your code.

Chapter 4

Control Structures

This chapter explores the various control structures in Perl, including conditional statements and loops. It provides detailed explanations of if-else statements, unless statements, switch statements, and the different types of loops such as for, foreach, while, and until. Additionally, the chapter covers loop control keywords and the use of nested control structures, offering a comprehensive understanding of flow control in Perl programming.

4.1 Introduction to Control Structures

Control structures form the foundational building blocks that dictate the flow of execution in Perl programs. These structures allow the programmer to dictate the sequence in which statements are executed, making it possible to create complex decision-making processes and repetitive tasks. In Perl, control structures can be primarily categorized into conditional statements and loops. Each of these categories provides a variety of mechanisms for managing execution flow.

Conditional statements in Perl execute code blocks based on specific conditions. The most common conditional statement is the if-else statement. There are also unless statements, which execute code when a condition is false, and switch statements, which provide a streamlined way to execute one code block out of multiple options based on the value of a variable.

Loops are another critical control structure, enabling the execution of a code block multiple times. Perl provides various types of loops, including for, foreach, while, and until loops. Each type of loop serves a different purpose and offers unique flexibility. Additionally, loop control keywords such as next, last, and redo provide further control over loop execution.

To begin, let's consider a simple if-else statement. The syntax is as follows:

```
if (condition) {
    # Code to execute if condition is true
} else {
    # Code to execute if condition is false
}
```

In this example, the code within the if block executes only when the condition evaluates to true. If the condition is false, the code within the else block executes instead. This fundamental structure allows the programmer to branch execution paths based on specific conditions.

The unless statement provides a convenient way to execute code when a condition is false. Its syntax is similar to the if statement, but inverted:

```
unless (condition) {
    # Code to execute if condition is false
}
```

This statement reduces the need for lengthy negation logic within if conditions, leading to clearer and more readable code.

Furthermore, Perl offers the switch statement, officially called given-when. This approach is syntactically appealing when dealing with multiple conditions. The switch statement's format looks like this:

```
use feature 'switch';

given ($variable) {
    when (condition1) {
        # Code to execute for condition1
    }
    when (condition2) {
        # Code to execute for condition2
    }
    default {
        # Code to execute if none of the above conditions are met
    }
}
```

The given-when construct simplifies handling multiple conditional branches, making the code more concise and organized.

Next, loops allow repetitive execution of code blocks as long as a specified condition holds true. A basic for loop's structure in Perl is:

```
for (my $i = 0; $i < 10; $i++) {
    # Code to execute for each iteration
}
```

In this loop:

1. Initialization (my $i = 0) occurs once before the loop starts. 2. Condition ($i < 10) is checked before each iteration—if true, the loop continues. 3. Increment ($i++) happens after the execution of the loop's body.

The foreach loop is particularly useful for iterating over arrays and lists:

```
my @array = (1, 2, 3, 4, 5);

foreach my $element (@array) {
    # Code to execute for each element in the array
}
```

Here, the foreach loop iterates over each element of the @array, assigning the current element to $element during each iteration.

The while loop continues to execute its block as long as its condition is true:

```
while (condition) {
    # Code to execute while the condition is true
}
```

Contrastingly, the until loop functions like a while loop but repeats until the condition becomes true:

```
until (condition) {
    # Code to execute until the condition is true
}
```

Lastly, loop control keywords—next, last, and redo—add further control within loops:

```
for (my $i = 0; $i < 10; $i++) {
    if ($i == 2) {
        next; # Skip the rest of the loop iteration
    }
    if ($i == 5) {
        last; # Exit the loop
    }
    if ($i == 7) {
        redo; # Restart the loop iteration without incrementing
    }
}
```

This loop control mechanism ensures that specific iterations or the entire loop can be managed dynamically based on conditions within the loop's body.

By understanding and effectively utilizing these foundational control structures, Perl programmers can compose code that is both efficient and maintainable, precisely directing the flow of their scripts as required by the task at hand.

4.2 Conditional Statements

Conditional statements are fundamental to controlling the flow of execution in any programming language, including Perl. They enable a program to execute different code blocks based on boolean expressions. Perl's implementation of conditional statements is versatile and includes several variations that cater to various programming needs. This section focuses on the primary conditional structures, providing an in-depth look at their syntax and usage.

Perl offers multiple ways to write conditional statements, each providing a different syntactical or semantic angle that can be advantageous depending on the context. The primary forms of conditional statements in Perl are the if, unless, and given-when structures. Furthermore, Perl supports ternary operators, which offer a more concise way to express simple conditional logic.

```
# Basic if statement syntax
if (condition) {
    # code to execute if condition is true
}

# Example
my $a = 10;
if ($a > 5) {
    print "a is greater than 5\n";
}
```

In the above example, the block of code inside the if statement is executed only if the condition $a > 5 evaluates to true. The condition is a boolean expression, which can utilize comparison operators such as ==, !=, >, <, >=, and <=.

```
# if-else statement syntax
if (condition) {
    # code to execute if condition is true
} else {
    # code to execute if condition is false
}
```

```
# Example
if ($a > 5) {
    print "a is greater than 5\n";
} else {
    print "a is not greater than 5\n";
}
```

The if-else statement extends the basic if construct by allowing alternative code to run when the condition evaluates to false. This is essential when the program needs a default action if the primary condition is not met.

```
# if-elsif-else statement syntax
if (condition1) {
    # code to execute if condition1 is true
} elsif (condition2) {
    # code to execute if condition2 is true
} else {
    # code to execute if none of the above conditions are true
}

# Example
if ($a > 5) {
    print "a is greater than 5\n";
} elsif ($a == 5) {
    print "a is exactly 5\n";
} else {
    print "a is less than 5\n";
}
```

The if-elsif-else construct allows for multiple conditional checks sequentially. Perl evaluates each condition in the order they appear and executes the corresponding block of code for the first true condition encountered. If none of the conditions are true, then the code inside the else block is executed.

Unless Statement

The unless statement in Perl is logically opposite to the if statement. It executes the block of code only if the condition evaluates to false. This can sometimes make the code more readable when the intent is to check for the negation of a condition.

```
# unless statement syntax
unless (condition) {
    # code to execute if condition is false
}

# Example
unless ($a > 5) {
    print "a is not greater than 5\n";
}
```

While the original if-else structure remains the predominant method for conditional logic in Perl, unless offers a syntactically neat alternative for negation conditions without using the ! operator.

Ternary Operator

Perl also supports a ternary conditional operator ? :, which offers a compact syntax to perform simple conditional evaluations. The ternary operator evaluates a boolean expression and returns one of two values depending on whether the expression is true or false.

```
# Ternary operator syntax
condition ? true_value : false_value;

# Example
my $b = ($a > 5) ? "greater" : "not greater";
print "b is $b\n";
```

In the example above, the variable $b is assigned the string "greater" if the condition $a > 5 is true, otherwise it is assigned "not greater". The ternary operator is particularly useful for simple assignments and inline conditional logic without the verbosity of multiple if-else blocks.

Given-When (Switch) Statements

Perl's given-when construct, similar to the switch statement in other languages, allows multiple conditions to be evaluated against a single expression or value. The given block evaluates a variable, and each when block specifies a condition to match against that value. The first when condition that evaluates to true executes its corresponding block of code.

```
# given-when statement syntax
use feature "switch";

given ($a) {
    when ($_ > 5) {
        print "a is greater than 5\n";
    }
    when (5) {
        print "a is exactly 5\n";
    }
    default {
        print "a is less than 5\n";
    }
}

# Example
use feature "switch";
given ($a) {
    when ($_ > 5) {
        print "a is greater than 5\n";
    }
    when (5) {
        print "a is exactly 5\n";
    }
```

```
    default {
        print "a is less than 5\n";
    }
}
```

The given-when construct enhances readability and organization when dealing with multiple conditions.

Overall, conditional statements play a crucial role in shaping the flow and logic of Perl scripts, offering flexibility and precision in programming. Proper understanding and utilization of these constructs can significantly streamline code efficiency and readability.

4.3 if-else Statements

The if-else statement is foundational in Perl for creating conditional logic, where the execution of specific blocks of code depends on the evaluation of one or more conditions. An if-else statement allows the programmer to specify a block of code that will execute if a given condition evaluates to true, and another block of code that will execute if the condition evaluates to false.

The syntax for a simple if-else statement in Perl is as follows:

```
if (condition) {
    # Code to execute if condition is true
} else {
    # Code to execute if condition is false
}
```

Here, the condition is any expression that Perl can evaluate as true or false. If the condition is true, the block of code within the first set of curly braces is executed. If the condition is false, the block of code within the else statement's curly braces is executed.

Consider the following example, which determines if a number is positive or not:

```
my $number = 10;

if ($number > 0) {
    print "$number is positive.\n";
} else {
    print "$number is not positive.\n";
}
```

When the above code is executed, the output will be:

```
10 is positive.
```

The if-else structure can be extended with the elsif keyword to handle multiple conditions. The elsif keyword allows for evaluation of additional expressions when the previous conditions have evaluated to false. The syntax for including elsif in an if-else statement is:

```
if (condition1) {
    # Code to execute if condition1 is true
} elsif (condition2) {
    # Code to execute if condition2 is true
} else {
    # Code to execute if neither condition1 nor condition2 is true
}
```

Let's expand the previous example to classify the number as positive, negative, or zero:

```
my $number = -5;

if ($number > 0) {
    print "$number is positive.\n";
} elsif ($number < 0) {
    print "$number is negative.\n";
} else {
    print "$number is zero.\n";
}
```

Executing this code produces the output:

```
-5 is negative.
```

Perl, being a flexible scripting language, offers a more concise way to write conditional statements using postfix if. This is particularly useful for simple conditions, where brevity is an advantage. For example:

```
print "$number is positive.\n" if $number > 0;
```

However, this succinct form becomes less readable when dealing with complex, nested or multiple conditions, and therefore is used sparingly and only when appropriate.

The concept of truth in Perl is worth emphasizing here. Perl evaluates many values as false, including 0, the empty string '', the string '0', undef, and empty lists. All other values are considered true. This behavior has implications in conditional statements and should be considered when writing if-else logic.

Additionally, Perl supports the use of logical operators to combine multiple conditions within an if or elsif statement. Logical operators include and, or, and not, which can be used to create complex conditional expressions. For instance:

```
if ($number > 0 and $number < 10) {
    print "$number is a single-digit positive number.\n";
} elsif ($number <= 0 or $number >= 10) {
    print "$number is either non-positive or double-digit.\n";
}
```

Combining conditions can provide additional control over the flow of the program, enabling more nuanced execution of code blocks based on multiple criteria.

In the context of file existence and readability, one might use an if-else statement as follows:

```
my $filename = 'example.txt';

if (-e $filename) {
    print "$filename exists.\n";
    if (-r $filename) {
        print "$filename is readable.\n";
    } else {
        print "$filename is not readable.\n";
    }
} else {
    print "$filename does not exist.\n";
}
```

In this example, the code first checks if the file exists using the -e file test operator. If the file exists, it then checks whether the file is readable using the -r operator, demonstrating nested conditional statements.

Mastering if-else statements and understanding the nuances of condition evaluation in Perl are crucial skills for scripting and automation tasks. These control structures enable the creation of dynamic, flexible, and responsive scripts that can handle a wide variety of conditions and scenarios.

4.4 unless Statements

The unless statement is a control structure in Perl that functions as the logical inverse of the if statement. It allows for the execution of a block of code only if a specified condition evaluates to false. This can be particularly useful for enhancing code readability and making logic more intuitive when dealing with conditions that are naturally expressed in negative form.

The general syntax for an unless statement is as follows:

```
unless (condition) {
```

```
    # Code to execute if condition is false
}
```

Here, condition is a Boolean expression. If condition evaluates to false, the code block within the curly braces is executed. If condition evaluates to true, the block is skipped. This is analogous to an if statement with a negated condition.

Consider the following example that demonstrates the use of an unless statement:

```
my $age = 17;
unless ($age >= 18) {
    print "You are not old enough to vote.\n";
}
```

In this example, the message "You are not old enough to vote." is printed because the condition $age >= 18 evaluates to false when $age is 17. This usage is often more readable than writing the equivalent if statement:

```
my $age = 17;
if (!($age >= 18)) {
    print "You are not old enough to vote.\n";
}
```

The unless statement can also be used with an else block, similar to the if statement with the else clause. The syntax is as follows:

```
unless (condition) {
    # Code to execute if condition is false
} else {
    # Code to execute if condition is true
}
```

Here is an example of using unless with else:

```
my $temperature = 30;
unless ($temperature < 32) {
    print "The water is not frozen.\n";
} else {
    print "The water is frozen.\n";
}
```

When $temperature is 30, the condition $temperature < 32 evaluates to true, so the control flow enters the else block, printing "The water is frozen." This combination of unless and else makes the logic concise and clear.

For even more concise code, Perl allows the use of the unless statement in a postfix form, where the condition follows a statement. The syntax is as follows:

```
# Action statement unless condition
print "File does not exist.\n" unless -e 'example.txt';
```

In this case, the message "File does not exist." will be printed only if the file example.txt does not exist (i.e., -e 'example.txt' evaluates to false). This form is particularly useful for simple, straightforward checks.

It is essential to use unless judiciously to ensure code readability. While it can succinctly express negative conditions, overuse or misuse can lead to confusing double negatives and obscure the intended logic. Therefore, it is important to evaluate whether the use of unless genuinely clarifies the code's intention.

For complex conditions or when both branches of the control flow contain significant logic, consider whether an if statement with a negated condition might enhance clarity. In general, unless is best employed in scenarios where its natural negative condition improves the readability and flow of the code.

4.5 Switch Statements

The ‘switch‘ statement in Perl, introduced in Perl 5.10 via the ‘given-when‘ construct, provides an efficient and readable way to perform multiple conditional checks. Unlike a series of ‘if-elsif‘ statements, the ‘switch‘ statement allows for a more structured and clear approach to evaluating a single variable against multiple potential values. The syntax is highly inspired by ‘switch-case‘ constructs found in other programming languages like C, C++, and Java.

The implementation of ‘switch‘ statements in Perl utilizes two keywords: ‘given‘ and ‘when‘. The ‘given‘ block takes a scalar value and tests it against a series of ‘when‘ conditions. If a match is found, the corresponding block of code is executed.

To begin, consider the canonical structure of a ‘given-when‘ construct:

```
use feature 'switch';

given ($variable) {
    when ($value1) {
        # Code to execute if $variable matches $value1
    }
    when ($value2) {
        # Code to execute if $variable matches $value2
    }
```

```
    default {
        # Code to execute if no when condition matches
    }
}
```

In the above example, $variable is the scalar value being evaluated. Each 'when' condition compares $variable to a specified value ($value1, $value2, etc.). The 'default' block executes if none of the 'when' conditions match, analogous to the 'else' block in an 'if-elsif' statement.

It's essential to enable the 'switch' feature with use feature 'switch';. Without this, the 'given-when' syntax will not be recognized by the Perl interpreter.

Detailed Example

To illustrate this with a practical example, let's consider a scenario where a program categorizes numerical scores into grading buckets (A, B, C, D, F).

```
use feature 'switch';

my $score = 85;

given ($score) {
    when ($_ >= 90) {
        print "Grade: A\n";
    }
    when ($_ >= 80) {
        print "Grade: B\n";
    }
    when ($_ >= 70) {
        print "Grade: C\n";
    }
    when ($_ >= 60) {
        print "Grade: D\n";
    }
    default {
        print "Grade: F\n";
    }
}
```

This structure evaluates the score against the given ranges and prints the corresponding grade. Note that the special topic variable $_ is implicitly used within the 'given' block to refer to the variable being evaluated, which in this case is $score.

Advanced Usage

- **Combining Conditions**: Multiple conditions can be checked within a single 'when' clause by using Perl's logical operators. For example, to identify whether a number is either negative or greater than 100, you can use:

```
use feature 'switch';

my $number = -10;

given ($number) {
    when ($_ < 0 || $_ > 100) {
        print "Out of range\n";
    }
    default {
        print "Within range\n";
    }
}
```

- **Smart Matching**: The 'given-when' construct leverages Perl's smart match operator (' '), which provides versatile comparison mechanisms beyond simple equality. The smart match operator adapts its comparison behavior based on the data types involved.

```
use feature 'switch';

my $item = "apple";

given ($item) {
    when ("apple") {
        print "It's an apple\n";
    }
    when ("banana") {
        print "It's a banana\n";
    }
    default {
        print "Unknown fruit\n";
    }
}
```

In the above snippet, the smart match operator checks for string equality.

- **Compound Statements**: Complex expressions can be succinctly evaluated within a 'when' clause using compound statements.

```
use feature 'switch';

my $age = 25;

given ($age) {
    when ($_ < 18) {
        print "Minor\n";
    }
    when ($_ >= 18 && $_ <= 64) {
        print "Adult\n";
    }
    when ($_ > 64) {
        print "Senior\n";
    }
}
```

Important Considerations

- **Fall-through Behavior**: Unlike many other languages, Perl's 'when' statements do not automatically "fall through" to subsequent blocks. Each 'when' block is isolated unless control explicitly transfers using constructs like 'continue'.
- **Legacy Code**: The 'switch' feature must be explicitly enabled as it is not part of Perl's default feature set. As a result, older Perl code may not recognize the 'given-when' syntax without the appropriate declaration.
- **Compatibility**: The 'given-when' construct is available from Perl 5.10 onward. It's essential to ensure compatibility if the code is expected to run on environments with older Perl versions.

Incorporating 'switch' statements via the 'given-when' construct into Perl programs enhances code readability and provides a structured mechanism for executing conditional logic based on multiple potential values.

4.6 Loops in Perl

In Perl, loops are essential constructs that facilitate repeated execution of code blocks. Understanding loops is critical for handling repetitive tasks efficiently. Perl supports several loop constructs, namely for loops, foreach loops, while loops, and until loops, each of which serves specific purposes and has unique syntax. This section provides an in-depth analysis of these loop constructs to equip you with the knowledge to utilize them effectively.

for loops are typically used when the number of iterations is known before entering the loop. The for loop syntax is similar to that in other programming languages:

```
for (my $i = 0; $i < 10; $i++) {
    print "Iteration number: $i\n";
}
```

In this example, the loop initializes a variable $i to 0. Then, as long as the condition $i < 10 is true, it executes the loop's body and increments $i after each iteration. The increment operator $i++ is shorthand for $i = $i + 1.

foreach loops, on the other hand, are ideal for iterating over lists or arrays. The syntax of a foreach loop is straightforward and expressive:

```
my @array = (1, 2, 3, 4, 5);
foreach my $element (@array) {
    print "Element: $element\n";
}
```

Here, @array contains a list of elements, and the loop iterates over each element, assigning it to $element on each iteration. The loop will continue until all elements in @array have been processed.

while loops are appropriate when the number of iterations isn't known upfront and the loop should continue running as long as a specified condition remains true:

```
my $counter = 0;
while ($counter < 5) {
    print "Counter is at: $counter\n";
    $counter++;
}
```

In this while loop, the condition $counter < 5 is evaluated before each iteration. As long as the condition is true, the loop body executes, incrementing $counter by 1 after each repetition. When $counter reaches 5, the loop terminates.

For scenarios where the loop should run until a certain condition becomes true, until loops are used. An until loop is essentially the opposite of a while loop:

```
my $countdown = 10;
until ($countdown == 0) {
    print "Countdown: $countdown\n";
    $countdown--;
}
```

In this example, the loop executes as long as the condition $countdown == 0 is not true. The variable $countdown is decremented by 1 in each iteration, and when it reaches 0, the loop stops.

Nested loops involve placing one loop inside another loop. They are useful in multidimensional data structures, for example, processing each row and column in a matrix. Consider the following nested for loops:

```
for my $i (0 .. 2) {
    for my $j (0 .. 2) {
        print "Processing element at row $i, column $j\n";
    }
}
```

Here, the outer loop iterates over the range 0 to 2, and for each iteration of the outer loop, the inner loop also iterates over the same range. Consequently, the total number of iterations is the product of the ranges of the two loops.

Loop control keywords such as next, last, and redo enhance the flexibility of loop constructs by altering the loop's flow. The next keyword is used to skip the rest of the current iteration and move to the next one:

```
for my $num (1 .. 10) {
    next if $num % 2 == 0; # Skip even numbers
    print "Odd number: $num\n";
}
```

The last keyword immediately exits the loop, irrespective of the loop condition:

```
my $i = 0;
while (1) {
    last if $i > 5; # Exit loop if $i greater than 5
    print "$i\n";
    $i++;
}
```

The redo keyword restarts the current iteration without evaluating the loop condition, useful in scenarios where you want to reprocess the same iteration:

```
my $j = 0;
while ($j < 5) {
    if ($j == 2) {
        $j++;
        redo;
    }
    print "$j\n";
    $j++;
}
```

In this example, redo causes the loop to reprint the value of $j immediately after incrementing it, effectively restarting the iteration.

Mastering these loop constructs and control keywords is fundamental for efficient scripting and automation in Perl, offering precise flow control and the ability to handle complex iterative processes.

4.7 for Loops

A for loop in Perl is a control structure that allows you to repeatedly execute a block of code for a specified number of times. This type of loop is especially useful when the number of iterations is known before entering the loop. The for loop in Perl is versatile and can be used in several ways to achieve iteration through lists, arrays, and ranges of numbers.

The syntax of the for loop is straightforward:

```
for (initialization; condition; increment) {
    # Block of code to be executed
}
```

The various components of the for loop syntax are:

- **Initialization**: This statement is used to set the initial condition of the loop and is executed once at the beginning of the loop. Typically, it involves the declaration and initialization of loop control variables.
- **Condition**: Before each iteration, the condition is evaluated. If the condition evaluates to true, the loop continues; if it evaluates to false, the loop terminates.
- **Increment**: This statement is executed at the end of each iteration and is typically used to update the loop control variables.

Consider the following example, which prints numbers from 0 to 9:

```
for (my $i = 0; $i < 10; $i++) {
    print "$i\n";
}
```

In this example:

- my $i = 0 initializes the loop control variable $i to 0.
- $i < 10 is the condition; the loop continues as long as $i is less than 10.
- $i++ increments the loop control variable by one after each iteration.

The output of this code is:

```
0
1
2
3
4
5
6
7
8
9
```

It is possible to omit the initialization, condition, or increment components if they are not needed. For example, the following loop iterates indefinitely because the condition is omitted:

```
for (;;) {
    print "This is an infinite loop\n";
    last; # Use 'last' to exit the loop
}
```

Here, the loop is exited with the last keyword to prevent an actual infinite loop during execution.

Looping through Lists and Arrays:

The for loop can also iterate through lists or arrays. This is sometimes referred to as the C-style for loop. The syntax and usage remain the same:

```
my @array = (1, 2, 3, 4, 5);
for (my $i = 0; $i < @array; $i++) {
    print "$array[$i]\n";
}
```

In this scenario:

- my @array = (1, 2, 3, 4, 5); initializes an array with five elements.
- for (my $i = 0; $i < @array; $i++) sets up the loop to iterate as long as $i is less than the number of elements in the array.
- Inside the loop, $array[$i] accesses each element of the array by index.

The output is:

```
1
2
3
4
5
```

Loop Modifiers:

Perl provides several loop control keywords that modify the behavior of loops. These include:

- last - Immediately exits the loop.
- next - Skips the remaining code in the current iteration and begins the next iteration.
- redo - Restarts the current iteration without evaluating the condition.

To illustrate these keywords, consider the following examples:

```
# Example using 'last'
for (my $i = 0; $i < 10; $i++) {
    last if $i == 5; # Exit loop when $i is 5
    print "$i\n";
}
```

The output ends prematurely:

```
0
1
2
3
4
```

```
# Example using 'next'
for (my $i = 0; $i < 10; $i++) {
    next if $i % 2; # Skip odd numbers
    print "$i\n";
}
```

The output includes only even numbers:

```
0
2
4
6
8
```

```
# Example using 'redo'
for (my $i = 0; $i < 10; $i++) {
    if ($i == 5) {
        $i--; # Adjust $i to redo the same iteration
        redo; # Restart the current iteration
    }
    print "$i\n";
}
```

The output reflects the redo action:

```
0
1
2
3
4
4
5
6
7
8
9
```

Understanding the for loop and its capabilities is essential for writing efficient and concise Perl code. These loops are fundamental tools that provide the requisite control to iterate through sequences and collections, ensuring that specific actions are repeated accurately based on defined criteria. Here is the corrected LaTeX text of the section with all errors fixed:

4.8 foreach Loops

The foreach loop in Perl provides a straightforward way to iterate over a list of values. This loop is particularly efficient when dealing with arrays or lists where each element needs to be processed in sequence. It is an excellent tool for performing repetitive tasks on datasets, ensuring the code remains readable and concise.

The basic syntax of the foreach loop is as follows:

```
foreach my $variable (@list) {
    # Code to execute for each element in the list
}
```

The @list represents the array or list to be iterated over, while $variable is the scalar variable that takes the value of each element in the list during each iteration. The block of code inside the curly braces {} is executed once for each element in the list. The my keyword is used to declare the loop variable's scope locally within the loop.

Consider the following example, which demonstrates the foreach loop by iterating through an array of numbers and printing each one:

```
my @numbers = (1, 2, 3, 4, 5);

foreach my $num (@numbers) {
    print "$num\n";
}
```

```
1
2
3
4
5
```

In this example, the @numbers array contains five elements. The foreach loop iterates over the array, assigning each element to the $num variable, and then prints it. The \n at the end of the print statement ensures that each number is printed on a new line.

The loop variable does not need to be newly declared within the foreach loop; it can be a previously existing variable. However, best practices in Perl recommend using my to avoid unintentional modification of previously declared variables and to limit the variable's scope to the loop.

Another example includes iterating over an array of strings and appending a suffix to each string:

```
my @words = ('apple', 'banana', 'cherry');

foreach my $word (@words) {
    $word .= '_fruit';
    print "$word\n";
}
```

```
apple_fruit
banana_fruit
cherry_fruit
```

Here, the foreach loop iterates through the @words array, appending '_fruit' to each element and printing the modified word.

The foreach loop can also work directly with the default variable $_, which implicitly holds each element of the list if no explicit loop variable is provided. This is illustrated in the example below:

```
foreach (@words) {
    $_ .= '_snack';
    print "$_\n";
}
```

```
apple_fruit_snack
banana_fruit_snack
cherry_fruit_snack
```

In this example, each element of the @words array is accessed via the $_ variable, making the code even more succinct.

When iterating over hashes, the foreach loop can be used in conjunction with the keys and values functions. For example, to iterate over the keys and values of a hash, a foreach loop can be used as follows:

```
my %fruit_colors = (
    apple => 'red',
```

```
    banana => 'yellow',
    cherry => 'red'
);

foreach my $key (keys %fruit_colors) {
    print "$key is $fruit_colors{$key}\n";
}
```

```
apple is red
banana is yellow
cherry is red
```

In this example, the keys function returns a list of keys from the %fruit_colors hash. The foreach loop iterates over these keys, and within the loop, we access the corresponding value using $fruit_colors{$key}.

The foreach loop also supports the use of complex expressions and function calls:

```
foreach my $elem (sort @numbers) {
    print "$elem\n";
}
```

```
1
2
3
4
5
```

In this instance, the sort @numbers expression sorts the @numbers array before the foreach loop iterates over this sorted list.

To control loop execution, Perl provides the next, last, and redo keywords. These can be used within a foreach loop to skip to the next iteration, exit the loop, or restart the loop block without advancing to the next element, respectively.

```
foreach my $number (1..10) {
    next if $number % 2; # Skip odd numbers
    print "$number\n";
}
```

```
2
4
6
8
10
```

In this code snippet, the next statement is used to skip odd numbers, printing only the even numbers from 1 to 10.

4.9 while Loops

The while loop is a fundamental construct in Perl used to repeatedly execute a block of code as long as a specified condition remains true. This construct allows for the execution of iterative operations, which are essential for tasks such as processing arrays, reading lines from files, and performing operations until a certain criterion is met.

The basic syntax of a while loop in Perl is as follows:

```
while (condition) {
    # Code to be executed while the condition is true
}
```

The condition is an expression that is evaluated before each iteration of the loop. If the condition evaluates to true, the code within the loop's block is executed. After the block has been executed, the condition is evaluated again, and this process repeats until the condition evaluates to false.

Consider the following example where we print numbers from 1 to 5:

```
my $count = 1;
while ($count <= 5) {
    print "$count\n";
    $count++;
}
```

```
1
2
3
4
5
```

In the example above, the variable $count is initialized to 1. The while loop checks if $count is less than or equal to 5. If true, it proceeds to execute the block where $count is printed and incremented. This continues until $count exceeds 5, causing the loop to terminate.

The while loop can also be used to read from input streams, such as from standard input or a file. Consider the following script, which reads lines from a file and prints them:

```
open(my $fh, '<', 'file.txt') or die "Cannot open file: \$!";
while (my $line = <$fh>) {
    print $line;
}
close($fh);
```

In this script, the while loop reads each line from the file handle $fh into the $line variable and then prints the line. The loop continues until there are no more lines to read, at which point <$fh> returns undef and the loop terminates.

Perl also supports the use of while modifiers to simplify code. A while modifier can be placed at the end of a statement. For example:

```
print "$_\n" while defined($_ = <STDIN>);
```

This reads from standard input and prints each line until there is no more input. The expression defined($_ = <STDIN >) ensures the loop continues as long as the input is defined.

Additionally, there are variations and enhancements to the while loop that provide more control over the execution flow. For instance, combining while with the last, next, and redo control keywords can manage the loop's behavior:

```
my $count = 1;
while ($count <= 10) {
    if ($count == 5) {
        $count++;
        next; # Skip the iteration when $count is 5
    }
    print "$count\n";
    $count++;
}
```

```
1
2
3
4
6
7
8
9
10
```

In this example, when $count equals 5, the next keyword skips the remainder of the loop block and proceeds directly with the next iteration. Consequently, the number 5 is not printed.

A common scenario involves nesting while loops to handle more complex data structures. Here is an example that processes a two-dimensional array:

```
my @array = (
    [1, 2, 3],
    [4, 5, 6],
    [7, 8, 9]
);

my $i = 0;
while ($i < @array) {
    my $j = 0;
    while ($j < @{$array[$i]}) {
```

```
        print $array[$i][$j] . " ";
        $j++;
    }
    print "\n";
    $i++;
}
```

```
1 2 3
4 5 6
7 8 9
```

In this nested while loop example, the outer loop iterates through each sub-array, while the inner loop iterates through the elements of each sub-array, printing them in a matrix format.

Understanding the nuances of while loops enhances the ability to create efficient and readable Perl scripts. This foundational construct is indispensable in scenarios requiring repeated execution based on dynamic conditions. Proper utilization of while loops, particularly in combination with other control structures and keywords, makes Perl programming more powerful and expressive.

4.10 until Loops

The until loop in Perl is a control structure that repeats a block of code until a specified condition is true. It is essentially the logical opposite of the while loop, which continues to execute as long as its condition remains true. The primary use case for until loops is when you want to execute a block of code as long as a condition is false.

The general syntax of an until loop is as follows:

```
until (condition) {
    # code block to be executed while condition is false
}
```

Within this syntax, the condition is a Perl expression that evaluates to a boolean value. The loop executes the code block repeatedly as long as the condition evaluates to false. Once the condition becomes true, the loop terminates.

Consider the following example that demonstrates an until loop counting from 1 to 5:

```
my $counter = 1;
until ($counter > 5) {
    print "Counter is at $counter\n";
    $counter++;
}
```

The output of this code will be:

```
Counter is at 1
Counter is at 2
Counter is at 3
Counter is at 4
Counter is at 5
```

In this example, the variable $counter is initially set to 1. During each iteration of the loop, the value of $counter is printed and then incremented by 1. The loop continues to execute until $counter exceeds 5. When $counter becomes 6, the until condition ($counter > 5) evaluates to true, and the loop terminates.

It is also possible to use the until loop in a postfix form. This can make the code more succinct and readable in scenarios where a simple operation is being performed repeatedly until a condition is met. The postfix syntax is written as follows:

```
print "Counter is at $counter\n" until $counter++ > 5;
```

This line achieves the same result as the previous example but condenses the loop into a single line. The block of code to execute is placed before the until, followed by the condition.

Another common usage of the until loop is in handling input. For example, you might want to keep prompting a user for input until they enter valid data:

```
my $input = "";
until ($input eq "exit") {
    print "Enter a command (type 'exit' to quit): ";
    $input = <STDIN>;
    chomp($input);
    print "You entered: $input\n";
}
```

Here, the user is prompted to enter a command repeatedly until they type the word "exit". Each entry is read from standard input, the newline character is removed using chomp, and the input is then printed back to the user. When the user types "exit", the until condition ($input eq "exit") evaluates to true, terminating the loop.

It is important to pay attention to the logic of the until condition to avoid creating infinite loops. Consider the following faulty example:

```
my $number = 10;
until ($number < 0) {
    print "$number\n";
}
```

In this scenario, the loop will execute indefinitely because the value of $number is never modified within the loop, leading to the condition ($number < 0) never becoming true. Always ensure that the condition will eventually be met by modifying the relevant variables appropriately within the loop.

The until loop can also be nested within other loops and control structures to create more complex programs. For instance, consider a scenario where you want to ask the user for numbers until they enter zero and then print those numbers until a sum exceeds a certain value:

```
my @numbers;
my $input;

# Collect numbers until the user enters zero
do {
    print "Enter a number (0 to finish): ";
    $input = <STDIN>;
    chomp($input);
    push(@numbers, $input) unless $input == 0;
} until ($input == 0);

# Print numbers until the sum exceeds 50
my $sum = 0;
foreach my $num (@numbers) {
    print "$num\n";
    $sum += $num;
    last if $sum > 50;
}
```

In this example, numbers are collected from the user and stored in an array until the user enters zero. Then, the numbers are printed in sequence until the cumulative sum of the numbers exceeds 50, demonstrating a practical nested utilization of the until loop within the broader context of Perl control structures.

4.11 Loop Control Keywords

Perl provides several loop control keywords that help manage the flow of loops. These keywords can drastically alter the behavior of loops by prematurely terminating, skipping parts of the iteration, or restarting the loop. The primary keywords involved in loop control are last, next, and redo. Understanding how and when to use these keywords is crucial for mastering the control of iterative processes in Perl programming.

The last Keyword

The last keyword functions similarly to the break statement in languages like C or Java. It immediately exits the loop, regardless of the loop's condition. The last keyword is particularly useful when a certain condition is met, and continuing the loop would be unnecessary or inefficient.

```
#!/usr/bin/perl
use strict;
use warnings;

my @array = (1, 2, 3, 4, 5);

foreach my $element (@array) {
    if ($element == 3) {
        last; # Exit the loop when $element is 3
    }
    print "$element\n";
}
```

In this example, the loop terminates when the variable $element equals 3, resulting in the output:

```
1
2
```

The next Keyword

The next keyword in Perl is equivalent to the continue statement in other programming languages. It causes the loop to skip the remainder of its block and immediately start the next iteration. This is useful for skipping over certain elements or conditions within the loop without exiting the loop completely.

```
#!/usr/bin/perl
use strict;
use warnings;

my @array = (1, 2, 3, 4, 5);

foreach my $element (@array) {
    if ($element % 2 == 0) {
        next; # Skip even numbers
    }
    print "$element\n";
}
```

The output of this script will skip the even numbers:

```
1
3
5
```

The redo Keyword

The redo keyword is somewhat unique to Perl, as it restarts the current iteration of the loop without testing the conditional statement again. This can be beneficial in situations where an iteration needs to be re-evaluated after correcting an error or handling a specific special case.

```
#!/usr/bin/perl
use strict;
use warnings;

my @array = (1, 2, 'error', 4, 5);

foreach my $element (@array) {
    if ($element eq 'error') {
        print "Error found. Redo the iteration.\n";
        $element = 3; # Correct the error
        redo;
    }
    print "$element\n";
}
```

The script detects a specific error condition, corrects it, and then redoes the current iteration, resulting in:

```
1
2
Error found. Redo the iteration.
3
4
5
```

Combining Loop Control Keywords

Perl also allows the combined use of these loop control keywords with labels. Labels are prefixed with a double colon and can help explicitly define which loop the control keywords should affect, especially in nested loops.

```
#!/usr/bin/perl
use strict;
use warnings;

my @matrix = (
    [1, 2, 3],
    [4, 'stop', 6],
    [7, 8, 9]
);

OUTER: foreach my $row (@matrix) {
    INNER: foreach my $element (@$row) {
        if ($element eq 'stop') {
            last OUTER; # Exit both loops
        }
        print "$element ";
    }
    print "\n";
}
```

By labeling the loops, the last keyword can be explicitly directed to terminate the OUTER loop, giving greater control over nested iterative structures. The output is:

Understanding and utilizing these loop control keywords enables efficient and effective flow control in Perl scripts, enhancing the programmer's ability to handle complex looping requirements with precision.

4.12 Nested Control Structures

Nested control structures in Perl are a powerful tool for creating complex logical flows within a program. They allow one control structure to be placed within another, leading to multifaceted conditions and loops that can accomplish sophisticated tasks.

At the core of nested control structures are the same fundamental elements discussed earlier in this chapter: conditional statements (such as if-else and unless) and looping constructs (like for, foreach, while, and until). When these elements are combined in a nested fashion, they enhance the script's ability to handle multiple layers of decision-making and iterative processes.

Consider first an example of nested if-else statements. Nested conditional statements are particularly useful when a decision depends on more than one condition.

```
#!/usr/bin/perl
use strict;
use warnings;

my $a = 10;
my $b = 20;

if ($a < $b) {
    print "a is less than b\n";
    if ($b > 15) {
        print "b is greater than 15\n";
    }
    else {
        print "b is not greater than 15\n";
    }
}
else {
    print "a is not less than b\n";
}
```

The outer if checks if $a is less than $b. If true, the code prints a is less than b and then proceeds to the inner if-else which further evaluates whether $b is greater than 15. This nesting allows for a more granular control over the conditions. The logical separation between the checks provides clarity and precision in the structure of the code.

Nested looping constructs are equally powerful. Here's an example where a for loop contains a nested while loop:

```
#!/usr/bin/perl
use strict;
use warnings;

for (my $i = 0; $i < 3; $i++) {
    print "Outer loop iteration: $i\n";
    my $j = 0;
    while ($j < 2) {
        print " Inner loop iteration: $j\n";
        $j++;
    }
}
```

In this example, the outer for loop runs three times. For each iteration of the outer loop, the inner while loop runs twice, printing the current iteration indices of both loops. This kind of structure can be used to traverse multidimensional datasets where each dimension requires a separate looping construct.

Let us now consider a scenario involving nested for loops where we need to traverse a two-dimensional array:

```
#!/usr/bin/perl
use strict;
use warnings;

my @matrix = (
    [1, 2, 3],
    [4, 5, 6],
    [7, 8, 9]
);

for (my $i = 0; $i < scalar @matrix; $i++) {
    for (my $j = 0; $j < scalar @{$matrix[$i]}; $j++) {
        print "Element [$i][$j]: $matrix[$i][$j]\n";
    }
}
```

In this program, we define a 2D array @matrix and utilize nested for loops to access each element. The outer loop iterates over rows, and the inner loop iterates over columns within each row. Such iterations are fundamental in applications that involve grid-based computations, such as image processing or matrix arithmetic.

Nested control structures are also deeply intertwined with loop control keywords such as next, last, and redo. Consider the following example:

```
#!/usr/bin/perl
use strict;
use warnings;

for (my $i = 0; $i < 4; $i++) {
```

```
    print "Outer loop: $i\n";
    for (my $j = 0; $j < 4; $j++) {
        if ($j == 2) {
            next;
        }
        print " Inner loop: $j\n";
    }
}
```

In this script, the inner loop skips the iteration where $j equals 2, continuing with the next value of $j. Such behavior is instrumental when certain conditions dictate the need to bypass iterations without breaking out of the loop entirely.

Finally, here is an illustration combining if statements with nested foreach loops:

```
#!/usr/bin/perl
use strict;
use warnings;

my @list1 = qw(a b c);
my @list2 = qw(1 2 3);

foreach my $element1 (@list1) {
    print "list1 element: $element1\n";
    foreach my $element2 (@list2) {
        if ($element2 == 2) {
            last;
        }
        print " list2 element: $element2\n";
    }
}
```

In this code, the inner foreach loop stops iterating when $element2 is 2 due to the last statement, which exits the smallest enclosing loop. This selective control is essential when working with nested data structures or conditions that require breaking out of loops based on specific criteria.

Mastering nested control structures is pivotal for writing efficient and understandable Perl programs, enabling complex logic implementations with clear, structured code.

Chapter 5

Subroutines and Functions

This chapter delves into subroutines and functions, explaining how to define, call, and pass arguments to subroutines in Perl. It covers the use of private variables, the 'my' and 'local' keywords, subroutine prototypes, and variable-length parameter lists. The chapter also addresses handling exceptions, recursion, and the differences between built-in functions and user-defined functions, providing a thorough understanding of modular Perl programming.

5.1 Introduction to Subroutines

In Perl programming, subroutines, also known as functions, are essential constructs that enable code modularity and reusability. A subroutine is a discrete block of code that performs a specific task and can be invoked from different parts of the program, allowing for better organization and management of code.

A subroutine in Perl is defined using the sub keyword, followed by an optional name and a block of code encapsulated within curly braces {}. The basic syntax for defining a subroutine is as follows:

```
sub subroutine_name {
    # code to be executed
}
```

Subroutines are not required to have a name; anonymous subroutines are also permissible in Perl, providing greater flexibility. An anonymous subroutine can be assigned to a variable for later execution:

```
my $anonymous_sub = sub {
    # code to be executed
};
```

Subroutines can be invoked or called from any part of the program using their name followed by parentheses. When a subroutine is called, the code within it executes, and control returns to the point where the call was made after execution:

```
subroutine_name();
```

One of the key advantages of using subroutines is the ability to divide a program into smaller, manageable units. This approach not only makes the code easier to understand but also facilitates debugging and testing. Furthermore, subroutines allow for code reuse, reducing redundancy. Code reuse is an important practice in programming as it enhances efficiency by minimizing the need to write the same code multiple times.

Subroutines can accept arguments, which are passed to them at the time of calling. These arguments are accessible within the subroutine via the special array @_, where each element corresponds to an argument passed:

```
sub greet {
    my ($name) = @_;
    print "Hello, $name!\n";
}

greet("Alice"); # Output: Hello, Alice!
```

In the example above, the subroutine greet accepts a single argument, name, and prints a greeting message. The @_ array holds the argument value, allowing it to be accessed and used within the subroutine.

It is crucial in Perl to understand the difference between the my and local keywords when dealing with variables inside subroutines. The my keyword creates private variables that are lexically scoped, meaning they are accessible only within the block where they are declared. On the other hand, the local keyword temporarily backs up the value of a global variable and restores it when the block exits, making changes to the variable only visible within the block.

Subroutines can also return values to the calling code using the return keyword, which explicitly specifies the value to be returned:

```
sub add {
    my ($a, $b) = @_;
    return $a + $b;
}

my $sum = add(2, 3); # $sum now holds the value 5
```

If the return keyword is omitted, the subroutine returns the value of the last evaluated expression. This feature is common in Perl and aligns with its context-sensitive behavior.

In summary, subroutines introduce a structured approach to organize code into functional units, significantly improving readability, maintainability, and reusability. Mastery of subroutines and their underlying principles is fundamental for any Perl programmer aiming to write efficient and modular Perl scripts. This foundation paves the way for leveraging more advanced features such as subroutine prototypes, variable-length parameter lists, and exception handling in subsequent sections.

5.2 Defining a Subroutine

To define a subroutine in Perl, the ‘sub‘ keyword is used followed by the subroutine name and a block of code within curly braces. This structure defines a subroutine that can be called later in the program to perform a specific task. A well-defined subroutine improves code modularity, readability, and reusability. The syntax is as follows:

```
sub subroutine_name {
  # Code to be executed by the subroutine
}
```

For example, a simple subroutine named greet that prints a greeting message can be defined as:

```
sub greet {
  print "Hello, world!\n";
}
```

Once a subroutine is defined, it can be invoked using its name followed by parentheses:

```
greet();
```

When this code is executed, the output will be:

```
Hello, world!
```

Subroutines in Perl can also return values. The 'return' keyword is used to specify the value to be returned to the caller. If no 'return' statement is provided, the last evaluated expression is returned by default. Consider the following subroutine that calculates and returns the sum of two numbers:

```
sub add {
  my ($a, $b) = @_;
  return $a + $b;
}

my $result = add(2, 3);
print "The sum is: $result\n";
```

In this example, the subroutine add takes two arguments, computes their sum, and returns the result. The output will be:

```
The sum is: 5
```

Perl also allows subroutine definitions to be anonymous. An anonymous subroutine is a subroutine without a name and is often used in dynamic contexts where a subroutine needs to be created on the fly, such as in higher-order programming or passing to other functions.

```
my $multiply = sub {
  my ($x, $y) = @_;
  return $x * $y;
};

print "Product: ", $multiply->(4, 5), "\n";
```

Here, the $multiply variable holds a reference to an anonymous subroutine that multiplies two numbers. The subroutine is called using the arrow operator '->', and the output is:

```
Product: 20
```

Subroutines in Perl can encapsulate complex functionalities and be reused across different parts of the program. Consider the following example, where a subroutine named factorial is defined to compute the factorial of a number recursively:

```
sub factorial {
  my ($n) = @_;
  if ($n == 0) {
    return 1;
  } else {
    return $n * factorial($n - 1);
  }
}

my $fact = factorial(5);
print "Factorial of 5 is: $fact\n";
```

The factorial subroutine calls itself recursively until the base case ($n == 0) is met. The output will be:

```
Factorial of 5 is: 120
```

When defining subroutines, it is important to understand the scope of the variables used. Using 'my' within a subroutine ensures that the variables are private to that subroutine, preventing unintended side effects in other parts of the program. Here is an example to illustrate the use of private variables within a subroutine:

```
sub increment {
  my $value = shift;
  my $result = $value + 1;
  return $result;
}

my $number = 10;
my $new_number = increment($number);
print "Original number: $number, Incremented number: $new_number\n";
```

In this example, the variable $value and $result are private to the increment subroutine due to the 'my' keyword. This ensures that changes to these variables do not affect other parts of the program. The output will be:

```
Original number: 10, Incremented number: 11
```

By clearly defining the structure and scope of subroutines, Perl allows developers to build organized and maintainable code. Properly defined subroutines serve as the fundamental building blocks for creating complex and efficient software systems.

5.3 Calling a Subroutine

Calling a subroutine in Perl is a fundamental operation that allows the reuse of code, making programs more modular and easier to maintain. A subroutine is invoked using its name, followed by optional arguments enclosed in parentheses. The simplest case of calling a subroutine involves merely using its name without any arguments:

```
greet();
```

This will call the greet subroutine, assuming it has been defined prior to this call. If the subroutine requires arguments, they can be passed inside the parentheses. For instance, consider a subroutine say_hello that prints a greeting:

```
sub say_hello {
    my ($name) = @_;
    print "Hello, $name!\n";
}

say_hello("Alice"); # This will print "Hello, Alice!"
```

Here, the subroutine say_hello is called with a single argument "Alice". The subroutine receives this argument in the special array @_, which is the default array for passing parameters to functions. In the example, my ($name) = @_; assigns the first element of @_ to the $name variable.

When calling subroutines, parentheses are optional if the subroutine has been declared before the point of invocation and there are no arguments:

```
greet; # Parentheses are optional for calling greet if it's already declared
```

However, for readability and to avoid ambiguity, it is good practice to use parentheses.

Subroutines can also be called using the & prefix. This was more common in older Perl code but is still supported:

```
&greet();
&say_hello("Bob");
```

One must be cautious when using the & operator. If parentheses are omitted after the & operator, Perl will pass the current @_ array implicitly:

```
sub display_items {
    foreach my $item (@_) {
        print "$item\n";
    }
}

@fruits = ("apple", "banana", "cherry");

&display_items; # Implicitly passes @_
```

In the snippet above, &display_items is called without parentheses, which results in the @_ of the current context being passed to the subroutine. It is advisable to avoid this form unless this behavior is specifically desired, as it can lead to unexpected results.

If a subroutine exists within another package, it is called by qualifying the subroutine name with the package name:

```
Package::subroutine_name();
```

Suppose we have a package MathOperations with a subroutine add:

```
package MathOperations;

sub add {
    my ($a, $b) = @_;
    return $a + $b;
}

package main;

my $sum = MathOperations::add(5, 3);
print "Sum: $sum\n"; # Outputs: Sum: 8
```

This fully-qualified name MathOperations::add ensures that the add subroutine from the MathOperations package is called, not from any other package.

Perl also supports function references, enabling subroutines to be called indirectly:

```
my $ref = \&say_hello;
$ref->("Charlie"); # This prints "Hello, Charlie!"
```

The above code snippet captures a reference to the say_hello subroutine in the $ref variable. The subroutine is then called indirectly using the -> operator.

For scenarios involving dynamic subroutine invocation based on the subroutine's name as a string, the use of the {} brackets with & is necessary:

```
my $sub_name = "say_hello";
&{$sub_name}("David"); # Prints "Hello, David!"
```

This approach is useful for situations where a subroutine's name might be determined at runtime.

By understanding the various ways to call subroutines in Perl, programmers can write flexible and maintainable code.

5.4 Passing Arguments to Subroutines

In Perl, arguments can be passed to subroutines in a straightforward manner. When calling a subroutine, the arguments are provided in parentheses following the subroutine name. These arguments are subsequently accessible within the subroutine via the special array $_. For example, consider the following Perl subroutine call:

```
sub example_sub {
    # Code to handle arguments
}

example_sub($arg1, $arg2, $arg3);
```

Within the example_sub subroutine, the arguments $arg1, $arg2, and $arg3 are accessible through $_[0], $_[1], and $_[2] respectively. Here is an extended example demonstrating this concept:

```
sub print_details {
    my ($name, $age, $occupation) = @_;
    print "Name: $name\n";
    print "Age: $age\n";
    print "Occupation: $occupation\n";
}

print_details('Alice', 30, 'Engineer');
```

In the above example, the subroutine print_details is designed to receive three arguments. Inside the subroutine, these arguments are extracted from the $_ array into more descriptively named variables using the list assignment. This effectively enhances the code's readability.

When the print_details subroutine is called with the arguments 'Alice', 30, and 'Engineer', the following output is generated:

```
Name: Alice
Age: 30
Occupation: Engineer
```

This demonstrates a clear and structured way to pass and access arguments within subroutines.

Handling Arbitrary Numbers of Arguments

Perl subroutines are inherently flexible, meaning they can handle an arbitrary number of arguments without requiring explicit prototypes. The $_ array can be directly iterated or processed, making the subroutine adaptable to varying input sizes. Here's an example of a subroutine that prints an arbitrary number of arguments:

```
sub print_all_arguments {
    foreach my $arg (@_) {
        print "Argument: $arg\n";
    }
}

print_all_arguments('apple', 'banana', 'cherry');
```

This will produce:

```
Argument: apple
Argument: banana
Argument: cherry
```

Such flexibility is particularly useful in scenarios where subroutine input may vary significantly, ensuring that the code remains robust and adaptable.

Using Hashes and Arrays as Arguments

Passing complex data structures like hashes and arrays to subroutines is a common necessity in Perl scripts. Perl facilitates this by allowing entire hash and array references to be passed as scalar values. Here is an example of passing an array reference:

```
sub print_array_elements {
    my ($array_ref) = @_;
    foreach my $element (@$array_ref) {
        print "Element: $element\n";
    }
}

my @fruits = ('apple', 'banana', 'cherry');
print_array_elements(\@fruits);
```

In this scenario, print_array_elements receives a reference to the fruits array. The array reference is accessed using the dereference operator ($array_ref), allowing the subroutine to iterate through the array elements.

Similarly, hashes can be passed using hash references:

```
sub print_hash_entries {
    my ($hash_ref) = @_;
    foreach my $key (keys %$hash_ref) {
        print "Key: $key, Value: $hash_ref->{$key}\n";
    }
}

my %person = (name => 'Alice', age => 30, occupation => 'Engineer');
print_hash_entries(\%person);
```

The subroutine print_hash_entries receives a reference to the %person hash. By dereferencing the hash reference (%$hash_ref), the subroutine accesses and prints each key-value pair.

Positional vs. Named Arguments

While passing positional arguments in lists is straightforward, it can sometimes lead to ambiguity, especially when dealing with numerous parameters. Named arguments can enhance clarity, avoiding confusion about the meaning of individual arguments. Named arguments are typically implemented by passing a hash or a hash reference, as shown below:

```
sub print_person_details {
    my %args = @_;
    print "Name: $args{name}\n";
    print "Age: $args{age}\n";
    print "Occupation: $args{occupation}\n";
}

print_person_details(name => 'Alice', age => 30, occupation => 'Engineer');
```

This method results in clearer and more maintainable subroutine calls, making the code easier to understand.

In the preceding example, print_person_details receives a hash containing named arguments. These arguments are accessed using their respective keys, which enhances code readability and makes the subroutine invocations more intuitive.

The various techniques for passing arguments to subroutines in Perl, ranging from simple positional arguments to more complex data structures and named arguments, provide Perl developers with powerful tools for writing modular, maintainable, and flexible code. The choice of method largely depends on the specific context and the desired clarity of the subroutine's interface.

5.5 Returning Values from Subroutines

In Perl, a subroutine can return values to the calling context using the return keyword. This feature enhances the reusability and modularity of code by allowing subroutines to compute results and hand them back to the part of the program that called them. Understanding the mechanisms for returning values from subroutines is crucial for effective Perl programming.

return can be used in different contexts and manners. By default, if a subroutine reaches the end without encountering an explicit return statement, it returns the value of the last expression evaluated. However, utilizing return makes the intention more explicit and often improves code readability.

```
sub add {
    my ($a, $b) = @_;
    return $a + $b;
}
```

In this example, the subroutine add takes two arguments and returns their sum. The return statement explicitly specifies the value to be returned.

Contexts of return

Perl subroutines can be used in different contexts: list, scalar, and void. The context in which a subroutine is called influences how the return value is interpreted.

When called in a scalar context, the expression returned is evaluated in a scalar context:

```
my $sum = add(2, 3); # $sum is now 5
```

In a list context, the subroutine can return a list of values:

```
sub create_list {
    my @list = (1, 2, 3, 4, 5);
    return @list;
}

my @numbers = create_list(); # @numbers is (1, 2, 3, 4, 5)
```

Returning an array in a list context encapsulates multiple values within a single return operation.

Scalar vs List Context

The ability to return different values based on the calling context makes Perl subroutines flexible. The wantarray function can be used within a subroutine to determine the context of the return.

```
sub list_or_scalar {
    return wantarray ? (1, 2, 3) : "scalar context";
}

my @array = list_or_scalar(); # @array is now (1, 2, 3)
my $scalar = list_or_scalar(); # $scalar is now "scalar context"
```

The wantarray function returns true if the subroutine is called in a list context, false if in a scalar context, and undef if in a void context.

Returning References

To return complex data structures such as arrays or hashes from a subroutine while maintaining simplicity in scalar context, references can be employed.

```
sub array_ref {
    my @array = (1, 2, 3);
    return \@array;
}

my $array_ref = array_ref(); # $array_ref is a reference to [1, 2, 3]
```

Utilizing references ensures that the returned data structure is treated as a single scalar value, making it easier to manage and manipulate.

Multiple Values

Perl subroutines can return multiple values directly, but the values are returned as a list, which can be captured into individual variables or an array.

```
sub split_name {
    my $full_name = shift;
    my ($first_name, $last_name) = split(' ', $full_name);
    return ($first_name, $last_name);
}

my ($first, $last) = split_name("John Doe"); # $first = 'John', $last = 'Doe'
```

Returning multiple values is useful for decomposing composite data into separate components.

Omitting return

When return is omitted, the subroutine implicitly returns the value of the last evaluated expression.

```
sub multiply {
    my ($x, $y) = @_;
    $x * $y; # Implicitly returns $x * $y
}

my $product = multiply(4, 5); # $product is now 20
```

While this can make the code more concise, explicit return statements are often preferred for clarity.

Understanding the nuances of returning values from subroutines enhances the ability to create versatile and reusable code components in Perl. Subroutines that effectively communicate their outcomes improve both maintainability and readability of the code.

5.6 Private Variables and the 'my' Keyword

In Perl, the use of private variables within subroutines is crucial for encapsulation and to prevent unintended interference with variables outside the subroutine. The my keyword is used to declare these private variables, restricting their scope to the enclosing block, file, or eval. This section explores the functionality and application of the my keyword, illustrating how to effectively utilize it to create private variables within subroutines.

When a variable is declared with the my keyword, it is confined to the scope in which it is defined. This means the variable cannot be accessed or modified outside of the block where it was declared. The syntax for declaring a private variable with my is as follows:

```
my $variable = value;
```

Consider the following example, which demonstrates the use of a private variable within a subroutine:

```
sub calculate_sum {
    my ($num1, $num2) = @_;
    my $sum = $num1 + $num2;
    return $sum;
}

my $result = calculate_sum(10, 5);
print "The sum is $result\n";
```

In this example, the variables $num1, $num2, and $sum are all declared using my, restricting their visibility to the calculate_sum subroutine. The variable $result is declared outside the subroutine and holds the returned value from the subroutine call. Thus, any attempt to access $num1, $num2, or $sum outside of the calculate_sum subroutine will result in an error because these variables do not exist in that scope.

The scoping rules for my can span across different constructs such as loops, conditionals, and other nested blocks. For instance:

```
sub iterate_and_sum {
    my (@numbers) = @_;
    my $total = 0;
    for my $num (@numbers) {
        $total += $num;
    }
    return $total;
}

my @values = (1, 2, 3, 4, 5);
my $sum = iterate_and_sum(@values);
print "The total sum is $sum\n";
```

Here, @numbers and $total are private to the iterate_and_sum subroutine, and $num is private to the for loop. The variable $num is redeclared for each iteration of the loop, and its scope is limited to within the loop itself.

Private variables can also be utilized in creating closures. A closure is a subroutine that captures variables from its scope at the time of its definition and retains access to those variables even when the scope has exited. Here is an example:

```
sub generate_counter {
    my $count = 0;
    return sub {
        $count += 1;
        return $count;
    };
}

my $counter1 = generate_counter();
print $counter1->(); # prints 1
print $counter1->(); # prints 2

my $counter2 = generate_counter();
print $counter2->(); # prints 1
```

In this code, generate_counter returns an anonymous subroutine (a closure) that increments the private variable $count each time it is called. The variable $count retains its state across calls to the inner anonymous subroutine but is kept private and cannot be accessed directly from outside.

Understanding the my keyword is fundamental for preventing accidental modification of variables and ensuring the robustness of the code. It promotes better coding practices by enforcing variable scope and reducing the risk of variable name collisions.

By using my to declare private variables within subroutines or other blocks, Perl programmers can achieve modular, reliable, and maintainable code.

5.7 Using local for Temporary Values

In Perl, the local keyword is utilized to temporarily override the value of a global variable within a designated dynamic scope, usually within a subroutine. This distinction is particularly critical in understanding how local differs from my, which restricts variable scope to the lexical block. The typical use case for local is to temporarily modify global variables like special variables ($_, _, etc.) or variables in other packages, without affecting the entire program execution.

The local keyword operates by saving the current value of a global variable and restoring it once the execution exits the scope where local is applied. This saving mechanism allows one to modify global state temporarily without permanent side effects.

Consider the following example, where the global package variable

$var is temporarily changed within a subroutine:

```
# Global variable
our $var = "Global";

sub modify_variable {
    local $var = "Local";
    print "Inside subroutine: $var\n"; # Outputs "Local"
}

print "Before subroutine: $var\n"; # Outputs "Global"
modify_variable();
print "After subroutine: $var\n"; # Outputs "Global"
```

```
Before subroutine: Global
Inside subroutine: Local
After subroutine: Global
```

The local keyword confines the temporary change to the dynamic scope of modify_variable, thus preserving the original global state before the subroutine call and automatically restoring it after execution completes.

One of the classic scenarios for local is manipulating special variables like $_, @_, and $/, which are used extensively by Perl's built-in functions. For instance, $/, the input record separator, can be localized to allow the reading of files in different modes within a subroutine:

```
sub read_paragraph {
    local $/ = "\n\n"; # Paragraph mode
    open my $fh, '<', 'file.txt' or die $!;
    while (my $paragraph = <$fh>) {
        print $paragraph;
    }
    close $fh;
}

# Outside the subroutine, the input record separator remains default
open my $fh, '<', 'file.txt' or die $!;
while (my $line = <$fh>) {
    print $line;
}
close $fh;
```

In this example, the input record separator $/ is set to "\n\n" (paragraph mode) within the read_paragraph subroutine. Outside this subroutine, $/ retains its default value of "\n", demonstrating localized changes without affecting the global state.

Another common usage is within exception handling blocks, where local modifies global special variables like $@, which holds error messages from eval blocks:

```
sub handle_exception {
    local $@;
    eval {
        die "An error occurred!";
```

```
    };
    if ($@) {
        print "Caught error: $@";
    }
}

handle_exception();
print "End of program\n";
```

Here, local $@ ensures that changes to $@ within the eval block do not persist beyond the subroutine, thereby maintaining the integrity of global error handling elsewhere in the program.

It is important to note that local applies to dynamic scoping, which differs from lexical scoping provided by my. Dynamic scoping considers the call stack, affecting all functions called from that point onward within the same dynamic scope, whereas lexical scoping is confined to the block where the variable is declared:

```
our $var = "Global";

sub outer {
    local $var = "Outer"; # Dynamic scope
    inner();
}

sub inner {
    print "Inside inner: $var\n"; # Affected by outer's local declaration
}

outer(); # Calls inner
print "Outside: $var\n"; # Outputs "Global"
```

```
Inside inner: Outer
Outside: Global
```

The use of local in the outer subroutine temporarily affects $var within the dynamic scope, including the execution of inner, demonstrating its utility for managing global states dynamically without affecting the broader program behavior beyond the specified scope.

5.8 Subroutine Prototypes

Subroutine prototypes in Perl provide a way to explicitly define the expected types and number of arguments for a subroutine. They allow the Perl interpreter to enforce context and argument count, thereby reducing the risk of errors. Prototypes can also influence how the arguments are passed to the subroutine.

A subroutine prototype is defined by specifying a string of special characters that represent argument types, placed in parentheses immediately after the subroutine name in the definition. Here are a few of the most commonly used characters in prototypes:

- `$` : Indicates a scalar value.
- `@` : Indicates an array.
- `%` : Indicates a hash.
- `&` : Indicates a subroutine reference.
- `*` : Indicates a typeglob (a reference to all symbol table entries of a given name).
- `;` : Separates mandatory arguments from optional ones.

Consider the following example to understand how subroutine prototypes work:

```
sub example_prototype($$@) {
    my ($mandatory_scalar1, $mandatory_scalar2, @optional_array) = @_;
    print "First scalar: $mandatory_scalar1\n";
    print "Second scalar: $mandatory_scalar2\n";
    print "Optional array: @optional_array\n";
}
```

In this example, `example_prototype` expects two mandatory scalar arguments followed by an optional array. The prototype `($$@)` ensures that the Perl interpreter enforces this argument structure.

When calling this subroutine, the argument list must conform to the specified prototype:

```
example_prototype('Hello', 'World', 1, 2, 3);
```

The output will be:

```
First scalar: Hello
Second scalar: World
Optional array: 1 2 3
```

Violating the prototype, such as passing fewer arguments than required, will result in an error.

Another important utility of prototypes is to influence the context in which their arguments are evaluated. For instance, consider a prototype that enforces scalar context:

```
sub sum_squared($$) {
    my ($a, $b) = @_;
```

```
    return ($a ** 2) + ($b ** 2);
}
```

The invocation of `sum_squared(3, 4)` expects precisely two scalar values, any deviation from this will result in context warnings or errors.

It's also possible to define prototypes for subroutines that can accept a variable number of scalars. Consider the following example:

```
sub average($@) {
    my ($count, @nums) = @_;
    my $sum;
    $sum += $_ for @nums;
    return $sum / $count;
}
```

Here, the prototype `($@)` means the subroutine expects one mandatory scalar followed by a list of values. This can be invoked as:

```
print average(4, 10, 20, 30, 40);
```

The output will be:

```
25
```

This illustrates how prototypes help structure the argument list, improving readability and reducing the chance of runtime errors.

Prototypes also facilitate the creation of subroutines that mimic the behavior of Perl built-in functions. Consider a subroutine designed to fetch the last element of an array, similar to the built-in `pop` function:

```
sub pop_like(\@) {
    my $array_ref = shift;
    return pop @$array_ref;
}
```

The reference `\@` prototype enforces that `pop_like` must be passed an array reference, ensuring that it operates as intended. The function can be called as follows:

```
my @array = (1, 2, 3, 4);
print pop_like(@array);
```

Resulting in the output:

```
4
```

This output demonstrates the subroutine's adherence to the expected behavior similar to `pop`, but within a user-defined context.

While prototypes can significantly enhance the robustness of your subroutines, they should be applied judiciously. Incorrect or overly rigid prototypes can constrain flexibility, potentially leading to an increased frequency of runtime errors or awkward coding patterns. Thorough testing is advised to ensure that the application of prototypes benefits the specific use cases of your Perl scripts.

5.9 Variable-Length Parameter Lists

In Perl, subroutines can be designed to accept a variable number of parameters, offering a more flexible approach compared to fixed parameter lists. This capability is particularly advantageous when dealing with functions that need to handle an unknown number or various types of input data.

To define a subroutine with variable-length parameter lists, Perl employs the special array $_, which captures all the arguments passed to the subroutine. This array provides developers the ability to dynamically access and manipulate each parameter. Consider the following example:

```
#!/usr/bin/perl
use strict;
use warnings;

sub print_values {
    foreach my $value (@_) {
        print "$value\n";
    }
}

print_values(1, 2, 3, 4, 5);
```

In this illustration, the subroutine print_values can accept any number of arguments. Here, @_ captures the integers 1 through 5, and each value is printed in a new line. Execution of this script produces:

```
1
2
3
4
5
```

When dealing with variable-length argument lists, it is often necessary to discern between different types or groups of arguments. Perl allows for array, scalar, hash, and reference parameters, enabling complex argument structures. For instance, consider a subroutine that computes the sum of a list of numbers:

```
#!/usr/bin/perl
```

```
use strict;
use warnings;

sub compute_sum {
    my $sum = 0;
    $sum += $_ for @_;
    return $sum;
}

my $total = compute_sum(10, 20, 30, 40);
print "Sum: $total\n";
```

The compute_sum subroutine aggregates the values passed through @_, returning the computed sum. Given the arguments 10, 20, 30, and 40, the output is:

```
Sum: 100
```

Further managing variable-length parameter lists can involve parsing the arguments based on positional or named parameters. A common convention is to use key-value pairs, typically passed as a hash:

```
#!/usr/bin/perl
use strict;
use warnings;

sub print_user_info {
    my %args = @_;
    print "Name: $args{name}\n";
    print "Age: $args{age}\n";
    print "Email: $args{email}\n";
}

print_user_info(
    name => 'John Doe',
    age => 30,
    email => 'john.doe@example.com'
);
```

This subroutine allows passing an arbitrary number of arguments in key-value pairs, making the parameter list more readable and maintainable. The execution of the script yields:

```
Name: John Doe
Age: 30
Email: john.doe@example.com
```

Considering performance, parameter handling using @_ does not incur significant overhead in most practical scenarios. Nevertheless, when operating with an exceedingly large number of parameters or in performance-critical applications, the overhead of copying @_ into another array or hash should be assessed. Employing references for arrays or hashes can mitigate such performance concerns:

```
#!/usr/bin/perl
```

```
use strict;
use warnings;

sub process_data {
    my ($data_ref) = @_;
    foreach my $item (@$data_ref) {
        print "$item\n";
    }
}

my @data = (1, 2, 3, 4, 5);
process_data(\@data);
```

In this variant, process_data accepts a reference to an array, thus circumventing the need to copy the entire data set into @_. The $data_ref is dereferenced within the subroutine to access and process each element, offering performance improvements for large datasets.

Error handling and input validation often become integral to managing variable-length parameter lists, ensuring the subroutine handles inputs correctly and gracefully manages unexpected scenarios. Utilizing Perl's croak from the Carp module can aid in generating informative error messages:

```
#!/usr/bin/perl
use strict;
use warnings;
use Carp;

sub validate_params {
    my %params = @_;
    croak "Missing name parameter" unless $params{name};
    croak "Missing age parameter" unless $params{age};

    print "Validated Parameters:\n";
    print "Name: $params{name}\n";
    print "Age: $params{age}\n";
}

validate_params(name => 'Alice', age => 28);
```

In this example, the validate_params subroutine checks for the presence of necessary parameters and utilizes croak to generate error messages if any mandatory parameter is missing. This proactive approach to validation enhances the robustness of the subroutine.

The flexibility afforded by variable-length parameter lists in Perl is a powerful feature, giving programmers the ability to write more adaptable and resilient subroutines. Understanding how to effectively handle and utilize these parameter lists is fundamental to mastering Perl subroutines.

5.10 Handling Exceptions in Subroutines

In robust Perl programming, handling exceptions within subroutines is crucial for reliable and maintainable code. Exception handling allows the script to manage errors gracefully and execute code specific to error resolution. Perl provides several built-in mechanisms for handling exceptions, including the use of eval blocks, the die function, and modules like Try::Tiny.

Using eval Blocks:

The eval block in Perl is a powerful tool for trapping errors that may occur during the execution of a block of code. When an error occurs within an eval block, the block returns undef, and the error message is placed in the special variable $@. This approach allows the script to handle errors without terminating unexpectedly.

```
sub divide {
    my ($numerator, $denominator) = @_;
    my $result = eval { $numerator / $denominator };

    if ($@) {
        warn "Division by zero error: $@";
        return undef;
    }
    return $result;
}

my $value = divide(10, 0);
print "Result: ", defined $value ? $value : "undefined", "\n";
```

In this example, the eval block catches the division by zero error. If an exception occurs, $@ contains the error message, and undef is returned, allowing the script to continue executing and issue a warning.

Using die Function:

The die function is used to raise an exception explicitly. It prints an error message to the standard error (STDERR) and terminates the current script unless caught by an eval block.

```
sub open_file {
    my ($filename) = @_;
    open my $fh, '<', $filename or die "Could not open file '$filename': $!\n";
    return $fh;
}

my $fh = eval { open_file("nonexistent_file.txt") };
if ($@) {
    warn "File operation failed: $@";
}
```

In this case, the attempt to open a non-existent file triggers die, which outputs an error message. The enclosing eval block captures this exception, and the script can gracefully handle the file operation failure.

Using Try::Tiny Module:

The Try::Tiny module provides a minimalist way to handle exceptions, avoiding some of the pitfalls of raw eval. It simplifies the syntax and ensures that exceptions are properly localized.

```
use Try::Tiny;

sub risky_operation {
    my ($value) = @_;

    try {
        die "Unacceptable value: $value" if $value < 0;
        print "Value is: $value\n";
    }
    catch {
        warn "Caught exception: $_";
    };
}

risky_operation(-1);
```

Here, the try block executes the code that may throw an exception. If an exception occurs, it is captured by the catch block, which makes the error handling process straightforward and readable.

Considerations for Effective Exception Handling:

- **Specific Error Messages:** Always provide clear and specific error messages to diagnose issues swiftly.
- **Minimal Scope for eval:** Limit the scope of eval blocks to just enough code to catch potential errors, minimizing unexpected behavior elsewhere in the script.
- **Avoid Silent Failures:** Ensure that exceptions are logged or reported appropriately. Silent failures can lead to difficult-to-trace bugs.
- **Contextual Handling:** Handle exceptions in a context-aware manner. For instance, differentiate between recoverable errors (like a file not found) and critical errors (such as data corruption), addressing them appropriately.

Through the integration of these techniques, Perl programmers can create resilient subroutines capable of managing both expected and unexpected conditions without compromising the overall stability of the script. Proper exception handling is an integral part of crafting high-quality, dependable Perl applications.

5.11 Recursive Subroutines

Recursive subroutines in Perl refer to subroutines that call themselves directly or indirectly to solve a problem by breaking it into smaller sub-problems of the same type. Recursion is a powerful tool in programming that enables the implementation of algorithms in a concise and readable manner.

The classic example of a recursive problem is calculating the factorial of a number. The factorial of a number n, denoted as $n!$, is the product of all positive integers less than or equal to n. It can be defined recursively as follows:

$$n! = \begin{cases} 1 & \text{if } n = 0 \\ n \times (n-1)! & \text{if } n > 0 \end{cases}$$

The following Perl code demonstrates a recursive subroutine for calculating the factorial of a number:

```
sub factorial {
    my ($n) = @_;
    return 1 if $n == 0;
    return $n * factorial($n - 1);
}

my $result = factorial(5);
print "The factorial of 5 is $result\n";
```

This subroutine, factorial, includes a base case and a recursive case. The base case is essential to terminate the recursive calls and avoid infinite recursion. Here, the base case is return 1 if $n == 0, which stops the recursion when n is zero. The recursive case return $n * factorial($n - 1) calls the subroutine itself with an argument decremented by one.

Another common example of a recursive problem is computing the Fibonacci sequence. The Fibonacci sequence is defined with the following base cases and recurrence relation:

$$F(n) = \begin{cases} 0 & \text{if } n = 0 \\ 1 & \text{if } n = 1 \\ F(n-1) + F(n-2) & \text{if } n > 1 \end{cases}$$

Here is the Perl implementation of a recursive subroutine to compute the Fibonacci number:

```
sub fibonacci {
    my ($n) = @_;
    return 0 if $n == 0;
    return 1 if $n == 1;
    return fibonacci($n - 1) + fibonacci($n - 2);
}

my $fib_number = fibonacci(10);
print "The 10th Fibonacci number is $fib_number\n";
```

In this code, the base cases are return 0 if $n == 0 and return 1 if $n == 1, ensuring the recursion terminates when n is 0 or 1. The recursive case return fibonacci($n - 1) + fibonacci($n - 2) defines the Fibonacci sequence as the sum of the two preceding numbers in the sequence.

Recursion is not always the most efficient way to solve problems due to its potential for significant overhead in time and memory, especially for problems with overlapping subproblems. For instance, the recursive Fibonacci algorithm above has exponential time complexity. Optimization techniques such as memoization can be used to address this:

```
my %fib_cache;
sub fibonacci_optimized {
    my ($n) = @_;
    return 0 if $n == 0;
    return 1 if $n == 1;
    return $fib_cache{$n} if exists $fib_cache{$n};
    $fib_cache{$n} = fibonacci_optimized($n - 1) + fibonacci_optimized($n - 2);
    return $fib_cache{$n};
}

my $fib_optimized = fibonacci_optimized(10);
print "The 10th Fibonacci number with optimization is $fib_optimized\n";
```

In the optimized version, we use a hash %fib_cache to store the results of Fibonacci calculations. Thus, whenever a Fibonacci number is needed, we first check if it is already computed and stored in %fib_cache. If not, we compute it, store it in the cache, and then return it. This reduces the time complexity to $O(n)$.

Another example where recursion is frequently used is tree traversal. Consider a binary tree where each node has at most two children. Recursive subroutines can traverse or search the tree in a natural and straightforward manner. Below is an example of an in-order traversal of a binary tree:

```
sub inorder_traversal {
    my ($node) = @_;
    return unless $node;
    inorder_traversal($node->{left});
    print "$node->{value} ";
    inorder_traversal($node->{right});
}

my $tree = {
    value => 1,
    left => {
        value => 2,
        left => undef,
        right => undef,
    },
    right => {
        value => 3,
        left => undef,
        right => undef,
    },
};

inorder_traversal($tree);
```

This example shows an in-order traversal where the subroutine first recursively traverses the left subtree, processes the current node, and then recursively traverses the right subtree. The base case here is `return unless $node`, which exits the subroutine if it encounters an undefined node. Such recursive techniques can be adapted for pre-order and post-order traversals by simply altering the order in which subroutine calls are made relative to the processing of the current node.

Recursive subroutines contribute to more readable and maintainable code, particularly when handling problems naturally defined in terms of smaller subproblems of the same type. It is crucial, however, to be mindful of the base case to prevent infinite loops and to consider optimization techniques like memoization for more efficient execution. Steps can be taken to convert recursive solutions into iterative ones using data structures like stacks, especially in environments where recursion might lead to stack overflow errors due to deep recursion levels.

5.12 Built-in Functions vs. User-Defined Functions

In Perl, understanding the distinction between built-in functions and user-defined functions is crucial for efficient scripting and automation. Built-in functions are native to the Perl language, providing a wide range of functionalities out-of-the-box, while user-defined functions offer custom solutions for specific problems.

Built-in functions are encapsulated pieces of code that are part of the Perl interpreter. They cover a myriad of tasks, including file handling, regular expressions, list and array manipulation, and string processing. Examples of frequently used built-in functions are print, chomp, length, and split. These functions are optimized for performance and correctness by the Perl developers and offer substantial benefits in terms of speed and reliability.

To illustrate, consider the length function, which returns the number of characters in a string. Its implementation in Perl is highly efficient:

```
my $string = "Hello, world!";
my $length = length($string);
print "The length of the string is $length.\n";
```

Output:

```
The length of the string is 13.
```

This example demonstrates how a built-in function can be invoked with minimal overhead, utilizing well-tested and optimized code paths within the Perl interpreter.

On the other hand, user-defined functions (or subroutines, as they are commonly named in Perl) are written by the programmer to perform specific, customized tasks that are not covered by built-in functions. These functions are essential for code modularity, reusability, and maintainability. A user-defined function in Perl is declared using the sub keyword, followed by the function name and a block of code encapsulated in braces.

Here is an example of a user-defined function that calculates the factorial of a number using recursion:

```
sub factorial {
    my ($n) = @_;
    return 1 if $n == 0;
    return $n * factorial($n - 1);
}
```

```
my $result = factorial(5);
print "The factorial of 5 is $result.\n";
```

Output:

```
The factorial of 5 is 120.
```

This example shows how user-defined functions allow programmers to tailor functionality to their specific needs. While user-defined functions provide flexibility, it is important to note that they may not always match the performance or reliability of built-in functions, especially for complex or resource-intensive operations.

When developing Perl scripts, it is often beneficial to leverage built-in functions wherever possible because they are optimized for performance and generally contain fewer bugs. However, there are scenarios where built-in functions may not suffice. For example, if a specific business logic needs to be implemented, or if a unique data processing requirement arises, user-defined functions become indispensable.

Additionally, user-defined functions can sometimes complement built-in functions. For example, if there is a need to perform multiple steps of data processing, integrating built-in functions within user-defined functions can provide a powerful combination. Consider the following example:

```
sub process_string {
    my ($input) = @_;
    $input = lc($input); # Convert to lowercase using built-in function
    $input =~ s/\s+/ /g; # Replace multiple spaces with a single space using regex
    return $input;
}

my $original = " Hello, World! ";
my $processed = process_string($original);
print "Original: '$original'\n";
print "Processed: '$processed'\n";
```

Output:

```
Original: '  Hello,   World!  '
Processed: ' hello, world! '
```

In this example, the user-defined function process_string integrates built-in functions like lc and regex substitution to achieve a desired outcome. This illustrates how combining both types of functions can enhance script functionality and readability.

Hopefully, the nuanced understanding of when and how to utilize built-in versus user-defined functions enables efficient and effective Perl programming. Emphasizing the strengths of each, while remaining aware of their respective limitations, allows for better design decisions and more robust code.

Chapter 6

Regular Expressions

This chapter provides a comprehensive guide to regular expressions in Perl, covering basic syntax, patterns, and metacharacters. It delves into character classes, quantifiers, anchors, grouping, capturing, and alternation. Additionally, the chapter addresses substitutions, modifiers, and common regex functions, complemented by practical examples and debugging techniques to effectively utilize regular expressions for text processing tasks.

6.1 Introduction to Regular Expressions

A regular expression (regex) is a powerful tool in programming and text processing that provides a concise and flexible means for matching strings of text, such as characters, words, or patterns of characters. In Perl, regular expressions are integral for tasks involving text manipulation, search, and data extraction. Understanding the fundamental concepts of regular expressions allows one to leverage their full potential effectively.

At its core, a regular expression is a sequence of characters that define a search pattern. Typically, this pattern is used by string-searching algorithms for "find" or "find and replace" operations on strings or for input validation. Perl's regular expression engine is one of the most robust and versatile available, facilitating complex pattern matching with ease.

To initiate the use of regular expressions in Perl, the primary operators are the binding operators = and ! , which are used to determine if a pattern matches a string. The match operator = checks the string on the left side against the regular expression on the right side, returning true if there's a match.

```
my $string = "Perl programming is powerful";
if ($string =~ /programming/) {
    print "Match found!\n";
}
```

The above code checks if the word "programming" exists within the string. If a match is found, it prints "Match found!". Conversely, the exclamation mark in the ! operator negates the match condition, thereby checking for non-matching strings.

```
if ($string !~ /python/) {
    print "No match found!\n";
}
```

Here, the script confirms that the word "python" is not present in the string, and prints "No match found!".

The slashes (/ /) surrounding the pattern are delimiters. Perl provides flexibility with other delimiters such as , [], and (), which are particularly useful when the pattern contains slashes.

```
if ($string =~ m{programming}) {
    print "Match found!\n";
}
```

This example demonstrates the use of {} as delimiters, yielding the same result as previously shown with slashes.

Regular expressions can include literal characters and metacharacters. Literal characters match themselves, whereas metacharacters are the building blocks for defining more complex patterns. The most commonly used metacharacters in regular expressions are:

- . – Matches any single character except newline
- ^ – Matches the beginning of a string
- $ – Matches the end of a string
- * – Matches zero or more occurrences of the preceding element
- + – Matches one or more occurrences of the preceding element
- ? – Matches zero or one occurrence of the preceding element

- | – Acts as a logical OR within patterns
- ( ) – Groups patterns and remembers the match for further use
- [ ] – Defines a character class
- \ – Escapes a metacharacter, causing it to be treated as a literal character

The use of metacharacters enhances the capability of regular expressions significantly. For instance, the dot (.) metacharacter is particularly versatile as it matches any single character. Consider the following example.

```
my $number_string = "1234";
if ($number_string =~ /1.3/) {
    print "Pattern matches!\n"; # This matches because "123" fits the pattern "1.3"
}
```

The pattern /1.3/ matches any three-character substring starting with '1' and ending with '3', with any single character in between.

Anchors are essential for matching patterns at specific positions within a string. The caret (^) specifies that the match must start at the beginning of the string, while the dollar sign ($) indicates that the match must occur at the end.

```
my $text = "The quick brown fox";
if ($text =~ /^The/) {
    print "Starts with 'The'\n"; # This matches because ^ asserts the start of the
        string
}
if ($text =~ /fox\$/) {
    print "Ends with 'fox'\n"; # This matches because $ asserts the end of the string
}
```

Quantifiers define the number of instances of a character or group. The asterisk (*) matches zero or more occurrences, the plus sign (+) matches one or more, and the question mark (?) matches zero or one.

```
my $data = "1024";
if ($data =~ /\d+/) {
    print "Contains one or more digits\n"; # \d+ matches one or more digits
}
if ($data =~ /\d*/) {
    print "Contains zero or more digits\n"; # \d* matches zero or more digits
}
```

Alternation with the pipe (|) allows for the matching of one pattern out of several. Grouping with parentheses (( )) enables capturing matched substrings for later reference and more complex patterns.

```
my $options = "cat";
if ($options =~ /(cat|dog)/) {
    print "Matched 'cat' or 'dog'\n"; # Matches either 'cat' or 'dog'
}
```

In this section, we have explored the foundational elements and primary operations of regular expressions in Perl. This understanding lays the groundwork for more advanced concepts, enabling the development of complex text processing routines efficiently.

6.2 Basic Syntax and Patterns

In Perl, regular expressions (regex) are implemented using the =~ binding operator and follow the syntax m/pattern/. A simple example would be:

```
my $string = "Hello, world!";
if ($string =~ m/Hello/) {
    print "Match found.\n";
}
```

The above code checks if the string "Hello, world!" contains the substring "Hello" and prints a message if the pattern matches.

Delimiters

Perl allows different delimiters for regex patterns. While the most common delimiter is the forward slash /, other characters can also be used for better readability, especially when the pattern itself contains slashes. For example:

```
my $url = "http://example.com";
if ($url =~ m{http://}) {
    print "URL found.\n";
}
```

Here, curly braces {} are used as delimiters. Similarly, you can use any non-alphanumeric, non-whitespace character:

```
if ($url =~ m#http://#) {
    print "URL found.\n";
}
```

Literal Characters

The simplest type of pattern is one that matches a literal string. This requires that the pattern literally matches the input text. For example, the pattern foo matches "foo" in "foobar":

```
my $text = "foobar";
if ($text =~ m/foo/) {
    print "Found 'foo'.\n";
}
```

Metacharacters

Regular expressions support a variety of metacharacters that facilitate matching complex patterns. The most common metacharacters include:

- . (dot): Matches any single character except newline.
- ^ (caret): Matches the start of the string.
- $ (dollar sign): Matches the end of the string or before the newline at the end.
- * (asterisk): Matches 0 or more occurrences of the preceding character.
- + (plus): Matches 1 or more occurrences of the preceding character.
- ? (question mark): Matches 0 or 1 occurrence of the preceding character.
- {n}: Matches exactly n occurrences of the preceding character.
- {n,m}: Matches between n and m occurrences of the preceding character.
- () (parentheses): Groups patterns together and captures part of the matching text.
- [] (square brackets): Denotes a character class to match any one of the enclosed characters.
- | (pipe): Acts as a logical OR to match one of multiple patterns.
- \ (backslash): Escapes a metacharacter to match the literal character.

Examples of Basic Patterns

Below are examples using metacharacters:

Dot (.) Matcher

The dot . matches any single character except a newline.

```
my $data = "abcd";
if ($data =~ m/a.c/) {
    print "Pattern matched any character between 'a' and 'c'.\n";
}
```

Caret (^) and Dollar ($) Anchors

Caret ^ and dollar $ are used as anchors to match the beginning and end of the string respectively.

```
my $sentence = "Hello Perl!";
if ($sentence =~ m/^Hello/) {
    print "Pattern found at the beginning of the string.\n";
}
if ($sentence =~ m/Perl!$/) {
    print "Pattern found at the end of the string.\n";
}
```

Star (*), Plus (+), and Question Mark (?) Quantifiers

These quantifiers specify the number of times a character or group may repeat.

```
my $repeat = "Helloooo";
# Match one or more 'o's
if ($repeat =~ m/Helloo+/) {
    print "Pattern matched with one or more 'o's.\n";
}
# Match zero or one 'o'
if ($repeat =~ m/Helloo?/) {
    print "Pattern matched with zero or one 'o'.\n";
}
# Match zero or more 'o's
if ($repeat =~ m/Helloo*/) {
    print "Pattern matched with zero or more 'o's.\n";
}
```

Braces ({n}, {n,m}) Quantifiers

Braces are used for specifying repetitions.

```
my $number = "12345";
# Match exactly three digits
if ($number =~ m/\d{3}/) {
    print "Pattern matched exactly three digits.\n";
}
# Match between two and four digits
if ($number =~ m/\d{2,4}/) {
    print "Pattern matched between two and four digits.\n";
}
```

Regular expressions in Perl provide powerful patterns for string matching. With basic syntax and patterns, various simple to complex text processing tasks can be efficiently handled.

6.3 Metacharacters

In Perl regular expressions, metacharacters are special characters that represent specific types of patterns. These characters are integral to the functionality and power of Perl's pattern matching capabilities. The primary metacharacters used in Perl regular expressions include: .,ˆ, $, *, +, ?, {}, [], ().

The Dot (.) The dot, or period, is a metacharacter that matches any single character except a newline.

```
# Example usage of the dot metacharacter
my $text = "abc";
if ($text =~ /a.c/) {
    print "Match found!\n";
}
```

In this example, a.c matches any character between a and c. As abc fits this pattern, the output will be:

```
Match found!
```

The Caret () The caret is used to match the beginning of a string.

```
# Example usage of the caret metacharacter
my $text = "hello";
if ($text =~ /^he/) {
    print "Starts with 'he'\n";
}
```

The pattern ĥe ensures that the string must start with "he". The output is:

```
Starts with 'he'
```

The Dollar Sign ($) The dollar sign matches the end of a string.

```
# Example usage of the dollar sign metacharacter
my $text = "hello";
if ($text =~ /lo$/) {
    print "Ends with 'lo'\n";
}
```

Here, lo$ ensures that the string ends with "lo". The output produced will be:

```
Ends with 'lo'
```

The Asterisk (*) The asterisk matches zero or more occurrences of the preceding element.

```
# Example usage of the asterisk metacharacter
my $text = "aaab";
if ($text =~ /a*b/) {
    print "Pattern A*B found\n";
}
```

This pattern matches any sequence of a's (including zero occurrences) followed by b. Since aaab fits, the output will be:

```
Pattern A*B found
```

The Plus (+) The plus matches one or more occurrences of the preceding element.

```
# Example usage of the plus metacharacter
my $text = "aaab";
if ($text =~ /a+b/) {
    print "Pattern A+B found\n";
}
```

In this case, a+b requires at least one a followed by b. Since the condition is satisfied by aaab, the output will be:

```
Pattern A+B found
```

The Question Mark (?) The question mark matches zero or one occurrence of the preceding element.

```
# Example usage of the question mark metacharacter
my $text = "ab";
if ($text =~ /a?b/) {
    print "Pattern A?B found\n";
}
```

Here, a?b matches b (with zero a) or ab. Since the string matches, the output will be:

```
Pattern A?B found
```

Curly Braces ({}) Curly braces allow for specifying the exact number or range of occurrences of the preceding element.

```
# Example usage of curly braces metacharacter
my $text = "aaaab";
if ($text =~ /a{3}b/) {
    print "Pattern A{3}B found\n";
}
```

This pattern a{3}b matches exactly three a's followed by b. The output will be:

```
Pattern A{3}B found
```

Ranges can also be specified, such as in:

```
# Example of range in curly braces
if ($text =~ /a{2,4}b/) {
    print "Pattern A{2,4}B found\n";
}
```

This pattern matches between 2 and 4 a's followed by b. The output will be:

```
Pattern A{2,4}B found
```

Square Brackets ([]) Square brackets define a character class to match any one of the characters within the brackets.

```
# Example usage of square brackets metacharacter
my $text = "face";
if ($text =~ /[aeiou]/) {
    print "Vowel found\n";
}
```

In this example, [aeiou] matches any single vowel. The output will be:

```
Vowel found
```

Ranges can also be specified within the brackets:

```
# Example of range in square brackets
if ($text =~ /[a-f]/) {
    print "Letter between A-F found\n";
}
```

This pattern matches any lowercase letter from a to f. The output will be:

```
Letter between A-F found
```

Parentheses (()) Parentheses are used for grouping and capturing. They create a capture group of the enclosed pattern.

```
# Example usage of parentheses metacharacter
my $text = "abcabc";
if ($text =~ /(abc)+/) {
    print "Pattern (ABC)+ found\n";
}
```

Here, (abc)+ matches one or more occurrences of "abc". Since the string contains "abcabc", the output will be:

```
Pattern (ABC)+ found
```

Metacharacters transform simple text matching into a versatile and powerful tool, enabling complex pattern handling and text manipulations efficiently. This understanding sets the groundwork for deeper exploration into Perl's regular expressions in subsequent sections.

6.4 Character Classes

Character classes in regular expressions (regex) are utilized to match any one of a specified set of characters. In Perl, character classes are enclosed within square brackets [] and allow you to specify a set of acceptable characters at a specific position in the input string. For instance, the character class [abc] will match any single character which is either a, b, or c.

Fundamentally, character classes provide a way of narrowing down possible matches, offering more precise search results. This section explores the usage and flexibility of character classes in Perl regular expressions by outlining their syntax, explaining their constructions, and providing practical code examples.

Basic Usage

A simple character class is a set of characters enclosed in square brackets. For example, [aeiou] defines a character class for vowels. Consequently, the regular expression /a[aeiou]k/ will match "aak", "aek", "aik", "aok", or "auk".

```
my $string = "hello fred";
if ($string =~ /fr[ei]/) {
    print "Match!\n";
}
```

```
Match!
```

This Perl script evaluates whether the string contains "fre" or "fri". Since the string does contain "fred", the script prints Match!.

Character Ranges

A range of characters can be specified using a hyphen - inside a character class. For example, [0-9] matches any digit from 0 to 9. Similarly, [A-Z] matches any uppercase letter, and [a-z] matches any lowercase letter.

```
my $entry = "Project E123";
if ($entry =~ /[A-Z][0-9]/) {
    print "Format matched!\n";
}
```

```
Format matched!
```

Here, the regex checks if there is an uppercase letter followed by a digit in the string "Project E123". The check is true because "E1" fits the pattern, hence it prints Format matched!.

Negated Character Classes

Negated character classes specify characters that should *not* be present. A caret ^ at the beginning of a character class signifies negation. For instance, [^aeiou] matches any character that is not a vowel.

```
my $code = "Var123";
if ($code =~ /[^0-9]{3}/) {
    print "Contains three non-digit characters at the start.\n";
}
```

```
Contains three non-digit characters at the start.
```

In this example, the regex checks if the string starts with exactly three non-digit characters. The string "Var123" matches this criteria.

Predefined Character Classes

Perl offers several predefined character classes for more succinct expressions:

- \d: Matches any digit (equivalent to [0-9]).
- \D: Matches any non-digit (equivalent to [^0-9]).
- \w: Matches any word character (alphanumeric plus _, equivalent to [a-zA-Z0-9_])
- \W: Matches any non-word character (equivalent to [^a-zA-Z0-9_]).

- \s: Matches any whitespace character (space, tab, newline).
- \S: Matches any non-whitespace character.

```
my $identifier = "var_name";
if ($identifier =~ /\w+/) {
    print "Valid identifier\n";
}
```

```
Valid identifier
```

This program checks if the string "var_name" is composed of word characters using the \w wildcard, and subsequently, it prints Valid identifier.

Combining Character Classes

Character classes can be combined by placing them within the same set of brackets. For instance, to match any letter or number, use [a-zA-Z0-9]. Similarly, character classes can reference predefined ranges like \d combined with specific sets [A-F].

```
my $hex_color = "#1A2B3C";
if ($hex_color =~ /#[0-9A-Fa-f]{6}/) {
    print "Valid hexadecimal color code\n";
}
```

```
Valid hexadecimal color code
```

This example confirms that the string "#1A2B3C" is a valid hexadecimal color code since the pattern #[0-9A-Fa-f]{6} looks for a hash followed by exactly six hexadecimal digits.

Character classes, both simplistic and complex, serve as foundational components in Perl regular expressions, enabling more structured and versatile text matches.

6.5 Quantifiers

Quantifiers in Perl regular expressions specify the number of times a character or group of characters should be matched. They are a powerful component of regular expressions, providing the ability to define repetitions with precision. This section covers the three main types of quantifiers: greedy, non-greedy (lazy), and possessive, detailing their syntax and behavior.

```
# Example of quantifiers in Perl
my $text = "xxxxxxxxx";
```

```
if ($text =~ /x{5}/) {
    print "Found five consecutive 'x's.\n";
}
```

```
Found five consecutive 'x's.
```

Greedy Quantifiers:

Greedy quantifiers match as many occurrences of the pattern as possible. The following are the common greedy quantifiers in Perl:

- * - Matches 0 or more occurrences.
- + - Matches 1 or more occurrences.
- ? - Matches 0 or 1 occurrence.
- {n} - Matches exactly n occurrences.
- {n,} - Matches n or more occurrences.
- {n,m} - Matches between n and m occurrences.

Examples:

```
# Zero or more occurrences
if ($text =~ /x*9x*/) {
    print "Matched zero or more 'x's around a '9'.\n";
}

# One or more occurrences
if ($text =~ /x+/) {
    print "Matched one or more 'x's.\n";
}

# Zero or one occurrence
if ($text =~ /x?9x?/) {
    print "Matched zero or one 'x' around a '9'.\n";
}

# Exactly 3 occurrences
if ($text =~ /x{3}/) {
    print "Matched exactly three 'x's.\n";
}

# Three or more occurrences
if ($text =~ /x{3,}/) {
    print "Matched three or more 'x's.\n";
}

# Between 3 and 5 occurrences
if ($text =~ /x{3,5}/) {
    print "Matched between three and five 'x's.\n";
}
```

```
Matched zero or more 'x's around a '9'.
Matched one or more 'x's.
Matched zero or one 'x' around a '9'.
Matched exactly three 'x's.
Matched three or more 'x's.
Matched between three and five 'x's.
```

Non-Greedy Quantifiers:

Non-greedy quantifiers, also known as lazy quantifiers, match as few occurrences as needed. They are similar to greedy quantifiers but with a ? appended:

- *? - Matches 0 or more occurrences, as few as possible.
- +? - Matches 1 or more occurrences, as few as possible.
- ?? - Matches 0 or 1 occurrence, as few as possible.
- {n,}? - Matches n or more occurrences, as few as possible.
- {n,m}? - Matches between n and m occurrences, as few as possible.

Examples:

```
# Zero or more occurrences (non-greedy)
if ($text =~ /x*?9x*?/) {
    print "Non-greedy match: zero or more 'x's around a '9'.\n";
}

# One or more occurrences (non-greedy)
if ($text =~ /x+?9x+?/) {
    print "Non-greedy match: one or more 'x's around a '9'.\n";
}

# Zero or one occurrence (non-greedy)
if ($text =~ /x??9x??/) {
    print "Non-greedy match: zero or one 'x' around a '9'.\n";
}

# Three or more occurrences (non-greedy)
if ($text =~ /x{3,}?/) {
    print "Non-greedy match: three or more 'x's.\n";
}

# Between 3 and 5 occurrences (non-greedy)
if ($text =~ /x{3,5}?/) {
    print "Non-greedy match: between three and five 'x's.\n";
}
```

```
Non-greedy match: zero or more 'x's around a '9'.
Non-greedy match: one or more 'x's around a '9'.
Non-greedy match: zero or one 'x' around a '9'.
Non-greedy match: three or more 'x's.
Non-greedy match: between three and five 'x's.
```

Possessive Quantifiers:

Possessive quantifiers match as many occurrences as possible, without backtracking. They are similar to greedy quantifiers but with a + appended:

- *+ - Matches 0 or more occurrences without backtracking.
- ++ - Matches 1 or more occurrences without backtracking.
- ?+ - Matches 0 or 1 occurrence without backtracking.
- {n}+ - Matches exactly n occurrences without backtracking.
- {n,}+ - Matches n or more occurrences without backtracking.
- {n,m}+ - Matches between n and m occurrences without backtracking.

Examples:

```
# Zero or more occurrences (possessive)
if ($text =~ /x*+9x*+/) {
    print "Possessive match: zero or more 'x's around a '9'.\n";
}

# One or more occurrences (possessive)
if ($text =~ /x++9x++/) {
    print "Possessive match: one or more 'x's around a '9'.\n";
}

# Zero or one occurrence (possessive)
if ($text =~ /x?+9x?+/) {
    print "Possessive match: zero or one 'x' around a '9'.\n";
}

# Three or more occurrences (possessive)
if ($text =~ /x{3,}+/) {
    print "Possessive match: three or more 'x's.\n";
}

# Between 3 and 5 occurrences (possessive)
if ($text =~ /x{3,5}+/) {
    print "Possessive match: between three and five 'x's.\n";
}
```

```
Possessive match: zero or more 'x's around a '9'.
Possessive match: one or more 'x's around a '9'.
Possessive match: zero or one 'x' around a '9'.
Possessive match: three or more 'x's.
Possessive match: between three and five 'x's.
```

Understanding the distinctions between these quantifiers is crucial for effective use of regular expressions. Greedy quantifiers often suffice for general purpose matching. Non-greedy quantifiers are optimal for parsimonious patterns. Possessive quantifiers ensure efficiency in specific contexts where backtracking is unnecessary or detrimental. Through practical applications, mastery of quantifiers enhances scripting and automation capabilities in Perl.

6.6 Anchors

Anchors are special metacharacters in regular expressions that assert specific positions in the input string. They do not match any character but are used to define the boundaries or positions within the string where a match must occur. Understanding anchors is crucial for constructing precise and efficient regular expressions. Here, we will explore the primary anchors: the caret (^) for the start of a string, and the dollar sign ($) for the end of a string, along with their practical usage in Perl.

Caret (^): Start of String Anchor

The caret (^) is used to assert the position at the start of a string or a line (depending on the mode). When this anchor is used at the beginning of a regular expression, it ensures that the subsequent pattern must match at the start.

```
# Perl example to match a pattern at the start of a string
my $string = "Hello World!";
if ($string =~ /^\w+/) {
    print "Match found at the start of the string.\n";
}
# This will match "Hello" since the pattern \w+ matches one or more word characters
    at the start.
```

```
Match found at the start of the string.
```

Dollar Sign ($): End of String Anchor

The dollar sign ($) is used to assert the position at the end of a string or a line. When placed at the end of a regular expression, it ensures that the previous pattern must match right up to the end.

```
# Perl example to match a pattern at the end of a string
my $string = "file.txt";
if ($string =~ /\.txt$/) {
    print "Match found at the end of the string.\n";
}
# This will match ".txt" at the end of the string.
```

```
Match found at the end of the string.
```

Combining Start and End Anchors

Often, it is necessary to ensure that an entire string conforms to a pattern from start to end. This can be accomplished by combining both the start (^) and end ($) anchors in the expression.

```
# Perl example for exact match using both start and end anchors
my $string = "12345";
if ($string =~ /^\d+$/) {
    print "The entire string is a number.\n";
}
# The pattern ensures that the entire string consists of one or more digits.
```

```
The entire string is a number.
```

Using Anchors in Multiline Mode

By default, the caret (^) and dollar sign ($) anchors only match the start and end of the entire string. However, when the multiline mode is enabled (using the m modifier), these anchors match the start and end of each line within the string.

```
# Multiline Mode Example
my $string = "first line\nsecond line";
if ($string =~ /^second/m) {
    print "Match found at the start of a line in multiline mode.\n";
}
# The pattern matches "second" at the start of the second line.
```

```
Match found at the start of a line in multiline mode.
```

Advanced Anchoring Techniques

In addition to the simple use of ^ and $, more advanced anchoring techniques involve zero-width assertions like word boundaries () and non-word boundaries (\B).

```
# Word Boundary Example
my $string = "The price is $100.";
if ($string =~ /\b\d+\b/) {
    print "Match found at word boundary.\n";
}
# Here, \b ensures the digits are matched as a separate word.
```

```
Match found at word boundary.
```

Anchors are a fundamental aspect of regular expressions, enabling precise control over where patterns match within strings. Their accurate use enhances the flexibility and robustness of text processing tasks in Perl.

6.7 Grouping and Capturing

Grouping and capturing are indispensable features when utilizing regular expressions in Perl. They enable the organization and extraction of specific subpatterns within a regular expression, facilitating complex text processing tasks.

Grouping is achieved by enclosing subpatterns within parentheses '()'. This feature allows us to treat a group of characters or a subpattern as a single unit. For example, the pattern '(abc)' will match the sequence 'abc' within the target string. To illustrate:

```
my $string = "abc def abc";
if ($string =~ /(abc)/) {
    print "Match found: $1\n";
}
```

In the code snippet above, the regular expression '(abc)' groups the characters 'abc', and upon a successful match, $1 captures and references this group. The output will be:

```
Match found: abc
```

Capturing, the second aspect of parentheses, refers to the process of storing the matched subpattern for later use. Perl automatically assigns captured groups to special variables, starting from $1 for the first capture group, $2 for the second, and so forth. Consider the following example:

```
my $string = "My phone number is 123-456-7890";
if ($string =~ /(\d{3})-(\d{3})-(\d{4})/) {
    print "Area Code: $1\n";
    print "Prefix: $2\n";
    print "Line Number: $3\n";
}
```

Here, the regular expression (\d{3})-(\d{3})-(\d{4}) utilizes three capturing groups, each corresponding to segments of the phone number. The output will be:

```
Area Code: 123
Prefix: 456
Line Number: 7890
```

Beyond mere grouping, parentheses also enable backreferences within the same regular expression. Backreferences allow us to refer to previously matched subpatterns, ensuring consistency within the match. For instance:

```
my $string = "abab";
```

```
if ($string =~ /(ab)\1/) {
    print "Match with backreference: $string\n";
}
```

In this example, \1 refers to the subpattern (ab), ensuring that the matched string repeats ab. The output will be:

```
Match with backreference: abab
```

Non-capturing groups, indicated by (?:...) allow subpattern grouping without capturing. This feature is useful for performance optimization and when the group is not required for further reference. For example:

```
my $string = "hello123";
if ($string =~ /hello(?:\d+)/) {
    print "Non-capturing group matched.\n";
}
```

Even though the digits following hello are matched, they are not stored in capture variables, ensuring an efficient match operation.

Alternation, represented by the pipe character |, works seamlessly with grouping to match one of several patterns. Each alternative should be enclosed in parentheses to form distinct subpatterns. For example:

```
my $string = "cat or dog";
if ($string =~ /(cat|dog)/) {
    print "Found a pet: $1\n";
}
```

The expression (cat|dog) captures either cat or dog, depending on which substring is found. The output will be:

```
Found a pet: cat
```

Grouping and capturing extend to the substitution operator s/// as well. Captured groups can be referenced in the replacement string using the same $1, $2, etc. variables. For instance:

```
my $string = "Perl is great";
$string =~ s/(Perl) is (great)/$1 is awesome/;
print $string;
```

The capturing groups (Perl) and (great) are referenced in the replacement, resulting in:

```
Perl is awesome
```

Nested capturing groups are permissible, with each pair of parentheses representing a distinct capture group. The numbering follows the order of the opening parenthesis, inside out. For example:

```
my $string = "food";
if ($string =~ /((f)o)(od)/) {
    print "Full match: $&\n";
    print "Group 1: $1\n";
    print "Group 2: $2\n";
    print "Group 3: $3\n";
}
```

Here, (f)o forms the first group, capturing fo, the second group captures o, and the third group captures od. The output will be:

```
Full match: food
Group 1: fo
Group 2: o
Group 3: od
```

Understanding grouping and capturing deepens the ability to manipulate and analyze textual data proficiently in Perl. These concepts provide the foundation for more advanced regular expression techniques, fostering greater precision in text processing tasks.

6.8 Alternation

In Perl regular expressions, alternation is a powerful feature that allows for the matching of multiple patterns within a single regex. The vertical bar '|' serves as the alternation operator. It functions much like a logical OR, enabling the regex engine to match one pattern or another.

When using alternation, it is crucial to understand how the regex engine processes these patterns. The engine evaluates patterns from left to right and attempts to match each part of the alternation in sequence. Once a match is found, the engine stops and does not continue to evaluate the subsequent alternatives.

The syntax for using alternation is straightforward:

```
pattern1|pattern2|pattern3
```

Each part separated by the vertical bar '|' is considered an alternative pattern.

Consider the following examples:

```
$sample_string = "apples and oranges";
if ($sample_string =~ /apples|oranges/) {
    print "Match found!\n";
}
```

In this case, the regex '/apples|oranges/' checks if the string contains either "apples" or "oranges". Since "apples" is present in the string, the condition evaluates to true, and "Match found!" is printed.

It is important to note the precedence of alternation in relation to other regex operators. Without explicit grouping, alternation affects the smallest possible subpatterns. Parentheses can be used to group alternatives and define the scope of the '|' operator.

Consider the following example:

```
$sample_string = "cat";
if ($sample_string =~ /c(at|ot|ut)/) {
    print "Match found!\n";
}
```

Here, the regex '/c(at|ot|ut)/' matches "cat", "cot", or "cut". The parenthesis enforce the grouping of 'at', 'ot', and 'ut' as a single sub-pattern. Thus, if $sample_string contains any of these combinations after the character "c", the condition is met and "Match found!" is printed.

The following example illustrates the default behavior without parentheses:

```
$sample_string = "cats";
if ($sample_string =~ /cat|s/) {
    print "Match found!\n";
}
```

In this scenario, the regex '/cat|s/' matches either "cat" or "s". Therefore, the string "cats" matches due to the presence of the substring "cat".

Perl also supports nested alternation, where alternations are placed within other alternations, enhancing the complexity and accuracy of pattern matching.

```
$sample_string = "I have a bat and a hat.";
if ($sample_string =~ /b(at|ell|at)|h(at|ell)/) {
    print "Match found!\n";
}
```

The regex '/b(at|ell|at)|h(at|ell)/' checks for combinations of substrings "bat" or "bell" or "hat" or "hell". Since "bat" is present in $sample_string, the condition will evaluate to true.

A practical application of alternation is evident in scenarios involving the validation or parsing of input data where multiple formats or values are acceptable. For example, matching various date formats can be achieved using alternation.

```
$date_string = "2023-10-05";
if ($date_string =~ /(\d{4}-\d{2}-\d{2})|(\d{2}\/\d{2}\/\d{4})/) {
```

```
    print "Valid date format!\n";
}
```

In this example, the regex '/(4-2-2)|(224)/' matches dates in both "YYYY-MM-DD" and "MM/DD/YYYY" formats. The presence of either format in $date_string results in "Valid date format!" being printed.

Bearing in mind the efficiency, placement, and order of alternative patterns can markedly influence the performance and accuracy of the regex:

- Avoid overly broad patterns that can lead to unwanted matches and increase processing time.
- Aim for specificity in each alternative to narrow down the possible matches effectively.

Through careful and strategic usage of alternation combined with other regex constructs, developers can create highly flexible and powerful regular expressions to handle a wide array of text processing tasks.

6.9 Substitutions

Substitutions in Perl's regular expressions allow for the modification of text by replacing matched patterns. The primary tool for substitutions is the s/// operator. This operator takes the form s/oldpattern/newpattern/ and serves to match portions of a string against oldpattern, replacing them with newpattern.

The syntax for a basic substitution is straightforward:

```
$s = "cat";
$s =~ s/cat/dog/;
print $s; # prints 'dog'
```

Here, the string "cat" is changed to "dog" as the pattern /cat/ is replaced with /dog/. The substitution operator operates in the context of bindings, commonly with the $_ variable, which means that if the variable is omitted, $_ is implicitly used.

Substitution can be controlled using modifiers. The most common ones include:

- /g (global): Replaces all occurrences of the pattern in the string.

- /i (case insensitive): Makes the pattern matching case insensitive.
- /e (evaluate): Treats the replacement string as Perl code and evaluates it.
- /m (multiline): Changes the behavior of ^ and $ so that they match at the start and end of each line within a string.
- /s (single line): Alters how the . character matches newline characters.

The global modifier is used to substitute all occurrences of a pattern in a string:

```
$s = "abcdef abcdef abcdef";
$s =~ s/abc/xyz/g;
print $s; # prints 'xyzdef xyzdef xyzdef'
```

The case-insensitive modifier allows a substitution to ignore case when matching:

```
$s = "AbCdEf";
$s =~ s/abc/xyz/i;
print $s; # prints 'xyzdEf'
```

Using the evaluate modifier allows dynamic computation of the replacement string:

```
$s = "123";
$s =~ s/[0-9]/$&*2/ge;
print $s; # prints '246'
```

In this example, the [0-9] pattern matches each digit in "123". The $& retains the matched digit, and $& *2 evaluates to the digit multiplied by 2.

For cases that involve multiline strings, the /m modifier helps to match patterns at the beginning or end of lines:

```
$s = "first line\nsecond line";
$s =~ s/^/start /gm;
print $s; # prints 'start first line\nstart second line'
```

With the /s modifier, the . character matches newline characters as well:

```
$s = "first line\nsecond line";
$s =~ s/first.*second/all/m;
print $s; # no match found, because '.*' does not include '\n'
```

```
$s =~ s/first.*second/all/s;
print $s; # prints 'all line'
```

Employing capture groups in substitutions enables referencing portions of the matched pattern in the replacement string via variables like $1, $2, etc.:

```
$s = "Name: John Doe";
$s =~ s/Name: (\w+) (\w+)/Name: $2, $1/;
print $s; # prints 'Name: Doe, John'
```

Nested substitutions permit layered and conditional modifications. Consider this example, which first capitalizes the initial letter(s) of words:

```
$s = "hello world";
$s =~ s/\b(\w)/\U$1/g;
print $s; # prints 'Hello World'
```

Here, \b asserts a word boundary, and (\w) captures the first character of each word. The replacement expression \U$1 converts it to uppercase.

Error detection and debugging in substitutions can be intricate. Therefore, employing the warn keyword can assist in troubleshooting:

```
$s = "a1b2c3";
$s =~ s/[a-z]/warn "Replaced $& with X"; "X"/ge;
print $s; # prints 'X1X2X3' and issues warnings for each substitution
```

By methodically leveraging these features, substitutions offer a robust toolkit for dynamic and complex text transformations in Perl, enhancing text processing capabilities comprehensively.

6.10 Modifiers

Modifiers in Perl regular expressions, also known as flags, modify the behavior of the pattern matching operations. They can be placed directly after the pattern's delimiters to extend or alter how the regular expression is interpreted. Understanding and utilizing these modifiers is crucial for optimizing regex operations and ensuring they perform precisely as intended. Below, we will explore the primary modifiers in Perl regex through detailed explanations and examples.

/i: Case-Insensitive Matching

The /i modifier makes the regular expression case-insensitive. Thus, it matches letters irrespective of their casing.

```
my $text = "Hello World";
if ($text =~ /hello/i) {
    print "Match found.\n";
}
```

```
Match found.
```

In this example, the Perl regex /hello/i matches the string "Hello" despite the case difference.

/m: Multi-line Mode

The /m modifier treats the input string as multiple lines. By default, the caret (^) and dollar ($) metacharacters match the start and end of the entire string, respectively. When the /m modifier is used, these metacharacters match the start and end of each line within the string.

```
my $text = "First line\nSecond line";
if ($text =~ /^Second/m) {
    print "Match found.\n";
}
```

```
Match found.
```

Here, the /Ŝecond/m pattern matches the string "Second" at the beginning of the second line due to the /m modifier.

/s: Single-line Mode

The /s modifier changes the behavior of the dot metacharacter (.). Normally, the dot matches any character except the newline. When the /s modifier is applied, the dot also matches newline characters.

```
my $text = "Line one.\nLine two.";
if ($text =~ /one.*two/s) {
    print "Match found.\n";
}
```

```
Match found.
```

In this code snippet, the /one.*two/s regular expression successfully matches across multiple lines due to the /s modifier.

/x: Extended Mode

The /x modifier allows for whitespace and comments within the regular expression, improving readability. Whitespace characters (excluding those within character classes or escaped with a backslash) are ignored.

```
my $text = "sample123text";
if ($text =~ /sample \s* 123 \s* text/x) {
```

```
    print "Match found.\n";
}
```

```
Match found.
```

Here, the /sample
s* 123
s* text/x regex includes spaces for clarity, thanks to the /x modifier.

Comments within the pattern can be added using the #.

```
if ($text =~ /
    sample # Match the word 'sample'
    \s* # Any whitespace
    123 # Followed by '123'
    \s* # Any whitespace
    text # Ending with 'text'
/x) {
    print "Match found.\n";
}
```

```
Match found.
```

/g: Global Matching

The /g modifier finds all occurrences of the pattern within the string, not just the first one. This is especially useful for iterative operations on all matches.

```
my $text = "Repeat Repeat Repeat";
my @matches = $text =~ /Repeat/g;
print "Matches found: " . scalar(@matches) . "\n";
```

```
Matches found: 3
```

The /Repeat/g regex counts all instances of "Repeat" in the string.

/o: Compile Once

The /o modifier instructs Perl to compile the regular expression only once. It is best used when the pattern is a constant, avoiding recompilation on subsequent uses.

```
my $pattern = "fixed";
my $text = "fixed pattern";
if ($text =~ /$pattern/o) {
    print "Match found.\n";
}
```

```
Match found.
```

This ensures the regex is compiled a single time, enhancing performance when the pattern does not change.

Combining Modifiers

Multiple modifiers can be combined by placing them together after the patterns' delimiters.

```
my $text = "Sample\nTEXT 123";
if ($text =~ /sample \s* TEXT/ix) {
    print "Match found.\n";
}
```

```
Match found.
```

In this example, both /i and /x modifiers work together to match the pattern ignoring case and allowing for embedded whitespace for readability.

6.11 Common Regex Functions in Perl

Perl provides a rich array of functions specifically designed to work with regular expressions. These functions facilitate pattern matching, substitution, and a variety of other text processing tasks. Understanding these functions is essential for effectively leveraging the power of regular expressions in Perl scripts.

The primary functions you'll encounter are:

- m// or //: Match Operator
- s///: Substitution Operator
- qr//: Quote Regular Expression Operator
- split: Split Function
- join: Join Function

These functions, when used correctly, enable efficient text manipulation, parsing, and data extraction. Below, we will discuss these functions in depth with examples to solidify their usage.

Match Operator (m// or //)

The match operator is used to search a string for a pattern. The syntax for the match operator is:

```
my $string = "Hello, world!";
if ($string =~ m/Hello/) {
    print "Match found.\n";
}
```

This example checks if the word "Hello" exists within the string `$string`. If a match is found, it prints "Match found." The match operator can also use delimiters other than slashes:

```
if ($string =~ m!Hello!) {
    print "Match found.\n";
}
```

When a match is successful, it stores the matched string in the special variable `$&`. Additionally, parentheses can be used for capturing:

```
if ($string =~ m/(Hello),/) {
    print "Captured: $1\n"; # Output: Captured: Hello
}
```

Substitution Operator (s///)

The substitution operator is used to replace parts of a string that match a regular expression. The syntax of the substitution operator is:

```
my $string = "cats";
$string =~ s/cats/dogs/;
print "$string\n"; # Output: dogs
```

In this example, the string "cats" is replaced with "dogs". The substitution operator can also use delimiters other than slashes:

```
$string =~ s!cats!dogs!;
```

Modifiers can be added to change the behavior of the substitution. For example, adding the `g` modifier will replace all occurrences:

```
my $string = "cats, cats, cats";
$string =~ s/cats/dogs/g;
print "$string\n"; # Output: dogs, dogs, dogs
```

Other common modifiers include `i` (case-insensitive), `e` (evaluate right side as an expression), and `o` (compile pattern only once).

Quote Regular Expression Operator (qr//)

The qr// operator compiles a regular expression and returns a regex object, which can then be reused. This is particularly useful for complex or frequently used patterns:

```
my $pattern = qr/Hello/;
if ("Hello, world!" =~ $pattern) {
    print "Match found.\n";
}
```

This approach enhances readability and allows for pattern reuse without recompilation.

Split Function

The split function divides a string into a list of substrings based on a specified pattern delimiter. The syntax for the split function is:

```
my $string = "apple,orange,banana";
my @fruits = split(/,/, $string);
print join(" - ", @fruits); # Output: apple - orange - banana
```

In this example, the string is split at each comma, resulting in a list containing "apple", "orange", and "banana". The delimiter can be any regular expression pattern:

```
my $line = "first\tsecond\tthird";
my @columns = split(/\t/, $line);
```

Using split with a capturing group will include the delimiter in the resulting list:

```
my $data = "a1b2c3";
my @parts = split(/(\d)/, $data);
print "@parts"; # Output: a 1 b 2 c 3
```

Join Function

The join function combines elements of a list into a single string, with each element separated by a specified delimiter. The syntax for the join function is:

```
my @words = ("The", "quick", "brown", "fox");
my $sentence = join(" ", @words);
print "$sentence\n"; # Output: The quick brown fox
```

The first argument to join is the separator, with the elements of the list being concatenated into a single string using this separator.

These Perl functions facilitate advanced text processing and data manipulation using regular expressions, enhancing automation capabilities and enabling intricate scripting solutions.

6.12 Practical Examples of Regular Expressions

In this section, we will explore several practical examples of regular expressions in Perl, illustrating how they can be employed to solve common text processing tasks. Each example will demonstrate the application of previously discussed concepts such as metacharacters, character classes, quantifiers, anchors, grouping, capturing, and alternation.

Example 1: Validating an Email Address

A typical requirement in many applications is to validate whether a given string is a valid email address. A simple regular expression for this purpose is:

```
my $email = 'example@example.com';
if ($email =~ /^[a-zA-Z0-9._%+-]+@[a-zA-Z0-9.-]+\.[a-zA-Z]{2,}$/) {
    print "Valid email address.\n";
} else {
    print "Invalid email address.\n";
}
```

Here, the pattern ^[a-zA-Z0-9._%
+-]+@[a-zA-Z0-9.-]+[a-zA-Z]{2,}$ is used to match a valid email address. The breakdown of the pattern is as follows:

- ^: Asserts position at the start of the string.
- [a-zA-Z0-9._%
+-]+: Matches one or more of any alphanumeric characters, or the symbols ".", "_", "%", "+", and "-".
- @: Matches the "@" symbol.
- [a-zA-Z0-9.-]+: Matches one or more of any alphanumeric characters, or the symbols "." and "-".

- [a-zA-Z]{2,}: Matches a literal ".", followed by two or more alphabetic characters.
- $: Asserts position at the end of the string.

Valid email address.

Example 2: Extracting URLs from Text

Another frequent task is extracting all URLs from given text. Consider the following Perl script:

```
my $text = 'Visit https://www.example.com and http://example.org for more
    information.';
my @urls = $text =~ /https?:\/\/[a-zA-Z0-9.-]+\.[a-zA-Z]{2,6}(\/\S*)?/g;
foreach my $url (@urls) {
    print "$url\n";
}
```

In this example, the regex pattern https?:[a-zA-Z0-9.-]+[a-zA-Z]{2,6}(
S)? is used to find URLs within the text. The elements of the pattern are:

- https?:: Matches "http" or "https".
- : Matches "//".
- [a-zA-Z0-9.-]+[a-zA-Z]{2,6}: Matches the domain name and top-level domain.
- (
  S)?: Optionally matches a path beginning with "/".

https://www.example.com
http://example.org

Example 3: Splitting a String by Delimiters

Assuming we have a string of comma-separated values (CSV), we might want to split this string into individual components. Here's how it can be done using a regular expression:

```
my $csv = 'apple,banana,orange,grape';
my @fruits = split(/,/, $csv);
foreach my $fruit (@fruits) {
    print "$fruit\n";
}
```

In this example, split(/,/, $csv) splits the string at each comma, producing an array of fruits.

```
apple
banana
orange
grape
```

Example 4: Reformatting Dates

To reformat dates from YYYY-MM-DD to DD/MM/YYYY format, consider the following script:

```
my $date = '2023-10-05';
if ($date =~ /(\d{4})-(\d{2})-(\d{2})/) {
    my $formatted_date = "$3/$2/$1";
    print "Reformatted date: $formatted_date\n";
}
```

Here, the regex pattern $(\{4\})$-$(\{2\})$-$(\{2\})$ captures the year, month, and day into separate groups. The captured groups are then rearranged to produce the desired format.

```
Reformatted date: 05/10/2023
```

Example 5: Finding and Replacing Text

To perform a find-and-replace operation, such as replacing all instances of "foo" with "bar", use the following script:

```
my $text = 'foo is a placeholder, foofoo is doubled, and foo is simple.';
$text =~ s/foo/bar/g;
print "$text\n";
```

In this example, s/foo/bar/g performs a global substitution, replacing every occurrence of "foo" with "bar".

```
bar is a placeholder, barbar is doubled, and bar is simple.
```

These practical examples demonstrate the versatility and power of regular expressions in Perl, providing solutions to common text processing tasks. By understanding and applying these patterns, one can effectively manipulate and analyze textual data.

6.13 Debugging Regular Expressions

Debugging regular expressions in Perl can be a challenging but crucial task. Regular expressions are powerful tools for text processing; however, their complexity can lead to subtle bugs that are difficult to identify and resolve. This section provides techniques and strategies to debug regular expressions effectively, ensuring they perform the desired text manipulation tasks.

One of the primary methods to debug regular expressions in Perl is using the `re` module, which provides detailed information about regex compilation and execution. This module can be enabled with the `use re 'debug';` statement, which outputs diagnostic messages.

```
use re 'debug';

my $string = "The quick brown fox jumps over the lazy dog";
my $pattern = qr/quick (fox)/;

if ($string =~ $pattern) {
    print "Match found!\n";
}
```

With `use re 'debug';` enabled, running this script outputs detailed information about the regex pattern, including compiled form, matching process, and backtracking steps. This level of detail can help identify issues like excessive backtracking or unexpected matches.

```
Compiling REx 'quick (fox)'
Final program size 10
   1: BOL (0)
   2: EXACT <quick> (4)
   4:   OPEN1 (5)
   5:     EXACT <fox> (7)
   7:   CLOSE1 (8)
  8: EOL (9)
Executing machine code
Freeing REx: 'quick (fox)'
Match found!
```

For a more granular look at pattern execution, use `use re 'debugcolor';` to color-code the output for better readability, if your terminal supports colors.

Another invaluable technique involves breaking down complex regular expressions into smaller, testable components. By isolating sections of a regex and validating their behavior independently, you can incrementally build towards the full pattern. Consider a regex intended to match an email address:

```
my $email = "example.email@domain.com";
my $username = qr/^[\w.-]+/; # Matches the username part
my $domain = qr/[\w.-]+\.[a-z]{2,6}$/; # Matches the domain part
my $email_pattern = qr/$username\@$domain/;

if ($email =~ $email_pattern) {
    print "Valid email address found!\n";
}
```

By first testing `$username` and `$domain` separately, you can confirm that each sub-pattern works correctly before combining them into the final pattern.

Perl's regular expression engine also supports the use of the (?...)| construct for conditional patterns, which can simplify debugging by allowing alternative sub-patterns without significant backtracking. For example:

```
my $string = "abc123def";
my $pattern = qr/(?:abc|def)\d+(?:ghi|jkl)/;

if ($string =~ $pattern) {
    print "Pattern matched!\n";
} else {
    print "Pattern did not match.\n";
}
```

Visual debugging with tools like Regex Coach or online regex testers (such as regex101.com) can also provide immediate feedback. These tools often include explanations for each part of the regular expression, visualization of the matching process, and sample input testing.

For dynamically constructed patterns or larger scripts, embedding debug print statements can help trace which parts of the pattern succeed or fail:

```
my $text = "Sample text";
my $pattern = qr/(sample)\s+(text)/i;

if ($text =~ $pattern) {
    print "Full match: $&\n";
    print "First group: $1\n";
    print "Second group: $2\n";
} else {
    print "No match found.\n";
}
```

Lastly, iterative refinement is essential for debugging. Test your regex patterns against a variety of cases, including edge cases that might reveal hidden bugs. This ensures robustness and reliability for production use.

By utilizing these debugging techniques and tools, you can methodically dissect regular expressions in Perl, improving their accuracy and performance for complex text processing tasks.

Chapter 7

File Handling

This chapter discusses file handling in Perl, detailing how to open, close, read from, and write to files. It covers file modes, permissions, and the use of filehandles. The chapter also includes file tests, directory operations, reading and writing binary files, and error handling in file operations. Practical examples illustrate the management of large files and efficient file handling techniques.

7.1 Introduction to File Handling

File handling is a fundamental aspect of programming that involves the manipulation of files and directories on a filesystem. Perl, as a robust scripting language, offers extensive support for file handling, providing numerous built-in functions that facilitate these operations efficaciously. In this section, we will delve into the basics of file handling in Perl, setting the stage for more advanced topics covered in subsequent sections.

In Perl, a file is accessed using a filehandle, which acts as a reference to the file in the filesystem. A filehandle is opened using the open function, through which the file can be read from or written to. Once operations on the file are completed, the filehandle should be closed using the close function to free up system resources.

To begin with basic file operations, consider the following Perl script which opens a file for reading:

```
# Example of opening a file for reading
open(my $fh, '<', 'input.txt') or die "Could not open file 'input.txt' $!";
while (my $line = <$fh>) {
    print $line;
}
close($fh);
```

In this script, the open function is invoked with three arguments: the filehandle $fh, the mode '<' indicating that the file is to be opened for reading, and the filename 'input.txt'. The or die statement ensures that if the file cannot be opened, the script will terminate, emitting an error message.

The $fh> syntax is used to read the file line-by-line. Each line read from the file is stored in the $line variable, which is then printed. Finally, the filehandle is closed with the close function.

Filehandles in Perl can also be used to open files for writing, appending, or updating. These operations are specified using different modes:

```
# Opening a file for writing
open(my $fh, '>', 'output.txt') or die "Could not open file 'output.txt' $!";
print $fh "This will overwrite the file content\n";
close($fh);

# Opening a file for appending
open(my $fh, '>>', 'output.txt') or die "Could not open file 'output.txt' $!";
print $fh "This will append to the file content\n";
close($fh);
```

Here, the mode '>' is used to open a file for writing. If the file 'output.txt' already exists, its content will be overwritten. The mode '»' is used for appending, meaning that new data is added to the end of the file, preserving existing content.

Perl provides a convenient and flexible way to handle errors during file operations. Using the or die construct, it is possible to output custom error messages that include the Perl special variable $!, which contains the latest error message from the operating system:

```
open(my $fh, '<', 'nonexistent.txt') or die "Could not open file 'nonexistent.txt': $!";
```

Incorporating error handling in scripts to manage file operations is crucial for developing robust applications that can handle unexpected scenarios gracefully.

File permissions and modes also play a vital role in controlling access to files. File modes such as read, write, and execute are determined by the permissions set on the file by the operating system. It is imperative that these permissions are appropriately managed to ensure secure and effective file handling.

Another important aspect of file handling in Perl is the use of built-in functions to test files. These functions can check for various file attributes such as existence (-e), readability (-r), writability (-w), executability (-x), and more. The following script demonstrates several file test functions:

```
my $file = 'test.txt';

if (-e $file) {
    print "$file exists\n";
}
if (-r $file) {
    print "$file is readable\n";
}
if (-w $file) {
    print "$file is writable\n";
}
if (-x $file) {
    print "$file is executable\n";
}
```

By utilizing these file test functions, scripts can perform checks before attempting operations on files, thus preventing errors and ensuring the desired outcomes.

Understanding the basics of file handling in Perl provides the foundation for more advanced topics such as directory operations, binary file processing, and efficient techniques for managing large files. This foundational knowledge is essential for leveraging Perl's full capabilities in scripting and automation tasks.

7.2 Opening and Closing Files

Opening and closing files in Perl are fundamental operations that form the basis for any file handling tasks. Understanding these operations enables us to read, alter, or store data in files efficiently.

In Perl, the open function is utilized to open a file, and the close function is used to close it. The syntax for the open function is as follows:

```
open(FILEHANDLE, MODE, EXPR)
```

Here, FILEHANDLE represents the filehandle, MODE specifies the mode in which the file is opened (such as read or write), and EXPR indicates the filename or path. The open function returns a true value upon a successful operation or undef if it fails. Typically, a scalar variable is used as the filehandle, though globally assigned barewords can also suffice.

Opening Files

To open a file in read mode:

```
open(my $fh, ’<’, ’filename.txt’) or die ”Could not open file: $!”;
```

In this example, the file filename.txt is opened for reading (<). The $fh is a scalar variable functioning as the filehandle, and the or die statement provides a simple error trap, outputting an error message if the file cannot be opened.

For writing to a file, use:

```
open(my $fh, ’>’, ’output.txt’) or die ”Could not open file for writing: $!”;
```

The mode > indicates writing to the file output.txt. The or die error trap ensures the program terminates with an informative message upon failure.

Appending data to a file is achieved by:

```
open(my $fh, ’>>’, ’logfile.txt’) or die ”Could not open file for appending: $!”;
```

Here, » specifies the append mode, allowing new data to be added to logfile.txt without overwriting existing information.

When working with filehandle variables, it is a common practice to use lexical variables (my $fh) as filehandles to limit their scope and avoid unintentional conflicts.

File Mode Flags

- <: Read mode (file must exist)
- >: Write mode (creates a new file or truncates an existing file)
- »: Append mode (creates a new file if it doesn’t exist)
- +<: Read/Write mode (file must exist)
- +>: Read/Write mode (creates a new file or truncates an existing file)
- +»: Read/Append mode (creates a new file if it doesn’t exist)

Closing Files

Closing a filehandle is equally important as it frees the associated system resources. The close function is used as follows:

```
close($fh) or warn "Could not close file: $!";
```

This close operation should be invoked once file operations are complete. If the close function fails, it returns undef, and in such scenarios, warn can include an error message.

Example

Let us consider a comprehensive example that demonstrates opening a file for reading, reading its contents, and then safely closing the filehandle:

```
# Opening the file for reading
open(my $input_fh, '<', 'input.txt') or die "Could not open input file: $!";

# Reading file contents
while(my $line = <$input_fh>) {
    print $line; # Processing each line
}

# Closing the filehandle
close($input_fh) or warn "Could not close input file: $!";
```

Here, open attempts to open input.txt in read mode. The while loop fetches each line, storing it in the $line variable and printing it to the standard output. Finally, close ensures the filehandle is closed effectively.

Importance of Error Handling

Error handling is crucial for robust file operations. The $! variable contains the error message from the last file operation, which aids in pinpointing issues. Commonly, error handling is embedded using:

```
open(my $fh, '<', 'file.txt') or die "Error opening file.txt: $!";
```

The use of or die or or warn constructs makes sure that the program behaves predictably and outputs readable error explanations when something goes wrong, aiding in debugging.

Regular practice should include checking the success of both opening and closing filehandles. By ensuring proper file operations and resource management, Perl scripts become reliable and maintainable, preventing file corruption and resource leaks.

7.3 Reading from Files

Reading data from files in Perl is a fundamental task that enables applications to process input from external sources. This section details the various methodologies for reading from files, ensuring that the reader understands the practical techniques and underlying mechanisms.

To read from a file in Perl, you must first open the file using the open function. The open function associates a filehandle with the file, providing a means to read the file's content. Consider the following example:

```
open(my $fh, '<', 'example.txt') or die "Could not open file 'example.txt' $!";
```

In this example, the open function associates the filehandle $fh with the file example.txt in read mode (indicated by the '<' symbol). If the file cannot be opened, the die function will terminate the program and print an error message.

Once the file is successfully opened, you can read data from it using several different methods. The most common methods are:

- Reading the entire file into a scalar variable.
- Reading the file line by line.
- Reading the file into an array.

To read the entire contents of a file into a scalar variable, you can use the following approach:

```
my $contents;
{
    local $/;
    $contents = <$fh>;
}
```

Here, we use a block to localize the special variable $/, which is the input record separator. By setting it to an undefined value, we enable Perl to read the entire file at once. The file's contents are then stored in the scalar variable $contents.

For most applications, reading a file line by line is more practical and memory-efficient. This can be done using a simple while loop:

```
while (my $line = <$fh>) {
    chomp $line;
    print "$line\n";
}
```

In this example, the input operator <$fh> reads the next line from the file. The chomp function removes the trailing newline character, and the line is then printed. This method is especially useful for processing text files where data is organized into lines.

To read the entire file into an array, where each element represents a line, you can use the following syntax:

```
my @lines = <$fh>;
close $fh;
foreach my $line (@lines) {
    chomp $line;
    print ”$line\n”;
}
```

In this approach, the input operator in list context reads all lines from the file into the array @lines. After closing the filehandle $fh, a foreach loop iterates over each line, chomping the newline character and printing the content.

It is critical to close the filehandle when you've completed reading:

```
close($fh) or warn ”Could not close file ’example.txt’ $!”;
```

Closing the filehandle ensures that resources are released and any pending data is properly flushed.

For situations requiring more control or processing, Perl also provides the ability to read files using explicit read operations. Consider the following example of reading a file in fixed-size blocks:

```
open(my $fh, ’<’, ’example.txt’) or die ”Could not open file ’example.txt’ $!”;
while (read($fh, my $buffer, 1024)) {
    print $buffer;
}
close $fh;
```

Here, the read function is called with the filehandle $fh, a buffer variable $buffer, and the length of bytes (1024 in this case) to read. This method is useful for binary files or situations requiring specific buffer sizes.

Another useful technique involves using Perl's IO::File module, which provides an object-oriented way to handle file operations:

```
use IO::File;
my $file = IO::File->new(’example.txt’, ’r’) or die ”Could not open file ’example.txt’ $!
    ”;
while (my $line = $file->getline) {
    chomp $line;
    print ”$line\n”;
}
$file->close;
```

The IO::File module streamlines file operations by encapsulating file-handle management within an object. This approach improves code readability and maintainability.

It is essential to handle any potential errors during file operations to make your script robust. Employing the or die construct ensures that the program notifies the user of any issues immediately. For extensive error handling, you can use the Try::Tiny module or similar approaches to manage exceptions and provide informative messages to the user.

Understanding different methods to read from files equips programmers with the flexibility to choose the most suitable approach for their specific needs, enhancing both performance and code clarity.

7.4 Writing to Files

Writing to files in Perl involves several key concepts and steps, including opening a file in write mode, appending data to an existing file, and correctly closing the file to ensure all data is properly saved. This section will explore the necessary syntax and best practices for writing data to files, focusing on different scenarios and examples to provide a comprehensive understanding.

To write to a file, the file must first be opened in the appropriate mode. Perl provides several modes for opening files, but for writing purposes, the most commonly used modes are > for writing (which truncates the file if it already exists) and » for appending (which leaves the existing data intact and appends new data at the end).

```
# Open a file for writing (truncates the file if it exists)
open(my $fh, '>', 'example.txt') or die "Could not open file 'example.txt' $!";

# Open a file for appending (preserves existing data)
open(my $fh_append, '>>', 'example.txt') or die "Could not open file 'example.txt' $!"
    ;
```

In the example above, the open function is used to open the file example.txt in two different modes. The first open command opens the file in write mode (>), which will overwrite any existing content. The second command opens the file in append mode (»), ensuring that new data is added to the end without disturbing the existing content.

Once the file is open, data can be written using the print function. It is essential to specify the filehandle when calling print, directing the output to the correct file.

```
# Writing data to a file
print $fh "This is a line of text.\n";

# Appending data to a file
print $fh_append "This is an appended line of text.\n";
```

In the above code, print $fh writes a line of text to example.txt, as specified when the file was opened in write mode. Similarly, print $fh_append appends a line of text to the same file, because the file was opened in append mode.

After writing or appending data, it is critical to close the file using the close function. This ensures that all data is correctly flushed to the file and no filehandles are left open unintentionally, which could lead to memory leaks or other issues.

```
# Close the filehandles
close($fh) or warn "Could not close file 'example.txt' $!";
close($fh_append) or warn "Could not close file 'example.txt' $!";
```

Handling errors in file operations is also essential. It is crucial to check whether the file operations (open, write, close) are successful and handle failures appropriately, such as by printing an error message or performing additional cleanup operations. Perl's special variable $! contains the error message if an operation fails.

```
# Open a file safely
open(my $safe_fh, '>', 'safe_example.txt') or die "Could not open file 'safe_example.
    txt' $!";

# Write data with error handling
print $safe_fh "Error handling example.\n" or die "Could not write to file '
    safe_example.txt' $!";

# Close the file safely
close($safe_fh) or warn "Could not close file 'safe_example.txt' $!";
```

Writing binary data to files involves a similar process but requires additional handling to ensure the data is not corrupted. The file should be opened in binary mode using the binmode function, which configures the filehandle to treat the file as binary and not perform any character encoding translations.

```
# Open a file in binary mode
open(my $bin_fh, '>:raw', 'binary_example.bin') or die "Could not open file '
    binary_example.bin' $!";

# Write binary data to the file
print $bin_fh "\xDE\xAD\xBE\xEF" or die "Could not write to file 'binary_example.
    bin' $!";

# Close the binary filehandle
```

```
close($bin_fh) or warn "Could not close file 'binary_example.bin' $!";
```

In practical applications, data to be written to files often comes from various sources, such as user inputs, computations, or other files. Careful handling and validation of this data are paramount to maintain data integrity and security.

Moreover, it is beneficial to consider buffering strategies and efficient file handling techniques, especially when dealing with large files. Utilizing memory-efficient approaches, such as writing data in chunks, can significantly enhance performance and resource management.

Effective writing to files is a vital skill in Perl programming, enabling the development of robust scripts and applications that handle data accurately and efficiently.

7.5 File Modes and Permissions

File modes and permissions are crucial in Perl for controlling how files are accessed and manipulated. Understanding these concepts ensures that scripts interact with files securely and correctly.

Perl utilizes multiple file modes to specify operations on a file, such as reading, writing, and appending. The file mode is defined within the open function, which associates the file with a filehandle. Filehandle management and the open function are discussed extensively in a preceding section. Here, we will focus specifically on the various file modes and permissions.

To open a file, the 'open' function uses the following syntax:

```
open(FILEHANDLE, MODE, FILENAME) or die "Cannot open file: $!";
```

Here, 'FILEHANDLE' is the filehandle we wish to associate with the file, 'MODE' specifies the manner in which we want to interact with the file, and 'FILENAME' is the name of the file we are opening. Let's discuss the common modes used in Perl.

Read-Only Mode ('<'):

Opening a file in read-only mode allows reading the file without modifying its contents. The syntax is as follows:

```
open(FILEHANDLE, "<", "input.txt") or die "Cannot open input.txt: $!";
```

This mode is appropriate when the file's content needs to be examined or processed without alterations.

Write-Only Mode (‘>‘):

Write-only mode is used when the intention is to write data to a file. If the file already exists, it will be truncated to zero length. If it does not exist, Perl will create it. The syntax is:

```
open(FILEHANDLE, ”>”, ”output.txt”) or die ”Cannot open output.txt: $!”;
```

This mode is suitable for creating new files or overwriting existing files with new content.

Append Mode (‘»‘):

For appending data to the end of an existing file, append mode is used. If the file does not exist, it will be created. The syntax is:

```
open(FILEHANDLE, ”>>”, ”logfile.txt”) or die ”Cannot open logfile.txt: $!”;
```

This mode is ideal for log files or any files where the previous content should not be replaced.

Read/Write Mode (‘+<‘):

To both read from and write to a file without truncating it, read/write mode is used:

```
open(FILEHANDLE, ”+<”, ”data.txt”) or die ”Cannot open data.txt: $!”;
```

This mode allows the script to modify existing content or add new content at any location within the file.

Write/Read Mode (‘+>‘):

Write/read mode is used when the file should be truncated upon opening, but both reading and writing capabilities are needed:

```
open(FILEHANDLE, ”+>”, ”data.txt”) or die ”Cannot open data.txt: $!”;
```

Append/Read Mode (‘+»‘):

Append/read mode is used for reading from and appending to a file, without truncating it:

```
open(FILEHANDLE, ”+>>”, ”data.txt”) or die ”Cannot open data.txt: $!”;
```

Permissions control access and modifications to files based on user roles and ownership. In UNIX-like systems, file permissions are managed via three types of permissions: read (r), write (w), and execute (x), applied to three categories: user (u), group (g), and others (o).

Permissions are viewed and modified using the command 'chmod' from the terminal. For example, the command

```
chmod u+x filename
```

adds execute permission to the file for the user. Correspondingly, in Perl, file permissions can be managed using the 'chmod' function:

```
chmod 0755, "script.pl";
```

Here, '0755' sets the permissions. The four-digit octal number indicates permissions: the first digit defines special flags, the second defines the user's permissions, the third for the group's permissions, and the fourth for others. The permission '0755' translates to 'rwxr-xr-x', granting the user full permissions and read/execute permissions for group and others.

Understanding file modes and permissions in Perl provides enhanced control over file handling operations, ensuring that files are accessed and modified securely and appropriately, in alignment with the script's requirements. This foundational knowledge is essential for developing robust and reliable Perl scripts that interact with the file system effectively.

7.6 Working with Filehandles

Filehandles are fundamental in Perl for performing file operations such as reading, writing, and appending. A filehandle is a special type of scalar used to associate a file with operations defined in your script. Assigning a filehandle to a file allows functions and commands to interact with it seamlessly. There are several aspects to working with filehandles that you need to understand to effectively handle files in Perl.

Filehandles are typically created using the open function. To open a file and create a filehandle, you can use the following syntax:

```
open(my $filehandle, $mode, $filename) or die "Cannot open file: $!";
```

- The first argument is a scalar variable, often preceded by my to restrict its scope to the block in which it is declared.
- The $mode specifies the file mode which can be read, write, or

append.

- The $filename is the name of the file you wish to operate on.

Here is an example to open a file for reading:

```
open(my $fh, '<', 'input.txt') or die "Cannot open file: $!";
```

This command opens the file input.txt in read mode. The angle bracket $<$ represents the read mode.

To open a file for writing, you replace the mode with a greater-than sign $>$:

```
open(my $fh, '>', 'output.txt') or die "Cannot open file: $!";
```

This example opens output.txt in write mode. If the file does not exist, Perl creates it. If it does exist, the file is truncated.

For appending, where data must be added to the end of the file without truncating it, you use the double angle bracket »:

```
open(my $fh, '>>', 'append.txt') or die "Cannot open file: $!";
```

After opening a file and associating it with a filehandle, you can perform various operations. For example, reading from a file line by line and printing the contents can be done using the angle bracket operator $<>$:

```
while (my $line = <$fh>) {
    print $line;
}
```

In this snippet, $line reads each line from the filehandle $fh. The while loop iterates over the file, processing it line by line. For each iteration, the current line is stored in $line and printed.

To write to a file, you can use the print function, directing its output to the filehandle:

```
print $fh "Hello, World!\n";
```

When done with file operations, it is essential to close the filehandle to free up system resources. The close function is used:

```
close($fh) or die "Cannot close file: $!";
```

Working with filehandles efficiently also involves employing error checking. This ensures that your program can handle situations where file operations fail, such as when a file is not found or cannot be written to.

The or die statement provides this basic error handling by terminating the program with an error message if the preceding operation fails.

In addition to standard file modes, Perl supports the use of more advanced mechanisms like file locking, which is crucial in concurrent environments to avoid race conditions. File locking can be implemented using the flock function:

```
use Fcntl qw(:flock);

open(my $fh, '>>', 'file.txt') or die "Cannot open file: $!";
flock($fh, LOCK_EX) or die "Cannot lock file: $!";

print $fh "Some data\n";

flock($fh, LOCK_UN) or die "Cannot unlock file: $!";
close($fh) or die "Cannot close file: $!";
```

In this example, the flock function locks the file for exclusive access using LOCK_EX, then performs the write operation and finally unlocks the file using LOCK_UN.

Another useful technique is tying a filehandle to a variable, which allows you to use familiar filehandle operations directly with scalars. The Tie::File module enables such functionality, particularly when you need random access to the lines of a file:

```
use Tie::File;

tie my @array, 'Tie::File', 'file.txt' or die "Cannot tie file: $!";

$array[0] = "New first line";
print $array[0];

untie @array;
```

In the snippet above, tie binds the @array to the file file.txt. You can then manipulate the file content as though you are directly manipulating an array. When done, untie is called to release the association.

Understanding and working correctly with filehandles ensures that your file operations in Perl are efficient, robust, and error-free. The careful selection of modes and effective error handling are critical steps in managing file I/O operations.

7.7 File Tests and Operations

File tests in Perl provide a highly efficient and straightforward mechanism to interrogate various attributes of files and directories. These tests can ascertain information such as file readability, existence, size, and other metadata. Operators such as '-e', '-r', '-w', '-x', and others enable such inquiries, providing a convenient means to programmatically verify file properties.

To illustrate the application of file test operators, consider the snippet below. This code evaluates whether a file named 'example.txt' exists and checks for its readability and writability:

```
my $filename = 'example.txt';

if (-e $filename) {
    print "$filename exists.\n";
}

if (-r $filename) {
    print "$filename is readable.\n";
}

if (-w $filename) {
    print "$filename is writable.\n";
}

if (-x $filename) {
    print "$filename is executable.\n";
}
```

Further file test operators are available, each serving a distinct purpose. Notable among these are:

- -e : Checks if the file exists.
- -r : Checks if the file is readable.
- -w : Checks if the file is writable.
- -x : Checks if the file is executable.
- -z : Checks if the file is empty.
- -s : Returns the size of the file.
- -f : Checks if it is a plain file.
- -d : Checks if it is a directory.
- -l : Checks if it is a symbolic link.
- -T : Checks if the file is a text file.
- -B : Checks if the file is a binary file.

For example, the '-s' operator returns the size of a file in bytes. Here is a Perl snippet demonstrating its usage:

```
my $filesize = -s $filename;
print "Size of $filename is $filesize bytes.\n";
```

To perform some practical file test operations, combining multiple tests can streamline comprehensive checks. For instance, an effective pattern for ensuring a file's suitability for reading and writing might look like this:

```
if (-e $filename && -r $filename && -w $filename) {
    print "$filename is both readable and writable.\n";
} else {
    print "$filename does not have the required permissions.\n";
}
```

Beyond testing, file and directory operations provide mechanisms to manipulate and manage file system objects. Actions such as renaming, deleting, and copying files integrate seamlessly using Perl's built-in functions. To rename a file, the 'rename' function is used, as shown:

```
my $oldname = 'oldfile.txt';
my $newname = 'newfile.txt';
rename($oldname, $newname) or die "Cannot rename $oldname to $newname: $!";
```

For file deletion, the 'unlink' function is employed:

```
my $file_to_delete = 'deletefile.txt';
unlink($file_to_delete) or warn "Could not delete $file_to_delete: $!";
```

To create directories, Perl provides the 'mkdir' function:

```
my $directory = 'new_dir';
mkdir($directory) or die "Cannot create directory $directory: $!";
```

Similarly, directories can be removed using the 'rmdir' function:

```
my $directory_to_remove = 'remove_dir';
rmdir($directory_to_remove) or warn "Could not remove directory
      $directory_to_remove: $!";
```

For more complex operations, such as copying files, the File::Copy module is appropriate. Here is an example of using it to copy a file:

```
use File::Copy;
my $source = 'source.txt';
my $destination = 'destination.txt';
copy($source, $destination) or die "Copy failed: $!";
```

The ability to combine these file operations with tests creates powerful scripts capable of dynamic and responsive file handling. For example, a script designed to archive logs might ensure that the log file exists and then move it to an archive directory only if it is sufficiently large:

```
use File::Copy;

my $logfile = 'logfile.txt';
my $archive_dir = 'archive/';
my $threshold_size = 1024;

if (-e $logfile && -s $logfile > $threshold_size) {
    my $archive_filename = $archive_dir . time() . '_logfile.txt';
    move($logfile, $archive_filename) or die "Cannot move $logfile to $archive_filename
        : $!";
    print "Archived $logfile to $archive_filename.\n";
} else {
    print "$logfile does not exist or is too small to archive.\n";
}
```

Such file test and operation techniques are essential for effective automation scripting, providing reliability and efficiency in managing file systems.

7.8 Reading and Writing Binary Files

Binary files are typically used to store data that is not text-based, such as images, executables, and other media files. Working with binary files in Perl involves certain nuances due to the inherent differences in handling binary and text data. In this section, we will explore techniques to read from and write to binary files, ensuring data integrity during the file operations.

The first step in working with binary files is to open them in the appropriate mode. Perl uses the concept of file modes to determine how a file is accessed. For binary files, the binmode function is crucial as it ensures that the data is read or written without translation of any byte sequences.

```
# Opening a binary file for reading
open(my $fh, '<:raw', 'input.bin') or die "Cannot open file: $!";
binmode($fh);

# Opening a binary file for writing
open(my $fh, '>:raw', 'output.bin') or die "Cannot open file: $!";
binmode($fh);
```

The <:raw and >:raw file modes specify that the file is to be handled in binary mode, bypassing any end-of-line translation or encoding conversions. The binmode($fh) function is explicitly applied to ensure no unwanted transformations are done by the system.

Reading from a binary file involves reading a specific number of bytes at a time, often managed using the read function. This function allows you to read arbitrary-sized chunks of data from a file.

```
# Reading 1024 bytes from a binary file
my $buffer;
open(my $fh, '<:raw', 'input.bin') or die "Cannot open file: $!";
binmode($fh);
my $bytes_read = read($fh, $buffer, 1024);

if (!defined $bytes_read) {
    die "Read error: $!";
}

print "Read $bytes_read bytes from the file\n";
close($fh);
```

Here, the read function reads up to 1024 bytes from the file into the scalar variable $buffer. The function returns the number of bytes successfully read, which should be checked to ensure there were no errors during the operation. Always closing the filehandle with close($fh) is necessary to release system resources.

Writing to a binary file is similarly straightforward by using the print function. It is important to handle the binary data correctly to maintain the integrity of the data being written.

```
# Writing binary data to a file
my $data = "\x{00}\x{01}\x{02}\x{03}";
open(my $fh, '>:raw', 'output.bin') or die "Cannot open file: $!";
binmode($fh);
print $fh $data or die "Cannot write to file: $!";
close($fh);
```

In this example, the scalar $data contains raw binary data. The print function writes this data to the specified file. It is important to check the success of the print operation to confirm that data is correctly written.

Binary file operations often entail dealing with large amounts of data. Therefore, it is efficient to read and write in chunks rather than processing the entire file content in one go. Loop-based techniques are employed to handle such scenarios.

```
# Efficiently reading and processing a large binary file in chunks
open(my $fh, '<:raw', 'large_input.bin') or die "Cannot open file: $!";
binmode($fh);
while (my $bytes_read = read($fh, my $buffer, 4096)) {
    if (!defined $bytes_read) {
        die "Read error: $!";
    }

    # Process the buffer content
    process_binary_chunk($buffer);
}
```

```
close($fh);

sub process_binary_chunk {
    my ($chunk) = @_;
    # Placeholder for processing logic
    print "Processing chunk of size: ", length($chunk), "\n";
}
```

In this example, the file is read in chunks of 4096 bytes. The process_binary_chunk subroutine acts as a placeholder for the logic to process each chunk. Reading in smaller chunks helps in managing memory usage effectively while dealing with large files.

Overall, the handling of binary files requires careful attention to ensure that the data is read or written accurately without unintended transformations. Proper use of binmode and chunked processing ensures that the operations are performed efficiently and correctly.

7.9 Directory Operations

Directory operations in Perl encompass tasks such as creating, reading, and removing directories, as well as iterating over directory contents. Understanding how to manage directories is essential for organizing file systems and ensuring efficient access to files.

Creating a directory can be achieved using the mkdir function. This function requires the name of the directory to be created and an optional mode argument that specifies the permissions for the directory. The mode should be given in octal format:

```
# Create a directory named 'example_dir' with permissions 0755.
mkdir 'example_dir', 0755 or die "Cannot create directory: $!";
```

The or die clause is a common Perl idiom for handling errors, which will terminate the program and print an error message if the mkdir function fails.

Reading the contents of a directory involves opening the directory with opendir, reading entries with readdir, and then closing the directory with closedir. Below is an example that demonstrates how to read and print the contents of a directory:

```
# Open a directory
opendir(my $dir, 'example_dir') or die "Cannot open directory: $!";

# Read directory contents
my @files = readdir($dir);
```

```
# Print the names of the files
foreach my $file (@files) {
    print "$file\n";
}

# Close the directory
closedir($dir);
```

The readdir function returns all entries in the directory, including special entries . (current directory) and .. (parent directory). These can be filtered out if necessary:

```
# Filter out . and ..
foreach my $file (@files) {
    next if ($file eq '.' or $file eq '..');
    print "$file\n";
}
```

Removing a directory can be performed with the rmdir function. This function will only succeed if the directory is empty:

```
# Remove an empty directory named 'example_dir'
rmdir 'example_dir' or die "Cannot remove directory: $!";
```

To recursively delete a directory and its contents, a combination of directory reading and file handling functions is required. Below is an example of a Perl subroutine that deletes a directory and all its contents recursively:

```
use File::Path qw(rmtree);

# Recursively delete a directory and its contents
sub remove_directory {
    my ($dir) = @_;

    # Check if directory exists
    if (-d $dir) {
        rmtree($dir) or warn "Failed to remove directory $dir: $!";
    } else {
        warn "Directory $dir does not exist.";
    }
}

# Usage
remove_directory('example_dir');
```

Alternatively, the File::Path module's rmtree function simplifies the process of recursively deleting directories.

Directory iteration is also important when performing operations on multiple files. The File::Find module provides a convenient way to traverse directory trees. Below is an example of using File::Find to print the names of all files and directories within a specified directory tree:

```
use File::Find;

# Subroutine to be called for each file and directory
sub wanted {
    print "$File::Find::name\n";
}

# Start traversal from 'example_dir'
find(\&wanted, 'example_dir');
```

The wanted subroutine is called for every file and directory found within the specified directory tree. The $File::Find::name variable contains the complete path of the current file or directory.

Effective directory operations in Perl require careful error handling to manage permissions, non-existent directories, and other potential issues. The following example demonstrates robust error handling when opening and reading directory contents:

```
# Attempt to open directory and handle possible errors
my $directory = 'example_dir';
if (opendir(my $dh, $directory)) {
    while (readdir $dh) {
        # Process entries
        next if ($_ eq '.' or $_ eq '..');
        print "$_\n";
    }
    closedir($dh);
} else {
    warn "Could not open directory '$directory': $!";
}
```

This example ensures that the directory handle $dh is properly managed, and any issues with opening the directory are logged for further investigation.

For advanced directory manipulation, the use of modules such as File::Path, File::Find, and File::Basename can provide additional functionalities and simplify complex tasks. Understanding the basics of directory operations alongside these powerful modules allows for comprehensive and efficient directory management in Perl programming.

7.10 Error Handling in File Operations

Handling errors effectively during file operations is a crucial aspect of robust Perl programming. This section delves deeply into the tools and techniques embedded within Perl for managing errors that occur when interacting with files.

Perl provides the die function for handling errors in file operations. When die is called, it prints the error message to STDERR and exits the script. To illustrate error handling with die, consider the following code snippet:

```
open(my $fh, '<', 'file.txt') or die "Cannot open file.txt: $!";
```

The $! variable holds the error message related to the last system call or library function's failure. In this case, if Perl cannot open file.txt, it will terminate the script and print the associated error message.

To handle errors more gracefully, especially in larger scripts, one might want to manage exceptions rather than abruptly ending the program. This is achieved using eval blocks that trap errors and allow the program to continue executing properly, providing a way to handle errors without terminating the script:

```
eval {
    open(my $fh, '<', 'file.txt') or die "Cannot open file.txt: $!";
    # Read from file
    close($fh);
};
if ($@) {
    warn "An error occurred: $@";
    # Additional error handling
}
```

Here, the eval block attempts to open and read file.txt. If an error occurs, $@ captures the error message, allowing the script to warn the user and proceed with additional error handling, if necessary.

A key principle when working with files is ensuring resources are correctly released, even when errors occur. Use the finally equivalent by ensuring that filehandles are always closed using the END block or explicitly within the eval block:

```
eval {
    open(my $fh, '<', 'file.txt') or die "Cannot open file.txt: $!";
    # File operations...
};
if ($@) {
    warn "An error occurred: $@";
}
else {
    close($fh) or warn "Could not close file: $!";
}
```

In Perl, the autodie pragma simplifies error handling in file operations. When used, it automatically throws exceptions on failures related to file handling functions, obviating the need for explicit error checking with or die statements:

```
use autodie;

open(my $fh, '<', 'file.txt');
# File operations...
close($fh);
```

Here, autodie automatically handles errors from open and close functions, ensuring that errors raise exceptions directly. Error messages are managed through eval blocks, as demonstrated previously.

Another aspect of error handling involves using file tests to prevent attempting unsafe operations. Built-in file test operators such as -e, -r, -w, and -x check for file existence, readability, writability, and executability, respectively:

```
if (-e 'file.txt') {
    if (-r 'file.txt') {
        open(my $fh, '<', 'file.txt') or die "Cannot open file.txt: $!";
        # Read from file
        close($fh);
    } else {
        warn "file.txt exists but is not readable";
    }
} else {
    warn "file.txt does not exist";
}
```

Using these file test operators allows the script to pre-emptively check for potential issues before attempting file operations, thus reducing the likelihood of encountering runtime errors.

Implementing robust error logging is another key practice. By writing error messages to log files, the programmer maintains a record of problems that can be debugged later. This practice is essential in large-scale systems, where immediate problem diagnosis is critical:

```
open(my $log_fh, '>>', 'error.log') or die "Cannot open error.log: $!";

eval {
    open(my $fh, '<', 'file.txt') or die "Cannot open file.txt: $!";
    # File operations...
};
if ($@) {
    print $log_fh "[$$] An error occurred at ", scalar localtime(), ": $@";
    warn "An error occurred: $@";
}
else {
    close($fh) or warn "Could not close file: $!";
}

close($log_fh) or warn "Could not close log file: $!";
```

In this code, error.log maintains a log of error messages with timestamps and process IDs, enhancing the script's traceability and debuggability.

By integrating these techniques into Perl file handling scripts, a programmer ensures that error handling is both systematic and informative, promoting the development of reliable and maintainable code.

7.11 Working with Large Files

Handling large files efficiently is a critical aspect of file management in Perl. Files that are several gigabytes in size require careful memory management and efficient processing to avoid performance degradation or system crashes.

Large file processing entails reading and writing operations where the entire file may not fit into memory. Instead, chunks of the file are processed incrementally. This section explores methods for reading from and writing to large files efficiently, leveraging utility modules and Perl's in-built capabilities.

To start with, let us consider the incremental reading of a large file. The typical approach is to read the file line by line, ensuring that only a minimal portion of the file is held in memory at any one time. This approach is achieved using the special global variable $_.

```
open my $fh, '<', 'largefile.txt' or die "Cannot open file: $!";
while (<$fh>) {
    chomp;
    # Process each line
    # $_ contains the current line
}
close $fh or die "Cannot close file: $!";
```

The while(<$fh>) construct reads the file line by line into the default variable $_. Each line is processed and, optionally, chomp is used to remove the newline character.

For tasks where multiple lines or specific sections of the file need to be read, reading in blocks can be more efficient. The read function reads a specified number of bytes from the file, which can then be processed as required.

```
open my $fh, '<:raw', 'largefile.txt' or die "Cannot open file: $!";
my $buffer;
while (read($fh, $buffer, 8192)) {
    # Process 8KB of data from the file
}
close $fh or die "Cannot close file: $!";
```

The read function here reads 8192 bytes in each iteration, which corresponds to 8KB. Processing data in this manner allows the script to handle very large files without overwhelming the available memory.

Writing to large files can be approached similarly. Instead of writing large data chunks all at once, data can be written incrementally. For example, data generation and writing could happen in tandem:

```
open my $fh, '>', 'outputfile.txt' or die "Cannot open file: $!";
for (1..10_000_000) {
    print $fh "Line $_\n";
}
close $fh or die "Cannot close file: $!";
```

This loop simulates writing 10 million lines to outputfile.txt, each line constructed and written sequentially. This way, memory usage stays constant regardless of the file size.

In cases where it's necessary to delete or modify only specific chunks of a large file, using file operation functions along with a temporary file can prove efficient. Copy a segment to the temporary file, modify or omit specific parts, and then overwrite the original file. Here's an example scenario where lines containing a specific keyword are removed:

```
open my $in_fh, '<', 'largefile.txt' or die "Cannot open file: $!";
open my $out_fh, '>', 'tempfile.txt' or die "Cannot open temp file: $!";

while (<$in_fh>) {
    print $out_fh $_ unless /keyword/;
}

close $in_fh or die "Cannot close input file: $!";
close $out_fh or die "Cannot close temp file: $!";
rename 'tempfile.txt', 'largefile.txt' or die "Cannot rename file: $!";
```

This script reads the entire file and copies only the lines that do not contain the keyword to a temporary file. Once processing is complete, the original file is replaced by the processed temporary file using rename.

Another practical method involves mmap (memory-mapped) files using modules like Sys::Mmap. This allows part of the file to be mapped into memory, providing efficient random access without loading the entire file into memory.

Install the Sys::Mmap module via CPAN before usage as shown:

```
use Sys::Mmap;

open my $fh, '<', 'largefile.txt' or die "Cannot open file: $!";
mmap(my $data, 0, PROT_READ, MAP_SHARED, $fh) or die "Cannot mmap file: $!
    ";

# $data now contains the contents of the file, accessible like a string
```

```
close $fh or die "Cannot close file: $!";
```

Accessing large files efficiently in Perl often involves combining these techniques to balance memory usage and processing speed. The following advanced example demonstrates using filehandles and memory-mapped files together.

```
use Sys::Mmap;

open my $fh, '<', 'largefile.txt' or die "Cannot open file: $!";
my ($file_size) = (stat $fh)[7];
mmap(my $data, $file_size, PROT_READ, MAP_SHARED, $fh) or die "Cannot
      mmap file: $!";

# Example: Summing up numerical values assuming each line contains a number
my $sum = 0;
while ($data =~ /(\d+)/g) {
   $sum += $1;
}
print "Sum: $sum\n";

close $fh or die "Cannot close file: $!";
```

Handling large files efficiently requires robust error checking and handling to ensure operations can gracefully handle unexpected conditions like file access issues or memory limitations. This includes verifying successful file opening, checking read and write permissions, and ensuring proper closing of filehandles. Such practices lead to more resilient and maintainable code.

7.12 Practical Examples of File Handling

Understanding file handling is crucial for efficient Perl programming. This section illustrates practical examples to solidify your comprehension of concepts like file operations, modes, and error handling discussed previously.

Example 1: Reading a File Line by Line

This example demonstrates reading a file line by line. Assume we need to process a log file, extracting and printing lines that contain the word "ERROR".

```
#!/usr/bin/perl
use strict;
use warnings;

# Open the file for reading
my $filename = 'logfile.txt';
open(my $fh, '<', $filename) or die "Could not open file '$filename' $!";
```

```
# Read file line by line
while (my $line = <$fh>) {
    if ($line =~ /ERROR/) {
        print $line;
    }
}

# Close the file
close($fh);
```

In this script, the filehandle $fh is used to open logfile.txt in read mode. The while loop reads each line, checks for the presence of "ERROR", and prints matching lines. Finally, the file is closed with close($fh).

Example 2: Writing to a New File

Creating a new file and writing content to it is another common task. Here, we create a file output.txt and write some example content.

```
#!/usr/bin/perl
use strict;
use warnings;

# Open the file for writing
my $filename = 'output.txt';
open(my $fh, '>', $filename) or die "Could not open file '$filename' $!";

# Write some content to the file
print $fh "This is the first line of the file.\n";
print $fh "This is the second line of the file.\n";

# Close the file
close($fh);
```

Here, the filehandle $fh is associated with output.txt in write mode (>). The print function writes lines to the file, and the file is then properly closed.

Example 3: Appending Data to an Existing File

Appending data to an existing file is common in logging applications. This example shows how to open a file in append mode and add new lines to it.

```
#!/usr/bin/perl
use strict;
use warnings;

# Open the file in append mode
my $filename = 'output.txt';
open(my $fh, '>>', $filename) or die "Could not open file '$filename' $!";

# Add new content
print $fh "This is an appended line.\n";
print $fh "Another appended line.\n";
```

```
# Close the file
close($fh);
```

The filehandle $fh is used to append (») to output.txt. The print function adds the specified text to the end of the file.

Example 4: Reading and Writing Binary Files

Handling binary files requires reading and writing in binary mode. Below is an example of copying a binary file.

```
#!/usr/bin/perl
use strict;
use warnings;

# Source and destination files
my $source = 'source.bin';
my $destination = 'destination.bin';

# Open source file for reading in binary mode
open(my $in, '<:raw', $source) or die "Cannot open '$source' $!";

# Open destination file for writing in binary mode
open(my $out, '>:raw', $destination) or die "Cannot open '$destination' $!";

# Copy the file
my $buffer;
while (read($in, $buffer, 4096)) {
    print $out $buffer;
}

# Close the files
close($in);
close($out);
```

Both source and destination files are opened in binary mode using <:raw and >:raw. The while loop reads 4096-byte chunks from $in and writes them to $out, effectively copying the file.

Example 5: Directory Operations

Creating scripts that interact with directories can be essential. This example demonstrates listing all files in a directory.

```
#!/usr/bin/perl
use strict;
use warnings;
use File::Basename;

# Directory to list
my $dir = '/some/directory/';

# Open directory
opendir(my $dh, $dir) or die "Cannot open directory '$dir' $!";

# Read files from directory
while (my $file = readdir($dh)) {
    next if ($file =~ m/^\./); # Skip hidden files
```

```
    print "Found file: $file\n";
}

# Close directory
closedir($dh);
```

The opendir function opens the directory handle $dh, and readdir reads each file/directory name. The next statement skips hidden files starting with a dot. Each file name is printed until all files have been processed.

These examples aim to consolidate your understanding of file handling in Perl, equipping you to manage text and binary files effectively. Moving forward, these skills will enable you to implement more complex file-based operations in your Perl scripts.

Chapter 8

Perl Modules

This chapter introduces Perl modules, guiding readers on how to use built-in modules and install CPAN modules. It covers creating custom modules, understanding module namespaces, and loading modules with 'use' and 'require'. The chapter also explains exporting functions and variables, module documentation, versioning, and dependency management, supplemented with practical examples of module utilization.

8.1 Introduction to Perl Modules

Perl modules encompass a robust system that allows for code reusability and modularity, integral to efficient scripting and automation. At the core, a Perl module is a collection of Perl functions and variables housed in a separate file with a .pm extension. This file can then be included and used in other Perl scripts or modules to facilitate code reuse and organization.

A Perl module typically contains package declarations, which define its namespace. This namespace acts as a container for related subroutines and variables, helping to avoid conflicts with other parts of a program or other modules. For instance, a file named MathTools.pm would conventionally begin with a package MathTools; statement, setting up a distinct namespace.

To declare a module, place the following code in a file named MathTools.pm:

```
# MathTools.pm
package MathTools;

use strict;
use warnings;

sub add {
    my ($x, $y) = @_;
    return $x + $y;
}

sub subtract {
    my ($x, $y) = @_;
    return $x - $y;
}

1; # End of MathTools
```

Here, MathTools.pm defines a MathTools package with two functions: add and subtract. Every Perl module must end with a 1; statement to indicate successful loading.

Modules can be incorporated into a Perl script using the use or require directives. The use directive imports the module at compile time and also implicitly calls the import method, facilitating the automatic loading of exported functions and variables. Conversely, require loads the module at runtime and does not call the import method automatically.

An example using the MathTools module in a Perl script:

```
#!/usr/bin/perl
use strict;
use warnings;
use MathTools;

my $sum = MathTools::add(10, 5);
print "Sum: $sum\n"; # Outputs: Sum: 15

my $difference = MathTools::subtract(10, 5);
print "Difference: $difference\n"; # Outputs: Difference: 5
```

In this script, the use MathTools; statement treats MathTools.pm as a library, importing its functions into the script. Functions from MathTools are invoked with their fully qualified names, ensuring that they do not collide with functions from other namespaces.

Another key advantage of Perl modules is their role in supporting Perl's object-oriented programming constructs. Traditional object-oriented methods involve defining a class with methods and attributes encapsulated within a module. For instance, a Person class can be defined as follows:

```
# Person.pm
```

```
package Person;

use strict;
use warnings;

sub new {
    my ($class, %args) = @_;
    my $self = {
        name => $args{name} || 'Anonymous',
        age => $args{age} || 0,
    };
    bless $self, $class;
    return $self;
}

sub get_name {
    my ($self) = @_;
    return $self->{name};
}

sub get_age {
    my ($self) = @_;
    return $self->{age};
}

1; # End of Person
```

This Person.pm file defines a Person class with a constructor new, and methods get_name and get_age. The bless function associates the anonymous hash $self with the class Person, transforming it into an object.

Implementing and using the Person class in a Perl script illustrates object-oriented integration:

```
#!/usr/bin/perl
use strict;
use warnings;
use Person;

my $person = Person->new(name => 'Alice', age -> 30);
print "Name: ", $person->get_name(), "\n"; # Outputs: Name: Alice
print "Age: ", $person->get_age(), "\n"; # Outputs: Age: 30
```

This section provides the foundational understanding needed to work with Perl modules, both in procedural and object-oriented paradigms. Subsequent sections will build on these principles, encompassing practical applications and advanced features such as versioning, dependency management, and documentation.

8.2 Using Built-in Modules

Perl comes with a variety of built-in modules that provide essential functions and simplify complex tasks. Understanding how to utilize these built-in modules effectively enriches your Perl programming capabilities and enhances code modularity and reusability. Built-in modules can be loaded using the use or require statements. The use statement is typically preferred for compile-time loading and importing symbols into the current namespace. Here is an example of using a built-in module:

```
use strict;
use warnings;

use Data::Dumper;

my %hash = (
    name => "John Doe",
    age => 42,
    occupation => "Engineer"
);

print Dumper(\%hash);
```

The Data::Dumper module is used here to print the contents of a hash reference in a readable format. By using the use statement, we are ensuring that the module is loaded at compile-time, and its functions are available for immediate use in the script.

Another commonly used built-in module is File::Basename. This module allows the extraction of file paths, names, and extensions, which is particularly useful for file manipulation tasks. Below is an example demonstrating its usage:

```
use strict;
use warnings;
use File::Basename;

my $file_path = "/home/user/documents/report.txt";

my $basename = basename($file_path);
my $dirname = dirname($file_path);

print "File name: $basename\n";
print "Directory: $dirname\n";
```

In this snippet, basename returns the file name from the given path, while dirname returns the directory.

The List::Util module provides a suite of utilities for performing common operations on lists. Here's an example:

```
use strict;
```

```
use warnings;
use List::Util qw(min max sum);

my @numbers = (1, 2, 3, 4, 5);

my $min_value = min(@numbers);
my $max_value = max(@numbers);
my $total_sum = sum(@numbers);

print "Minimum: $min_value\n";
print "Maximum: $max_value\n";
print "Sum: $total_sum\n";
```

In the above code, the min, max, and sum functions from List::Util are used to find the minimum value, maximum value, and sum of the list, respectively.

When a Perl script is run, it searches for modules in directories specified in the INC array. You can view and modify this array within your script. For instance:

```
use strict;
use warnings;

print "Initial \@INC paths:\n";
print "$_\n" for @INC;

# Modify \@INC to include a new directory
use lib '/path/to/your/modules';

print "Modified \@INC paths:\n";
print "$_\n" for @INC;
```

This script displays the initial paths in INC, adds a new directory using use lib, and then displays the modified paths. This flexibility allows the inclusion of private module directories without altering the global Perl configuration.

It is also important to handle potential errors when using built-in modules. This can be done by carefully using eval blocks to catch any run-time errors that may occur. Here's an example:

```
use strict;
use warnings;

eval {
    require NonExistent::Module;
    NonExistent::Module->import();
};

if ($@) {
    print "Error loading module: $@\n";
}
```

In this example, require is used within an eval block to attempt to load a non-existent module. If an error occurs, it is captured in $@ and subsequently printed.

Using built-in modules effectively can significantly reduce the complexity of Perl programs by leveraging pre-tested and widely-used functionalities. Ensuring modules are loaded correctly, handling errors appropriately, and understanding the scope of available built-in functionalities are crucial aspects of mastering Perl built-in modules.

8.3 Installing CPAN Modules

The Comprehensive Perl Archive Network (CPAN) serves as an extensive repository of Perl modules, scripts, and distributions. CPAN simplifies the distribution and installation of Perl software across diverse environments. This section details steps to install CPAN modules, practical methods for managing these installations, and troubleshooting tips.

Prerequisites for CPAN Installation

Before installing CPAN modules, ensure that Perl and its core modules are correctly installed on your system. Most modern operating systems come preloaded with Perl. Verify Perl installation by executing:

```
$ perl -v
```

For Windows users, installing 'Strawberry Perl' or 'ActiveState Perl' is recommended for an environment equipped with a CPAN-compatible Perl installation.

CPAN Client Configuration

To install modules from CPAN, a CPAN client is required. Perl includes a default CPAN client, 'CPAN.pm', but the 'cpanminus' client (cpanm) is popular for its simplicity. First, configure 'CPAN.pm' if not already configured:

```
$ perl -MCPAN -e shell
o conf init
```

The configuration process prompts for inputs about repository mirrors, paths, and other settings. Typically, default options are suitable for most users.

Installing cpanminus

It is highly advisable to install cpanminus, which offers a more streamlined installation experience. Install cpanminus via the default CPAN client with:

```
$ cpan App::cpanminus
```

Post-installation, cpanm can be used to manage CPAN module installations.

Installing a CPAN Module

To install a module using cpanm, execute:

```
$ cpanm Module::Name
```

For example, to install the 'JSON' module, the command is:

```
$ cpanm JSON
```

The cpanm command will handle all dependencies and configurations, providing a user-friendly installation procedure.

Using the Default CPAN Client

Alternatively, the default CPAN client can install modules. Begin the CPAN shell and use the 'install' command. For instance:

```
$ perl -MCPAN -e shell
cpan> install JSON
```

Updating CPAN and Installed Modules

Regular updates of CPAN clients and installed modules ensure system robustness and security. Upgrade the CPAN client itself using:

```
$ cpanm -self-upgrade
```

Update all modules to their latest versions with:

```
$ cpanm --upgrade .
```

For the default CPAN client, updating involves:

```
$ perl -MCPAN -e shell
cpan> reload index
cpan> upgrade /
```

Troubleshooting Installation Issues

Inevitably, issues may arise during CPAN module installations. Common problems include missing dependencies, network errors, or incompatible module versions.

1. *Missing Dependencies*: CPAN clients typically report missing dependencies. Resolve these manually using:

```
$ cpanm Dependency::Name
```

2. *Network Errors*: Network issues may be mitigated by selecting different CPAN mirrors during client configuration. Change the configuration via:

```
$ perl -MCPAN -e shell
cpan> o conf urllist unshift http://cpan.example.mirror/
cpan> o conf commit
```

3. *Incompatibility*: Ensure compatibility by consulting module documentation for version constraints and adjusting installation commands accordingly. For instance:

```
$ cpanm 'Module::Name@=1.23'
```

Local::Lib for Local Module Installations

For environments where administrative privileges are restricted, 'local::lib' assists in installing modules to user-specific directories. Configure 'local::lib' with:

```
$ cpanm --local-lib=~/myperl5local Perl::Module
$ eval $(perl -I ~/myperl5local/lib/perl5/ -Mlocal::lib=~/myperl5local)
```

Adjust the command in '.bashrc' or similar shell configuration files to persist session changes:

```
$ echo 'eval $(perl -I ~/myperl5local/lib/perl5/ -Mlocal::lib=~/myperl5local)' >> ~/.
    bashrc
```

The usage of 'local::lib' allows for the installation of CPAN modules without root access, ensuring project-specific module management.

Understanding and utilizing CPAN provides extensive Perl module resources, enhancing scripts and automation tasks significantly. By mastering CPAN tools, installation processes, and best practices, Perl programmers can fully leverage the comprehensive module ecosystem CPAN offers.

8.4 Creating Your Own Modules

Creating modules in Perl is integral for code reusability and organization. A Perl module is essentially a package defined in a file, and these packages can contain functions, variables, and even other packages. To create a module, you will need to adhere to certain conventions for file naming, structure, and content.

A Perl module file should have a .pm extension to signify that it is a Perl module. For instance, if your module is named MyModule, the file would be MyModule.pm.

To begin, define a package in your module file. The package name should match the filename to maintain consistency. Below is a basic example of a module that defines a few simple functions:

```
# MyModule.pm
package MyModule;

use strict;
use warnings;

# Function to add two numbers
sub add {
    my ($a, $b) = @_;
    return $a + $b;
}

# Function to subtract two numbers
sub subtract {
    my ($a, $b) = @_;
    return $a - $b;
}

# End of package
1;
```

In the example above, MyModule::add and MyModule::subtract are functions defined within the MyModule package. The final 1; is crucial; it indicates that the module returns a true value, a requirement for a Perl module.

To use this module in a script, utilize the use or require statement:

```
#!/usr/bin/perl
use strict;
use warnings;

use MyModule;

my $sum = MyModule::add(10, 5);
my $difference = MyModule::subtract(10, 5);

print "Sum: $sum\n";
```

```
print "Difference: $difference\n";
```

In a more complex scenario, you might want your module to export certain functions automatically rather than calling them with the package name every time. The Exporter module facilitates this.

To export functions, incorporate the Exporter module and define the @ISA and @EXPORT arrays in your module:

```
# MyModule.pm
package MyModule;

use strict;
use warnings;
use Exporter 'import';

our @ISA = qw(Exporter);
our @EXPORT = qw(add subtract);

sub add {
    my ($a, $b) = @_;
    return $a + $b;
}

sub subtract {
    my ($a, $b) = @_;
    return $a - $b;
}

1;
```

With @EXPORT, functions add and subtract are automatically available in any script that uses MyModule:

```
#!/usr/bin/perl
use strict;
use warnings;

use MyModule;

my $sum = add(10, 5);
my $difference = subtract(10, 5);

print "Sum: $sum\n";
print "Difference: $difference\n";
```

For more granular control over exporting, use @EXPORT_OK instead of @EXPORT. This allows the caller to explicitly import only selected functions:

```
# MyModule.pm
package MyModule;

use strict;
use warnings;
use Exporter 'import';
```

```
our @ISA = qw(Exporter);
our @EXPORT_OK = qw(add subtract);

sub add {
    my ($a, $b) = @_;
    return $a + $b;
}

sub subtract {
    my ($a, $b) = @_;
    return $a - $b;
}

1;
```

Now, to import specific functions, you would modify the script to include an import list:

```
#!/usr/bin/perl
use strict;
use warnings;

use MyModule qw(add);

my $sum = add(10, 5);

print "Sum: $sum\n";
```

Once you have a module defined and your desired functions specified, document your module using POD (Plain Old Documentation). Documentation within the module file itself is beneficial for reference and maintenance:

```
=head1 NAME

MyModule - A simple module for arithmetic operations

=head1 SYNOPSIS

  use MyModule;
  my $sum = MyModule::add(10, 5);
  my $difference = MyModule::subtract(10, 5);

=head1 DESCRIPTION

This module provides basic arithmetic operations.

=head2 Functions

=over 4

=item add($a, $b)

Adds two numbers and returns the result.

=item subtract($a, $b)

Subtracts the second number from the first and returns the result.
```

```
=back

=cut
```

POD documentation helps clarify the module's purpose and usage, which is essential for both users and maintainers.

Developing Perl modules encourages the separation of concerns, where different functionalities are encapsulated in distinct modules. This makes the code more maintainable and reusable. As your project grows, organizing code into modules becomes indispensable.

8.5 Module Namespaces

In Perl, a namespace is a separate domain where variable and function names can be stored. Namespaces help avoid conflicts that can occur when different parts of a program or different modules use the same name for different purposes. By creating isolated namespaces, Perl modules can ensure that their internal symbols do not unintentionally interfere with symbols in other modules or in the main program.

A namespace is defined by the package keyword, which changes the current namespace to the specified name until another package statement is encountered. Namespaces can be thought of as the equivalent of modules or classes in other programming languages. Here is a basic example illustrating the use of the package keyword:

```
package MyModule;

sub hello {
    print "Hello, World!\n";
}

package main;

MyModule::hello(); # Fully qualified subroutine call
```

In this example:

- A namespace MyModule is specified using the package keyword.
- A subroutine hello is defined within the MyModule namespace.
- The script then switches back to the main package.
- Finally, the hello subroutine is called using its fully qualified name

MyModule::hello to avoid ambiguity with any other hello subroutines that may exist in other namespaces.

Namespaced symbols (variables and subroutines) can be referred to using their fully qualified names (e.g., MyModule::variable_name or MyModule::subroutine_name), ensuring isolation of module contents.

Use of Symbol Tables

Under the hood, Perl uses a hash to implement each namespace, known as a symbol table. The name of the symbol table for a package MyModule is %MyModule::. Each key in this hash is the name of a symbol, and the corresponding value is a typeglob (*) that holds references to the actual variable or subroutine.

For example:

```
package MyModule;

$MyModule::var = 10;

sub display_var {
    print "Value of var: $MyModule::var\n";
}

package main;

MyModule::display_var();
```

Here, var is a scalar variable stored in the symbol table %MyModule::. The symbol table allows Perl to maintain separate variables var in different namespaces without conflict.

Nested Namespaces

Names can also be hierarchical. This means you can have nested namespaces, providing additional levels of organization. These nested namespaces allow you to create more complex and descriptive module groupings:

```
package Main::SubModule;

sub greet {
    print "Greetings from Main::SubModule!\n";
}

package main;

Main::SubModule::greet();
```

In this code, we define a submodule Main::SubModule with its own greet subroutine. Perl's namespace handling automatically creates the nested structure without requiring any special declarations.

Namespace Best Practices

- **Use Descriptive Names**: When creating a module, choose a name that clearly describes the module's purpose and context.
- **Avoid Common Names**: Avoid using common names that might collide with existing modules on CPAN or built-in Perl functions.
- **Hierarchical Naming**: Structure your module namespaces hierarchically, particularly for a suite of related modules. This aids in organization and decreases the likelihood of name conflicts.
- **Minimal Export**: Ensure that your modules export only what is necessary. Over-exporting can lead to namespace pollution, causing unexpected conflicts.
- **Documentation**: Always document the namespace and the functions/variables it contains, making it clear for other developers how to use the module correctly.

Symbol Alias

Sometimes, you may want to create shortcuts or aliases for symbols in a namespace. This can be done using the built-in * operator to create typeglobs. Here is an example:

```
package MyModule;

sub original_function {
    print "This is the original function.\n";
}

*alias_function = \&original_function;

package main;

MyModule::alias_function();
```

In this example, *alias_function is an alias to *original_function in the MyModule namespace. Calling MyModule::alias_function invokes original_function, demonstrating how aliasing can simplify references within complex namespaces.

Understanding and properly implementing namespaces in Perl allows you to structure and organize your code effectively, facilitating maintenance and enhancing readability, especially in larger and more complex projects.

8.6 Loading Modules with 'use' and 'require'

In Perl, managing and organizing code via modules is a powerful technique. Modules are brought into a Perl script using either the `use` or `require` statements. Understanding the distinctions between these two mechanisms is fundamental for efficient usage.

The `use` statement imports the specified module at compile time, i.e., before the script starts running. This behavior ensures that any syntax errors or missing modules are identified early in the execution process. Additionally, `use` automatically calls the `import` method from the module being used, which can further facilitate the exportation of symbols such as functions and variables.

In contrast, the `require` statement loads the module at runtime, which can be useful in situations where execution flow determines the necessity of a specific module. This dynamic loading mechanism enables lazy inclusion of modules, potentially enhancing performance by deferring the load until it is absolutely required.

Consider the following example, showcasing the usage of `use`:

```
use strict;
use warnings;
use Some::Module;
```

In this case, the `use strict` and `use warnings` are Perl pragmas that help enforce good coding practices by generating compile-time warnings. The line `use Some::Module` imports `Some::Module` at compile time and calls its `import` method if it exists, bringing any exported symbols into the current namespace.

Now, look at a counterpart example using `require`:

```
require Some::Module;
Some::Module->import();
```

Here, `require` loads `Some::Module` at runtime, and the explicit call to `Some::Module->import();` mimics the behavior of `use` by calling the module's `import` method.

When to use `use` versus `require` depends on the specific needs of the script. Utilizing `use` is generally preferred for most scenarios as it provides early error detection and convenience by automating the import mechanics. However, `require` demonstrates its utility when modules need to be conditionally loaded based on certain runtime conditions.

Consider the following Perl script which conditionally loads a module using require.

```
my $module_name = "Some::Module";

if (some_condition()) {
    eval {
        require $module_name;
        $module_name->import();
        1;
    } or do {
        my $error = $@;
        print "Failed to load $module_name: $error";
    };
}

sub some_condition {
    # Some logic to determine if the module should be loaded
    return 1; # Assuming the condition returns true for the sake of demonstration
}
```

In this example, require is wrapped in an eval block to capture any errors that might occur during the dynamic loading of Some::Module. If the module fails to load, it prints an error message instead of terminating the program, which illustrates a graceful degradation approach.

Consider also the scenarios where require can be useful in reducing memory footprint or optimizing initialization time by loading only the necessary modules. For instance, in a large application with multiple functionalities, each part might depend on different modules. Using require, modules can be loaded only when their particular functionality is invoked:

```
sub process_data {
    require Data::Dumper;
    my $data = shift;
    print Data::Dumper::Dumper($data);
}

sub perform_database_operation {
    require DBI;
    my $dbh = DBI->connect('DBI:mysql:database=test;host=localhost','user','
        password');
    # Perform database operations...
}
```

In this segment, Data::Dumper and DBI modules are loaded only within their respective subroutines, optimizing memory usage and start-up times of the application.

Avoiding module load conflicts is another practical aspect when dealing with Perl modules. If different parts of an application inadvertently load different versions of a module, unforeseen behaviors and conflicts may arise. Both use and require can specify a minimum version number to alleviate such issues:

```
use Some::Module 1.20;
require Some::Module 1.20;
```

In essence, the choice between use and require is situationally determined, with use being beneficial for compile-time checks and implicit imports, while require provides runtime flexibility and conditional module loading capabilities. Both mechanisms play vital roles in the structured and efficient development of Perl applications.

8.7 Exporting Functions and Variables

In Perl, modules often need to share functions and variables with other parts of a program. This sharing process, known as "exporting", enables the integration and reuse of code across different scripts. The Exporter module provides a straightforward mechanism for exporting variables and functions from a module.

To begin with exporting, it is essential to understand the role of the Exporter module. Exporter is a core Perl module that facilitates the importation of symbols (functions and variables) into a user's namespace. This prevents the repetitive use of fully qualified names and makes the code more concise.

To use Exporter, include it in your module and define an @EXPORT array, an @EXPORT_OK array, or both. @EXPORT lists the symbols that will be automatically exported when the module is used, while @EXPORT_OK lists symbols available for export upon request.

Consider the following example of a custom Perl module:

```
package MyModule;

use strict;
use warnings;
use Exporter 'import';

# Symbols to be automatically exported
our @EXPORT = qw(hello);

# Symbols to be exported on demand
our @EXPORT_OK = qw(goodbye);

# Function definitions
sub hello {
    return "Hello, World!";
}
```

```
sub goodbye {
    return "Goodbye, World!";
}

1;
```

In this example, the hello function is automatically exported, meaning that any script that uses MyModule will import the hello function by default. The goodbye function, on the other hand, can be imported upon request.

To use this module in a script, you can simply write:

```
use strict;
use warnings;
use MyModule;

print hello(); # Automatically exported
# print goodbye(); # Uncommenting this line will cause an error
```

The script will output:

```
Hello, World!
```

To import the goodbye function explicitly, modify the use statement to include an import list:

```
use strict;
use warnings;
use MyModule qw(hello goodbye);

print hello();
print goodbye();
```

Executing this script will produce:

```
Hello, World!
Goodbye, World!
```

Sometimes, you may want more granular control over what gets exported. For instance, you can make use of the special tags to group a set of functions and export them collectively.

```
package MyModule;

use strict;
use warnings;
use Exporter 'import';

our @EXPORT_OK = qw(hello goodbye);
our %EXPORT_TAGS = (
    all => [qw(hello goodbye)],
    greetings => [qw(hello)],
);

sub hello {
```

```
    return "Hello, World!";
}

sub goodbye {
    return "Goodbye, World!";
}

1;
```

This configuration allows users to import all or specific sets of functions:

```
use strict;
use warnings;
use MyModule qw(:all); # or
# use MyModule qw(:greetings); # to import only the 'hello' function

print hello();
print goodbye();
```

Using tags grants users the flexibility to manage namespace pollution effectively.

By maintaining organized export lists and default exports judiciously, you can prevent unintentional importation of unnecessary symbols and improve code clarity. Adopting this approach ensures that only the needed functions are made available, preserving the encapsulation of your module's internal logic.

Remember that excessive use of the @EXPORT array might lead to conflicts, especially when different modules export functions with the same name. Therefore, consider using @EXPORT_OK and explicit import lists as best practices for robust module design.

Lastly, when developing a module that coordinates various exports, comprehensive documentation is indispensable. Properly documented export lists, descriptions of functions, and examples of module usage significantly enhance the module's usability and foster safer use by other developers and users. This module management strategy enables the seamless integration of reusable code components into complex Perl applications.

8.8 Module Documentation

Module documentation is a critical aspect of Perl module development, ensuring that other developers, as well as future instances of yourself, can understand and efficiently use your module. Perl uses Plain Old Documentation (POD) format to incorporate documentation within the code. POD is simple and allows for easy embedding of documentation directly in Perl scripts and modules.

To begin documenting a module, POD commands are embedded in the code. The basic structure of a POD document includes headings, paragraphs, lists, and code segments. Here is a simple example of how POD might look in a Perl module.

```
package My::Module;

use strict;
use warnings;

=head1 NAME

My::Module - Example module for demonstrating POD

=head1 SYNOPSIS

  use My::Module;
  my $result = My::Module::example_function();

=head1 DESCRIPTION

This module provides example functionalities to demonstrate
how POD documentation is embedded within a Perl module.

=head2 example_function

  my $result = example_function();

This function returns a sample string.

=cut

sub example_function {
    return "This is an example function from My::Module.";
}

1; # End of My::Module
```

POD directives begin with '=' and end with '=cut'. Above, several key POD sections are used:

=head1 NAME: This section typically contains the name of the module followed by a brief description. This is crucial for identifying the purpose of the module.

=head1 SYNOPSIS: This section provides short code examples that demonstrate how to use the module. This is often the first place a developer will look to understand how to quickly get started with the module.

=head1 DESCRIPTION: Here detailed information about the module's functionality is documented. This can include how the module works, its features, and any important background information.

=head2: Subsections within the description are commonly delineated using '=head2'. This organizes the documentation hierarchically.

=cut: This directive ends the POD section, returning the parser to the Perl code.

POD supports additional formatting commands such as '=over', '=item', and '=back' for lists, 'B<text>' for bold text, 'I<text>' for italic text, and 'L<text>' for links. Developers should leverage these features to make documentation readable and informative.

```
=over 4

=item *

Use 'example_function' to obtain a sample string response.

=cut
```

Converting POD into other documentation formats can be done using several tools such as 'perldoc', 'pod2man', 'pod2html', and 'pod2text'. These tools provide flexibility in how documentation is distributed and consumed.

```
# To read POD documentation for My::Module in the terminal
perldoc My::Module

# To convert POD to HTML
pod2html MyModule.pm > MyModule.html

# To convert POD to plain text
pod2text MyModule.pm > MyModule.txt
```

Properly documented modules not only enhance readability but also drive better adoption and usage by other developers. Including comprehensive examples, detailed descriptions, and clear usage guidelines are essential.

Writing complete documentation results in long-term maintenance benefits and reinforces best practices in software development.

8.9 Versioning in Modules

Versioning in Perl modules is a critical aspect of module development and maintenance. It provides a mechanism to track changes, ensure compatibility, and manage dependencies effectively. This section delves into the nuances of versioning within Perl modules, covering the declaration of version numbers, the use of version control systems, and best practices for maintaining version consistency.

Declaring Version Numbers: In Perl, declaring a module's version number is typically done using the $VERSION variable. This variable is most commonly set near the beginning of the module file. The $VERSION variable is a package-scoped global variable and is often declared as follows:

```
package My::Module;
our $VERSION = '1.00';
```

In the above example, the version number is set to 1.00. It is essential to use a consistent format for version numbers. The commonly accepted practice is to use a decimal number format, which allows for straightforward version comparison.

Using version Module: Perl provides the 'version' module, which offers additional functionality for handling and comparing version numbers. Using the 'version' module, you can specify version numbers and perform comparison operations with enhanced precision.

Consider the following example:

```
use version;
our $VERSION = version->declare('v1.2.3');
```

In this example, the version number is declared in a more readable and structured manner using the 'version->declare' function. It standardizes version numbers as version objects that provide a robust mechanism for version comparison.

Version Control Systems: Effective module versioning also involves using Version Control Systems (VCS) like Git. VCS are crucial for tracking changes, rolling back to previous versions, and collaborating with other developers. Each commit or change in the module can be tagged with a specific version number, providing a history of module versions.

For instance, in Git, tagging a commit with a version number can be done as:

```
git tag v1.0.0
git push origin v1.0.0
```

Here, the version 'v1.0.0' is tagged to a specific commit in the repository, and this tag is pushed to the remote repository.

Maintaining Version Consistency: Consistency in versioning practices is imperative for module stability and user trust. Each release of a module should increment the version number following a defined scheme. Semantic Versioning (Semver) is a widely adopted convention for version numbering, comprising three numbers: Major.Minor.Patch.

- **Major** version increments when there are incompatible API changes. - **Minor** version increments when functionality is added in a backwards-compatible manner. - **Patch** version increments when backwards-compatible bug fixes are made.

Following the Semver convention assists users in understanding the nature of changes between different versions of the module.

Practical Versioning Example: Implementing practical versioning involves combining the above concepts into a cohesive version management strategy. Below is an example of how a developer might manage versioning for a Perl module:

```
package Utilities::StringProcessing;

use version;
our $VERSION = version->declare('v2.3.1');

# Module code follows...

1;
```

Here, the module 'Utilities::StringProcessing' has its version number declared as 'v2.3.1'. This designation helps users and package managers identify which version of the module is currently in use and what kind of changes or updates can be expected from it.

Additionally, maintaining a 'Changes' file in the module's directory, which documents the changes made in each version, proves beneficial for users. A typical entry in the 'Changes' file may look like this:

```
Revision history for Utilities::StringProcessing

v2.3.1  2023-10-15
        - Fixed bug in string reversal function
        - Improved performance of substring extraction

v2.3.0  2023-09-30
        - Added new function for case-insensitive search
```

Utilizing 'version' Objects in Code: It is also possible to use version objects directly within the code to enforce specific version requirements. This can be done using the 'use' keyword:

```
use Utilities::StringProcessing 2.3.1;
```

Such a statement ensures that the 'Utilities::StringProcessing' module loaded is at least version '2.3.1'. Failing to meet this requirement will result in a compilation error, thereby safeguarding against compatibility issues.

Overall, careful versioning within Perl modules enhances module reliability, manages compatibility gracefully, and ensures that developers and users can work with the right versions of dependencies effectively.

8.10 Managing Dependencies

Managing dependencies is a fundamental aspect of Perl module development and usage. Dependencies ensure the required modules and libraries are available for your Perl script to function correctly. Efficient management of these dependencies ensures that your scripts are portable, maintainable, and less prone to errors.

A common practice is to list your module dependencies in a special file so that they can be easily installed by others using automated tools. The primary tools used for managing dependencies in Perl include cpan, cpanm, and tools provided by Perl itself such as ExtUtils::MakeMaker and Module::Build.

Dependencies in a Makefile.PL

When distributing your Perl module, you will often include a Makefile.PL script. This script uses ExtUtils::MakeMaker to generate a Makefile, which in turn guides the building, testing, and installation of your module and its dependencies.

To specify required modules, you include a PREREQ_PM key in the WriteMakefile call. This key maps module names to version numbers. Below is an example:

```
use ExtUtils::MakeMaker;

WriteMakefile(
    NAME => 'My::Module',
    VERSION_FROM => 'lib/My/Module.pm',
    PREREQ_PM => {
        'List::Util' => 0, # Any version
        'DBI' => 1.631,
        'LWP::UserAgent'=> 6.15,
    },
);
```

When users run perl Makefile.PL, it checks for these modules and their versions, ensuring all prerequisites are met before proceeding with the build process.

Dependencies in Build.PL

Another common tool for managing dependencies is Module::Build. Similar to Makefile.PL, Build.PL defines the dependencies using the requires and build_requires keys. Here is an example using Module::Build:

```
use Module::Build;

my $builder = Module::Build->new(
    module_name => 'My::Module',
    license => 'perl',
    requires => {
        'List::Util' => 0,
        'DBI' => 1.631,
        'LWP::UserAgent'=> 6.15,
    },
    build_requires => {
        'Test::More' => 0.98,
    },
    create_makefile_pl => 'traditional',
);

$builder->create_build_script();
```

This script serves a similar function as Makefile.PL but offers more flexibility. When the user runs perl Build.PL, it generates a Build script that manages the module's lifecycle.

CPANfile and cpanm

Some developers prefer to use cpanm (App::cpanminus) for simplicity and its modern approach. With cpanm, you can specify dependencies in a cpanfile. The cpanfile syntax is simpler and more readable:

```
requires 'List::Util', '0';
requires 'DBI', '1.631';
requires 'LWP::UserAgent', '6.15';

on 'test' => sub {
    requires 'Test::More', '0.98';
};
```

To install the dependencies listed in the cpanfile, you simply run:

```
cpanm --installdeps .
```

This command installs all required modules specified in the cpanfile without the overhead of maintaining a Makefile.PL or Build.PL. It is particularly useful in continuous integration (CI) environments.

Ensuring Compatibility

When specifying dependencies, it's crucial to ensure compatibility across different Perl versions and environments. This often involves specifying minimum versions of your dependencies. You might need to verify that there are no breaking changes between different versions of dependencies. The Test::More module and other testing frameworks can be invaluable for this:

```
use Test::More tests => 3;

BEGIN { use_ok('List::Util') }
BEGIN { use_ok('DBI', '1.631') }
BEGIN { use_ok('LWP::UserAgent') }
```

Running these tests ensures that the specified modules and versions are available and correctly loaded.

Advanced Dependency Management with MetaCPAN and CPAN Meta Spec

To interact with broader Perl community tools like MetaCPAN, you can include metadata files like META.json or META.yml. These files provide extensive information about your module, including dependencies, configurations, and repository details. Here's an example of a META.json file:

```
{
    "name" : "My-Module",
    "version" : "0.01",
    "abstract" : "My Perl Module",
    "author" : [
        "John Doe <john.doe@example.com>"
    ],
    "prereqs" : {
        "runtime" : {
            "requires" : {
                "perl" : "5.10.0",
                "List::Util" : "1.24",
                "DBI" : "1.631",
                "LWP::UserAgent" : "6.15"
            }
        },
        "test" : {
            "requires" : {
                "Test::More" : "0.98"
            }
        }
    }
}
```

Tools like cpanm and minicpan will respect these definitions, ensuring that the correct dependencies are installed.

Understanding and managing dependencies is crucial for ensuring that your Perl scripts and modules are robust, portable, and easy to maintain. Proper dependency management not only facilitates smoother deployments and distribution but also aids in maintaining a cohesive development environment.

8.11 Practical Examples of Module Usage

To solidify the concepts presented in this chapter, we will explore practical examples illustrating the usage of various Perl modules. These examples encompass both built-in modules and those from the Comprehensive Perl Archive Network (CPAN), as well as demonstrate the creation and application of custom modules.

Consider a scenario where we need to manipulate XML data. For this purpose, we utilize the XML::Simple CPAN module, which provides an accessible interface to parse and create XML.

```
use strict;
use warnings;
use XML::Simple;
use Data::Dumper;

my $xml = XML::Simple->new();
my $data = $xml->XMLin('example.xml');
print Dumper($data);
```

The above code uses XML::Simple to read an XML file named example.xml and convert it into a Perl data structure. Data::Dumper is used to output the structured data, allowing for an easy inspection of the resultant Perl hash:

```
$VAR1 = {
          'item' => [
                      {
                        'name' => 'apple',
                        'type' => 'fruit'
                      },
                      {
                        'name' => 'carrot',
                        'type' => 'vegetable'
                      }
                    ]
        };
```

Next, let us explore a computational task using the built-in Math::Complex module. This module is used for performing operations with complex numbers.

```
# Including the Math::Complex module
```

```
use strict;
use warnings;
use Math::Complex;

# Define two complex numbers
my $z1 = Math::Complex->make(2, 3); # 2 + 3i
my $z2 = Math::Complex->make(1, -1); # 1 - 1i

# Perform operations
my $addition = $z1 + $z2;
my $multiplication = $z1 * $z2;

print "Addition: $addition\n";
print "Multiplication: $multiplication\n";
```

Executing the above script will yield:

```
Addition: 3+2i
Multiplication: 5+i
```

Next, we delve into filesystem manipulation using the File::Copy module, a built-in module for copying files or filehandles in Perl. This is particularly useful for scripts that manage file backups or duplication.

```
use strict;
use warnings;
use File::Copy;

my $source = 'source.txt';
my $destination = 'destination.txt';

# Copy source.txt to destination.txt
copy($source, $destination) or die "Copy failed: $!";
print "File copied successfully\n";
```

If source.txt exists in the current directory and is accessible, the script will copy its contents to destination.txt and print a confirmation message.

Another practical example involves network programming using the Socket module, a built-in module that facilitates creating and using sockets. Here, we will create a simple TCP client.

```
use strict;
use warnings;
use IO::Socket::INET;

# Creating a new socket
my $client_socket = new IO::Socket::INET (
    PeerHost => '127.0.0.1',
    PeerPort => '5000',
    Proto => 'tcp',
) or die "ERROR in Socket Creation: $!\n";

print "TCP Connection Success.\n";

# Send data to the server
$client_socket->send("Hello Server!");
```

```
# Receive response from the server
my $response = "";
$client_socket->recv($response, 1024);
print "Received from Server: $response\n";

# Close the socket
$client_socket->close();
```

This script demonstrates how to create a TCP client that connects to a server running on 127.0.0.1 at port 5000, sends a message, and receives a response. Proper error handling ensures that any issues during socket creation are captured and reported.

Finally, let us create and use a custom module. Suppose we have a module named Greet.pm containing a simple greeting function.

```
package Greet;

use strict;
use warnings;
require Exporter;

our @ISA = qw(Exporter);
our @EXPORT = qw(say_hello);

sub say_hello {
    my ($name) = @_;
    return "Hello, $name!";
}

1;
```

This module defines a function say_hello that returns a greeting message. Note the 1; at the end, which ensures the module returns a true value upon loading.

To use this module in a script:

```
use strict;
use warnings;
use lib '.';
use Greet;

my $name = 'Alice';
my $greeting = say_hello($name);
print "$greeting\n";
```

Here, we include the custom module by specifying the current directory with use lib '.';. The method say_hello is then used to greet Alice by name. Upon execution, the script prints:

```
Hello, Alice!
```

These practical examples demonstrate the flexibility and power that modules bring to Perl programming, enabling efficient and reusable code across a variety of tasks.

Chapter 9

Object-Oriented Perl

This chapter explores object-oriented programming in Perl, covering the creation of classes and objects. It explains key concepts such as inheritance, encapsulation, polymorphism, and method overloading. The chapter also addresses the use of constructors and destructors, advanced object-oriented techniques, and practical examples to build robust and maintainable applications.

9.1 Introduction to Object-Oriented Perl

Object-oriented programming (OOP) is a paradigm centered around the concept of objects, which can contain both data and code that manipulate that data. Perl, being a highly versatile scripting language, supports OOP by enabling the definition of classes, creation of objects, and usage of essential OOP principles such as inheritance, encapsulation, and polymorphism.

Perl's support for OOP is provided through packages, which serve as building blocks for creating classes. A package in Perl is a separate namespace that allows variables and subroutines to be defined without conflicting with similarly named entities elsewhere in the program.

Objects in Perl are typically referred to as instances of a class. They are constructed using a special subroutine called a constructor. Upon creation, the object can be manipulated using methods, which are subroutines defined within the package representing the class.

To begin with, let's examine a basic class definition in Perl. Consider a simple class representing a Point in a two-dimensional space:

```
package Point;

sub new {
    my $class = shift;
    my $self = {
        x => shift,
        y => shift,
    };
    bless $self, $class;
    return $self;
}

sub get_x {
    my $self = shift;
    return $self->{x};
}

sub get_y {
    my $self = shift;
    return $self->{y};
}

sub set_x {
    my ($self, $value) = @_;
    $self->{x} = $value;
}

sub set_y {
    my ($self, $value) = @_;
    $self->{y} = $value;
}

1;
```

In this example, the Point class begins with the package keyword, identifying the namespace. The new subroutine acts as the constructor for the class. It receives arguments, creates an anonymous hash to store the object's attributes, and uses the bless function to turn this hash reference into an object of the class.

The get_x and get_y methods are accessor methods, used to retrieve the values of the x and y attributes, respectively. The set_x and set_y methods are mutator methods, enabling the modification of these attributes.

To utilize this Point class in a Perl script, one would do the following:

```
use Point;

my $point = Point->new(2, 3);
print "X coordinate: ", $point->get_x(), "\n";
print "Y coordinate: ", $point->get_y(), "\n";

$point->set_x(5);
```

```
$point->set_y(6);

print "Updated X coordinate: ", $point->get_x(), "\n";
print "Updated Y coordinate: ", $point->get_y(), "\n";
```

The script imports the Point class, creates a new Point object with initial coordinates (2, 3), prints these coordinates using the accessor methods, updates the coordinates using the mutator methods, and prints the updated values. The output of the script would be:

```
X coordinate: 2
Y coordinate: 3
Updated X coordinate: 5
Updated Y coordinate: 6
```

Perl's OOP model is flexible and dynamic, enabling the creation and manipulation of objects in a straightforward manner. Understanding the fundamentals of Perl's object-oriented system is essential for building robust and maintainable applications. As you progress through this chapter, you will build upon these basics, exploring more advanced techniques and concepts that will enhance your Perl programming skills through the lens of OOP.

9.2 Basic Concepts of OOP

Object-Oriented Programming (OOP) is a paradigm centered around the concept of "objects," which are instances of classes. A class defines a blueprint for objects, detailing their attributes (properties) and behaviors (methods). This fundamental shift in programming facilitates modularity, code reuse, and abstraction.

In Perl, OOP is not built into the language core as rigidly as in languages like Java or C++. Instead, Perl offers the flexibility to use OOP in a more ad-hoc manner, leveraging packages and references to achieve the same goals. Let's explore the central concepts of OOP, focusing on their implementation in Perl.

Classes and Objects: A class is defined as a package. To create a class, a package declaration is utilized, encapsulating the attributes and methods associated with the class. Attributes are typically stored in a hash reference, while methods are subroutines within the package.

```
package Animal;

sub new {
    my ($class, %args) = @_;
    my $self = {
```

```
        name => $args{name} || 'Unnamed',
        sound => $args{sound} || 'Silent',
    };
    bless $self, $class;
    return $self;
}

sub speak {
    my $self = shift;
    print $self->{name} . " says " . $self->{sound} . "\n";
}
```

In this example, Animal is a class with a constructor new and a method speak. The constructor initializes a new object and returns a blessed reference, linking the object to its class.

Inheritance: Inheritance enables a class (subclass or derived class) to inherit attributes and methods from another class (superclass or base class). This promotes code reuse and establishes a hierarchical relationship between classes.

```
package Dog;
use parent 'Animal';

sub speak {
    my $self = shift;
    print $self->{name} . " barks: " . $self->{sound} . "\n";
}

1;
```

Here, Dog inherits from Animal. The use parent 'Animal' statement ensures that Dog has access to Animal's attributes and methods. The speak method is overridden to provide specific behavior for Dog objects.

Encapsulation and Data Hiding: Encapsulation is the bundling of data (attributes) and methods that operate on the data into a single unit or class. Data hiding restricts direct access to some of an object's attributes, which is achieved in Perl by using naming conventions and access controls.

```
package Account;

sub new {
    my ($class, %args) = @_;
    my $self = {
        _balance => $args{balance} || 0,
    };
    bless $self, $class;
    return $self;
}

sub deposit {
    my ($self, $amount) = @_;
    $self->{_balance} += $amount;
```

```
}

sub get_balance {
    my $self = shift;
    return $self->{_balance};
}
```

In this example, the _balance attribute is intended to be private, indicated by the underscore prefix. The deposit and get_balance methods encapsulate the functionality to interact with _balance.

Method Overloading: Method overloading allows a class to define multiple methods with the same name but different signatures. Perl does not natively support method overloading based on signatures, but one can handle varying numbers and types of arguments within a method.

```
package MathOperations;

sub add {
    my $self = shift;
    my $sum = 0;
    $sum += $_ for @_;
    return $sum;
}
```

The add method adds a list of numbers passed as arguments, demonstrating a simplistic form of overloading by handling a variable number of arguments.

Polymorphism: Polymorphism allows objects of different classes to be treated as objects of a common superclass. This is closely tied to inheritance where subclasses override superclass methods.

```
package main;

my $animal = Animal->new(name => 'Generic Animal', sound => '...');
$animal->speak();

my $dog = Dog->new(name => 'Rex', sound => 'Woof');
$dog->speak();
```

In this script, both Animal and Dog objects are treated uniformly in terms of invoking methods, demonstrating polymorphism.

These basic concepts form the foundation upon which robust and maintainable OOP-based applications can be built in Perl. While Perl offers flexibility, adhering to these principles ensures structured and efficient code development.

9.3 Creating a Class in Perl

A class in Perl is essentially a package that indicates which code and data should be grouped together to form a coherent unit, encapsulating behavior and state. The first step in creating a class is defining a package. This package will contain the class's methods and attributes.

Begin by declaring a package with the package keyword:

```
package MyClass;
```

In this example, MyClass is the name of our class. Now, we will define the constructor, which in Perl is a subroutine named new. The new method instantiates an object of the class.

```
sub new {
    my $class = shift;
    my $self = {
        _attribute1 => shift,
        _attribute2 => shift,
    };
    bless $self, $class;
    return $self;
}
```

Next, we need to create accessor (get) and mutator (set) methods for the object's attributes to provide controlled access. These methods ensure encapsulation by controlling how attributes are read and modified.

```
sub get_attribute1 {
    my ($self) = @_;
    return $self->{_attribute1};
}

sub set_attribute1 {
    my ($self, $value) = @_;
    $self->{_attribute1} = $value;
}

sub get_attribute2 {
    my ($self) = @_;
    return $self->{_attribute2};
}

sub set_attribute2 {
    my ($self, $value) = @_;
    $self->{_attribute2} = $value;
}
```

Here, get_attribute1 and get_attribute2 are accessor methods, while set_attribute1 and set_attribute2 are mutator methods. With these methods in place, they allow modifying and retrieving attribute values post-instantiation.

After completing this, an instance of MyClass can be created and utilized. For illustration:

```
my $object = MyClass->new('value1', 'value2');
print "Attribute1: ", $object->get_attribute1(), "\n";
print "Attribute2: ", $object->get_attribute2(), "\n";

$object->set_attribute1('new_value1');
print "New Attribute1: ", $object->get_attribute1(), "\n";
```

The output will be:

```
Attribute1: value1
Attribute2: value2
New Attribute1: new_value1
```

This example demonstrates the foundation of creating a class, constructing objects, and utilizing both accessor and mutator methods.

For a more comprehensive illustration, let us define a class representing a Book. This class will have attributes such as title, author, and isbn.

```
package Book;

sub new {
    my $class = shift;
    my $self = {
        _title => shift,
        _author => shift,
        _isbn => shift,
    };
    bless $self, $class;
    return $self;
}

sub get_title {
    my ($self) = @_;
    return $self->{_title};
}

sub set_title {
    my ($self, $title) = @_;
    $self->{_title} = $title;
}

sub get_author {
    my ($self) = @_;
    return $self->{_author};
}

sub set_author {
    my ($self, $author) = @_;
    $self->{_author} = $author;
}

sub get_isbn {
    my ($self) = @_;
    return $self->{_isbn};
}
```

```
sub set_isbn {
    my ($self, $isbn) = @_;
    $self->{_isbn} = $isbn;
}
```

Using this Book class, we can create objects that represent individual books and manipulate their attributes.

```
my $book = Book->new("The Catcher in the Rye", "J.D. Salinger", "9780316769488");
print "Title: ", $book->get_title(), "\n";
print "Author: ", $book->get_author(), "\n";
print "ISBN: ", $book->get_isbn(), "\n";

$book->set_title("To Kill a Mockingbird");
print "New Title: ", $book->get_title(), "\n";
```

The output for this will be:

```
Title: The Catcher in the Rye
Author: J.D. Salinger
ISBN: 9780316769488
New Title: To Kill a Mockingbird
```

This example extends your understanding from a simple class with basic attributes to a more practical, real-world scenario demonstrating object creation and manipulation.

Understanding how to create a class in Perl forms the foundation of object-oriented programming in Perl and opens up possibilities for more complex design and organization of programs.

9.4 Creating and Using Objects

Creating objects in Perl involves defining a new instance of a class, typically through a special method known as a constructor. A constructor is a subroutine that initializes a newly created object from a class, preparing it for use. In Perl, the constructor is conventionally named new, although this is not a strict requirement.

To illustrate, let's define a simple class named Person. The Person class will have two attributes: name and age. Here is how we define the Person class and its new method:

```
package Person;

sub new {
    my ($class, $name, $age) = @_;
    my $self = {
        name => $name,
        age => $age
```

```
    };
    bless $self, $class;
    return $self;
}
```

The new method takes three parameters: the class name, and the values for name and age. It creates an anonymous hash reference to store the object's data, blesses this reference (associating it with the class), and finally returns the blessed reference, now representing an object of Person.

To create an instance (object) of the Person class, we invoke the new method:

```
my $person = Person->new("Alice", 30);
```

The variable $person now holds an object of the Person class, initialized with the name "Alice" and age 30. Accessing the object's attributes is done via methods. We can add getter methods for name and age:

```
package Person;

# Existing new method...

sub get_name {
    my $self = shift;
    return $self->{name};
}

sub get_age {
    my $self = shift;
    return $self->{age};
}
```

With these methods defined, we can retrieve the values of name and age:

```
print "Name: " . $person->get_name() . "\n";
print "Age: " . $person->get_age() . "\n";
```

The output of the above code will be:

```
Name: Alice
Age: 30
```

Perl allows modifying the object's state by defining setter methods. Let's add setters for name and age:

```
package Person;

# Existing methods...

sub set_name {
    my ($self, $name) = @_;
```

```
    $self->{name} = $name;
}

sub set_age {
    my ($self, $age) = @_;
    $self->{age} = $age;
}
```

This enhancement allows altering the name and age attributes of an object:

```
$person->set_name("Bob");
$person->set_age(35);

print "Updated Name: " . $person->get_name() . "\n";
print "Updated Age: " . $person->get_age() . "\n";
```

Executing the above code will produce the output:

```
Updated Name: Bob
Updated Age: 35
```

Additionally, it's possible to define methods that perform operations using the object's data. Suppose we want to create a display method that outputs the object's details:

```
package Person;

# Existing methods...

sub display {
    my $self = shift;
    print "Name: " . $self->{name} . "\n";
    print "Age: " . $self->{age} . "\n";
}
```

We can now call the display method on a Person object:

```
$person->display();
```

When the display method is invoked, it will output:

```
Name: Bob
Age: 35
```

To further enrich our Person class, we can incorporate additional methods and attributes, ultimately depending on the specific requirements of the program being developed. These foundational principles of object creation and utilization in Perl equip programmers to build complex, maintainable, and robust software architectures.

9.5 Class Inheritance

In object-oriented programming (OOP), inheritance is a fundamental concept that allows a class (termed as a subclass or derived class) to inherit attributes and methods from another class (referred to as a superclass or base class). In Perl, inheritance is implemented through a mechanism known as the @ISA array, which defines an is-a relationship between the classes. This section provides a comprehensive understanding of how to achieve inheritance in Perl, illustrating it with detailed examples and use-cases.

In Perl, a class is structured as a package, and inheritance is implemented by defining the @ISA array in the subclass. The @ISA array contains a list of the superclasses' names from which the subclass will inherit methods and attributes. When a method is called on an object, Perl looks for the method in the package of the object's class. If the method is not found, Perl then searches the packages listed in the class's @ISA array. This lookup process continues recursively up the inheritance chain until the method is found.

Consider the following example where we define a superclass Animal and a subclass Dog that inherits from Animal.

```
# Defining the superclass Animal
package Animal;

sub new {
    my $class = shift;
    my $self = {
        name => shift,
        sound => shift,
    };
    bless $self, $class;
    return $self;
}

sub speak {
    my $self = shift;
    print "A generic animal makes a sound.\n";
}

# Defining the subclass Dog that inherits from Animal
package Dog;
use parent -norequire, 'Animal';

sub new {
    my $class = shift;
    my $self = $class->SUPER::new(shift, 'Woof!');
    bless $self, $class;
    return $self;
}

sub speak {
```

```
    my $self = shift;
    print $self->{name}, " says ", $self->{sound}, "\n";
}

1; # End of the module
```

In this example, the Animal class defines a constructor new and a method speak. The Dog class uses the parent pragma to declare its inheritance from Animal. The parent pragma automatically sets the @ISA array for you, effectively adding Animal as a superclass of Dog.

The Dog class overrides the new constructor to initialize a Dog object with a specific sound ('Woof!') and also overrides the speak method to print the dog's name followed by the sound it makes. Even though Dog overrides the new and speak methods of Animal, it still retains access to any other methods or attributes defined in Animal that are not overridden.

Method overriding is a crucial aspect of inheritance, allowing a subclass to provide a specific implementation of a method that is already defined in its superclass. This can be seen in our example where the Dog class provides its version of the speak method.

To create an object of the subclass Dog and call its methods, we do the following:

```
use Dog;

my $pet = Dog->new('Buddy');
$pet->speak;
```

The output when running the above script is:

```
Buddy says Woof!
```

This demonstrates that the Dog class has successfully inherited from Animal and has overridden the necessary methods.

In some scenarios, it might be necessary to call a superclass method from within an overriding method in the subclass. This can be accomplished by using the SUPER keyword which directs Perl to look for the method in the superclass. For instance, if the Dog class wanted to extend the behavior of the speak method from the Animal class rather than completely overriding it, one could do as follows:

```
package Dog;

sub speak {
    my $self = shift;
    $self->SUPER::speak(); # Calls the speak method in Animal
    print $self->{name}, " really says ", $self->{sound}, "\n";
```

```
}
```

Calling $self->SUPER::speak() in the overriding method within the Dog class ensures that the original speak method from Animal is executed before the additional subclass-specific behavior. This is particularly useful for maintaining consistency and avoiding redundancy in code definitions.

Inheritance can be extended to multiple levels, resulting in a chain of derived classes each inheriting from its immediate predecessor. Careful design is essential to manage complexity and avoid unintended consequences such as the diamond problem, where an ambiguity arises in the method resolution order due to multiple inheritance paths.

Overall, by leveraging inheritance in Perl, one can build more modular, scalable, and maintainable code structures. This allows for reusability of common functionality in base classes while enabling specialized behavior in derived classes. When applied judiciously, inheritance is a powerful tool in the arsenal of Perl object-oriented programming.

9.6 Encapsulation and Data Hiding

Encapsulation is a fundamental concept in object-oriented programming, ensuring that the internal representation of an object is hidden from the outside world. This concept, often intertwined with data hiding, allows for an interface to interact with an object's data, without exposing the actual implementation details. In Perl, encapsulation is primarily achieved using packages and the manipulation of variables' scope.

To illustrate encapsulation in Perl, let us create a basic class representing a BankAccount.

```
package BankAccount;

# Constructor
sub new {
    my $class = shift;
    my $self = {
        _balance => shift,
    };
    bless $self, $class;
    return $self;
}

# Method to deposit amount
sub deposit {
```

```
    my ($self, $amount) = @_;
    $self->{_balance} += $amount;
    return $self->{_balance};
}

# Method to withdraw amount
sub withdraw {
    my ($self, $amount) = @_;
    if($self->{_balance} >= $amount) {
        $self->{_balance} -= $amount;
        return $self->{_balance};
    } else {
        warn "Insufficient funds";
        return $self->{_balance};
    }
}

# Method to get current balance
sub get_balance {
    my $self = shift;
    return $self->{_balance};
}

1;
```

In this example, the BankAccount class encapsulates the _balance attribute. The underscore prefix is a common convention in Perl to indicate that the variable is intended to be private. Although Perl lacks built-in mechanisms for strictly private variables, using underscores and disciplined access methods can mimic private behavior.

The BankAccount class includes accessor and mutator methods, such as deposit, withdraw, and get_balance, enabling controlled access to the _balance attribute. This approach adheres to the principle of encapsulation by providing a structured interface to interact with the data, while concealing the internal state.

Consider the following script that utilizes the BankAccount class:

```
#!/usr/bin/perl
use strict;
use warnings;
use BankAccount;

my $account = BankAccount->new(100); # Initial balance of 100 dollars

print "Initial balance: ", $account->get_balance(), "\n";
$account->deposit(50);
print "After depositing 50 dollars: ", $account->get_balance(), "\n";
$account->withdraw(30);
print "After withdrawing 30 dollars: ", $account->get_balance(), "\n";
$account->withdraw(150);
print "Attempt to withdraw 150 dollars: ", $account->get_balance(), "\n";
```

Running the above script will generate the following output:

```
Initial balance: 100
After depositing 50 dollars: 150
After withdrawing 30 dollars: 120
Attempt to withdraw 150 dollars: 120
```

This output demonstrates how encapsulation effectively manages access to the _balance variable. Direct manipulation of the internal _balance variable is avoided, and all interactions occur through well-defined methods.

In Perl, true data hiding can be further enforced using lexical scoping with the my keyword inside closures, combined with object references. This technique ensures that private attributes are not accessible outside the scope of the class. Below is an advanced implementation to enhance encapsulation by using lexical variables:

```
package BankAccount;

# Constructor using a lexical variable for enforcing strict encapsulation
sub new {
    my $class = shift;
    my $balance = shift;

    my $self = bless {
        _get_balance => sub { $balance },
        _set_balance => sub { $balance = shift },
    }, $class;

    return $self;
}

# Method to deposit amount
sub deposit {
    my ($self, $amount) = @_;
    my $balance = $self->{_get_balance}->();
    $self->{_set_balance}->($balance + $amount);
    return $self->{_get_balance}->();
}

# Method to withdraw amount
sub withdraw {
    my ($self, $amount) = @_;
    my $balance = $self->{_get_balance}->();
    if($balance >= $amount) {
        $self->{_set_balance}->($balance - $amount);
    } else {
        warn "Insufficient funds";
    }
    return $self->{_get_balance}->();
}

# Method to get current balance
sub get_balance {
    my $self = shift;
    return $self->{_get_balance}->();
}

1;
```

By adopting a closure-based approach, the _balance variable is genuinely private. Access to _balance is controlled by the closures _get_balance and _set_balance. This encapsulation technique precludes any possibility of external code accessing or modifying the internal state directly.

Finally, adopting encapsulation and data hiding practices in Perl not only protects the integrity of an object's state but also simplifies debugging and maintenance. By promoting modularity and reducing dependencies on implementation specifics, encapsulation fosters the development of robust and maintainable code.

9.7 Overloading Methods

Method overloading allows the use of multiple methods with the same name but different parameters within a single class. This concept is prevalent in object-oriented languages and can be implemented in Perl to create more flexible and intuitive interfaces.

Perl itself does not support method overloading out of the box in the same way languages like C++ or Java do. However, method overloading can be achieved through various techniques, particularly by using the capabilities of flexible function arguments and custom dispatch logic. This section covers how to implement method overloading in Perl using these techniques.

```
package MyClass;

# Constructor
sub new {
    my ($class, %args) = @_;
    my $self = {
        name => $args{name} || 'unknown',
        age => $args{age} || 0,
    };
    bless $self, $class;
    return $self;
}

# Overloaded method example
sub display {
    my ($self, @args) = @_;

    # Check the number of arguments and dispatch accordingly
    if (@args == 0) {
        return $self->_display0();
    } elsif (@args == 1) {
        return $self->_display1($args[0]);
    } elsif (@args == 2) {
        return $self->_display2(@args);
```

```
    } else {
        die "Invalid number of arguments for display";
    }
}

# Method with 0 arguments
sub _display0 {
    my ($self) = @_;
    return "Name: " . $self->{name} . ", Age: " . $self->{age};
}

# Method with 1 argument
sub _display1 {
    my ($self, $arg1) = @_;
    return "$arg1: " . $self->{name};
}

# Method with 2 arguments
sub _display2 {
    my ($self, $arg1, $arg2) = @_;
    return "$arg1 $arg2: " . $self->{name} . ", Age: " . $self->{age};
}
```

In this example, the display method is overloaded within the MyClass package. The display method takes a variable number of arguments and dispatches the call to the appropriate internal private method (_-display0, _display1, or _display2) based on the count of arguments.

Instances can use the overloaded display method as follows:

```
my $obj = MyClass->new(name => "Alice", age => 30);

print $obj->display(); # Calls _display0
print $obj->display("Info"); # Calls _display1
print $obj->display("Full", "Details"); # Calls _display2

# Output
Name: Alice, Age: 30
Info: Alice
Full Details: Alice, Age: 30
```

```
Name: Alice, Age: 30
Info: Alice
Full Details: Alice, Age: 30
```

This approach leverages Perl's flexibility in handling lists and arrays, allowing us to write intuitive, yet powerful code.

Method overloading enables code reusability and a cleaner class design, making it easier to maintain and extend. When implementing overloaded methods, it is crucial to provide meaningful method names that clearly indicate their purpose and to manage argument validation to avoid runtime errors.

Another way to achieve similar functionality is by using Perl's package Class::Multimethods, which provides a more formalized way to support multimethods and multiple dispatching.

```
use Class::Multimethods;

multimethod display => (
    qr/^MyClass;$/ => sub {
        my ($self) = @_;
        return "Name: " . $self->{name} . ", Age: " . $self->{age};
    },
    qr/^MyClass; SCALAR$/ => sub {
        my ($self, $arg1) = @_;
        return "$arg1: " . $self->{name};
    },
    qr/^MyClass; SCALAR; SCALAR$/ => sub {
        my ($self, $arg1, $arg2) = @_;
        return "$arg1 $arg2: " . $self->{name} . ", Age: " . $self->{age};
    }
);

my $obj = MyClass->new(name => "Alice", age => 30);

print $obj->display(); # Calls first multimethod
print $obj->display("Info"); # Calls second multimethod
print $obj->display("Full", "Details"); # Calls third multimethod

# Output
Name: Alice, Age: 30
Info: Alice
Full Details: Alice, Age: 30
```

```
Name: Alice, Age: 30
Info: Alice
Full Details: Alice, Age: 30
```

Method overloading in Perl can extend functionality and improve code maintainability, especially when combining Perl's features with packages like Class::Multimethods. This synergy provides a structured and efficient approach to managing multiple method signatures and behaviors within classes.

9.8 Polymorphism

Polymorphism is a fundamental concept in object-oriented programming that allows objects of different classes to be treated as objects of a common superclass. It facilitates the ability to define methods in a superclass and override them in derived classes, enabling a unified interface to interact with different object types.

In Perl, polymorphism can be achieved through various mechanisms, including method overriding and using specific Perl features such as @ISA arrays to manage inheritance.

To illustrate polymorphism in Perl, consider the following example. We will first define a superclass and then derive two subclasses from it. Each subclass will override a method defined in the superclass, demonstrating polymorphism in action.

```
# Define the superclass Animal
package Animal;
sub new {
    my $class = shift;
    my $self = {
        name => shift,
    };
    bless $self, $class;
    return $self;
}

sub speak {
    my $self = shift;
    return "An animal sound";
}
```

In the above code, the Animal class is defined with a constructor (new) and a method (speak). The speak method returns a generic message indicating an animal sound.

Next, let's define two subclasses, Dog and Cat, that inherit from the Animal class and override the speak method.

```
# Define the subclass Dog
package Dog;
our @ISA = qw(Animal); # Inherit from Animal

sub speak {
    my $self = shift;
    return "Woof! Woof!";
}

# Define the subclass Cat
package Cat;
our @ISA = qw(Animal); # Inherit from Animal

sub speak {
    my $self = shift;
    return "Meow! Meow!";
}
```

The @ISA array is used to establish the inheritance relationship with the superclass Animal. Both Dog and Cat override the speak method to provide specific implementations.

To demonstrate polymorphism, we will create objects of each class and call the speak method on them:

```
# Script to demonstrate polymorphism

# Create an array of Animal objects
```

```
my @animals = (
    Dog->new("Buddy"),
    Cat->new("Mittens"),
    Animal->new("Generic Animal"),
);

# Iterate over each animal and call its speak method
foreach my $animal (@animals) {
    print $animal->speak() . "\n";
}
```

When the above script is executed, the output will be:

```
Woof! Woof!
Meow! Meow!
An animal sound
```

In this example, the speak method call on each object invokes the appropriate implementation based on the object's class.

Another facet of polymorphism in Perl can be explored through method overloading, where multiple methods can have the same name but different parameter lists. While Perl inherently does not support traditional overloads as seen in strongly typed languages, it allows for dynamic method handling using the AUTOLOAD subroutine. The AUTOLOAD method can catch calls to undefined methods and dispatch them accordingly.

The following example demonstrates polymorphic behavior using the AUTOLOAD mechanism:

```
package Animal;

sub AUTOLOAD {
    my $self = shift;
    my $name = our $AUTOLOAD;
    $name =~ s/.*:://; # Remove package name portion

    if ($name eq 'speak') {
        return "An animal sound";
    } else {
        die "Method $name not implemented in class " . ref($self);
    }
}

# Define subclass Dog
package Dog;
our @ISA = qw(Animal);

sub speak {
    return "Woof! Woof!";
}

# Define subclass Cat
package Cat;
our @ISA = qw(Animal);

sub speak {
```

```
    return "Meow! Meow!";
}
```

In this example, the AUTOLOAD subroutine in the Animal class catches calls to undefined methods and provides a general response for the speak method if defined in neither Dog nor Cat. However, the subclass methods override the generic implementation by defining their own speak method, adhering to polymorphic principles.

Polymorphism provides flexibility and extensibility in writing Perl scripts. By allowing objects from various classes to be treated uniformly, software design becomes more intuitive, maintainable, and scalable. This facilitates the development of modular systems where disparate components can interact seamlessly through shared interfaces while preserving specialized behavior through class-specific method implementations.

9.9 Using Constructors and Destructors

In object-oriented programming (OOP), the concepts of constructors and destructors are crucial for proper management of object lifecycles. Constructors initialize new objects, while destructors handle the cleanup process when objects are no longer needed. This section delves into how constructors and destructors are implemented and utilized in Perl, enhancing your ability to maintain robust and efficient code.

A constructor is a special subroutine that prepares a new object. In Perl, constructors are typically named new, but this is a convention, not a requirement. The primary task of a constructor is to create a reference to an anonymous hash, array, or any other data structure and then bless it to turn it into an object. The bless function associates the reference with a specific class. Here's a basic example of a constructor in a Perl class:

```
package Animal;

# Constructor
sub new {
    my ($class, %args) = @_;
    my $self = {
        name => $args{name} || 'Unnamed',
        age => $args{age} || 0,
    };
    bless $self, $class;
    return $self;
```

```
}
```

In this example, the new subroutine is defined to accept a class name and a list of named arguments. It initializes the object with default values if arguments are not provided, blesses the reference to associate it with the Animal class, and finally returns the blessed reference.

When creating an object, invoke the constructor like this:

```
my $dog = Animal->new(name => 'Rex', age => 3);
```

This code snippet creates an Animal object representing a 3-year-old dog named Rex.

Destructors, on the other hand, handle cleanup operations before an object is destroyed. In Perl, destructors are subroutines named DESTROY. Perl automatically calls the DESTROY method when the last reference to an object is deleted. Here's an example of a destructor:

```
package Animal;

# Destructor
sub DESTROY {
    my ($self) = @_;
    print "Destroying Animal object: ", $self->{name}, "\n";
}
```

You don't explicitly call the DESTROY method; Perl does it when the object's reference count drops to zero. For example:

```
{
    my $cat = Animal->new(name => 'Whiskers', age => 5);
    # $cat goes out of scope, and DESTROY is called automatically
}
```

In this case, when $cat goes out of scope, Perl calls the DESTROY method to clean up the object, printing the message defined in the destructor.

Constructors can also initialize subclass objects through inheritance. Consider a subclass Dog that inherits from Animal:

```
package Dog;
use parent 'Animal';

# Constructor
sub new {
    my ($class, %args) = @_;
    $args{name} ||= 'Unnamed Dog';
    my $self = $class->SUPER::new(%args);
    bless $self, $class;
    return $self;
}
```

Here, Dog's constructor calls SUPER::new to inherit the Animal constructor's initialization code, adds subclass-specific initialization if needed, and blesses the reference to the subclass.

Complex objects may require more intricate initialization and cleanup. Consider a scenario where external resources need management:

```
package FileHandler;

# Constructor
sub new {
    my ($class, %args) = @_;
    my $self = {
        filename => $args{filename},
        filehandle => undef,
    };
    bless $self, $class;

    # Open file handle
    open($self->{filehandle}, '<', $self->{filename})
        or die "Cannot open file: $!";
    return $self;
}

# Destructor
sub DESTROY {
    my ($self) = @_;
    if (defined $self->{filehandle}) {
        close($self->{filehandle})
            or warn "Failed to close file handle: $!";
    }
}
```

In this FileHandler class, the constructor opens a file and stores the handle, while the destructor ensures the file is properly closed.

By understanding and implementing constructors and destructors, you effectively manage the initialization and cleanup processes in your Perl programs, enhancing stability and resource management.

9.10 Advanced Object-Oriented Techniques

In the previous sections, we have laid the groundwork for understanding the basic principles of object-oriented programming (OOP) in Perl, such as class creation, inheritance, encapsulation, and polymorphism. This section delves into more advanced techniques that leverage the full power of OOP in Perl, focusing on roles, traits, mixins, and meta-object protocols.

Roles in Perl provide a way to compose behaviors from different classes, bringing together the capabilities of multiple classes without resorting to traditional multiple inheritance. This mitigates the complexity often associated with multiple inheritance while promoting code reuse.

```
package AnimalRole;
use Moose::Role;

requires 'speak';

sub eat {
    my $self = shift;
    print "The animal is eating.\n";
}
```

In the above example, we define an "AnimalRole" with Moose. The 'requires' keyword specifies that any class consuming this role must implement the 'speak' method. The 'eat' method provides a default behavior that can be used without modification.

To consume a role in a Moose-based class:

```
package Dog;
use Moose;
with 'AnimalRole';

sub speak {
    print "Woof!\n";
}
```

To ensure better code modularity and maintainability, traits come into play, allowing small, reusable units of behavior to be composed into classes dynamically.

```
package Flying;
use Moose::Role;

sub fly {
    print "Flying high.\n";
}

package Swimming;
use Moose::Role;

sub swim {
    print "Swimming in the pool.\n";
}

package Bird;
use Moose;
with 'Flying', 'Swimming';

sub speak {
    print "Chirp!\n";
}
```

In this example, the 'Bird' class consumes both the 'Flying' and 'Swimming' roles, thereby composing behavior without the pitfalls of deep inheritance hierarchies.

Mixins are another advanced technique used in Perl to include methods from a module into a class. Unlike roles, which provide a cleaner, more formalized approach, mixins can be seen as a simpler means of method inclusion.

```
package Mixin;
sub mixin_method {
    print "This is a mixin method.\n";
}

package MyClass;
use base 'Mixin';

my $object = MyClass->new();
$object->mixin_method(); # Outputs: This is a mixin method.
```

While mixins allow for straightforward code reuse, caution is advised to avoid name clashes and ensure cohesive behaviors.

Moose also offers meta-object protocols (MOP), enabling developers to define custom behaviors and extend the metaclass itself. This allows fine-tuned manipulations of class behaviors at runtime, giving unparalleled flexibility and control.

To illustrate the use of MOP in defining and extending metaclasses:

```
package MetaExample;
use Moose;

before 'new' => sub {
    my $class = shift;
    print "Creating a new instance of $class\n";
};

package main;
my $obj = MetaExample->new();
```

By using the 'before' method modifier, we alter the behavior of the object's instantiation process, providing a hook to execute custom code before creating a new instance.

Moreover, overloading operators provides a means to redefine the behavior of operators for objects of user-defined classes, making objects interact more intuitively.

```
package Point;
use overload
    '+' => \&add,
    '""' => \&to_string,
    fallback => 1;

sub new {
    my ($class, $x, $y) = @_;
    return bless { x => $x, y => $y }, $class;
}
```

```
sub add {
    my ($self, $other) = @_;
    return Point->new($self->{x} + $other->{x}, $self->{y} + $other->{y});
}

sub to_string {
    my $self = shift;
    return "($self->{x}, $self->{y})";
}
```

In this example, we define a 'Point' class with overloaded addition and stringification operators. This enables the use of the '+' operator to sum points and automatic string conversion when needed.

The understanding and application of these advanced object-oriented techniques make it possible to create more robust, flexible, and maintainable Perl applications. The next phase involves integrating these techniques into real-world scenarios, demonstrating how they can simplify complex software development tasks.

9.11 Practical Examples of OOP in Perl

To solidify the understanding of object-oriented Perl, we will delve into practical examples that demonstrate the principles discussed throughout this chapter. These examples will cover the creation of classes, instantiation of objects, usage of inheritance, and application of encapsulation and polymorphism.

Example 1: Simple Animal Class

First, we will create a simple class, Animal, which will encapsulate basic properties and behaviors of an animal.

```
package Animal;

sub new {
    my $class = shift;
    my $self = {
        name => shift,
        sound => shift,
    };
    bless $self, $class;
    return $self;
}

sub make_sound {
    my $self = shift;
    return $self->{sound};
}

sub get_name {
```

```
    my $self = shift;
    return $self->{name};
}

1; # End of Animal package
```

Here, the Animal class is created with a constructor new which initializes the properties name and sound. The methods make_sound and get_name provide controlled access to these properties.

Example 2: Inheritance with Dog and Cat Classes

Next, we will extend the Animal class to create Dog and Cat classes, demonstrating inheritance.

```
package Dog;
use parent 'Animal';

sub new {
    my $class = shift;
    my $self = $class->SUPER::new(shift, 'Bark');
    bless $self, $class;
    return $self;
}

sub speak {
    my $self = shift;
    return $self->make_sound();
}

1; # End of Dog package

package Cat;
use parent 'Animal';

sub new {
    my $class = shift;
    my $self = $class->SUPER::new(shift, 'Meow');
    bless $self, $class;
    return $self;
}

sub speak {
    my $self = shift;
    return $self->make_sound();
}

1; # End of Cat package
```

In this example, both the Dog and Cat classes inherit from Animal. The SUPER::new call in their constructors ensures that the base class's constructor is invoked, setting the name property while each subclass sets its own sound property.

Example 3: Using the Classes

We will now instantiate objects of the Dog and Cat classes and utilize their methods.

```
use Dog;
use Cat;

my $dog = Dog->new('Buddy');
print $dog->get_name(), " says ", $dog->speak(), "\n";

my $cat = Cat->new('Whiskers');
print $cat->get_name(), " says ", $cat->speak(), "\n";
```

Here is the expected output when the above script is executed:

```
Buddy says Bark
Whiskers says Meow
```

Example 4: Encapsulation and Data Hiding

Implementing data hiding can protect the internal state of an object. Here we refine our Animal class to use private data:

```
package Animal;

sub new {
    my $class = shift;
    my $self = {
        _name => shift,
        _sound => shift,
    };
    bless $self, $class;
    return $self;
}

sub make_sound {
    my $self = shift;
    return $self->{_sound};
}

sub get_name {
    my $self = shift;
    return $self->{_name};
}

1; # End of Animal package
```

The properties _name and _sound are now prefixed with an underscore to suggest that they are private. Direct access to these properties from outside the object is thereby discouraged.

Example 5: Polymorphism in Object-Oriented Perl

Finally, we demonstrate polymorphism by allowing different classes to be treated through a common interface.

```
package Animal;

sub new {
    my $class = shift;
    my $self = {
```

```
        _name => shift,
        _sound => shift,
    };
    bless $self, $class;
    return $self;
}

sub make_sound {
    my $self = shift;
    return $self->{_sound};
}

sub get_name {
    my $self = shift;
    return $self->{_name};
}

1; # End of Animal package

package Dog;
use parent 'Animal';

sub new {
    my $class = shift;
    my $self = $class->SUPER::new(shift, 'Bark');
    bless $self, $class;
    return $self;
}

1; # End of Dog package

package Cat;
use parent 'Animal';

sub new {
    my $class = shift;
    my $self = $class->SUPER::new(shift, 'Meow');
    bless $self, $class;
    return $self;
}

1; # End of Cat package

# Script to demonstrate polymorphism
use Animal;
use Dog;
use Cat;

my @animals;
push(@animals, Dog->new('Buddy'));
push(@animals, Cat->new('Whiskers'));

foreach my $animal (@animals) {
    print $animal->get_name(), " says ", $animal->make_sound(), "\n";
}
```

Here is the expected output when the script is executed:

```
Buddy says Bark
Whiskers says Meow
```

This demonstrates that both Dog and Cat objects can be managed through a common Animal interface, showcasing polymorphism's power.

These examples illustrate the practical applications of object-oriented programming in Perl. By constructing classes, utilizing inheritance, ensuring encapsulation, and implementing polymorphism, one can create robust and maintainable Perl applications.

Chapter 10

Advanced Perl Programming

This chapter delves into advanced Perl programming topics, including references and complex data structures, advanced regular expressions, and autoloading. It also covers closures, anonymous subroutines, evaluation, exception handling, and interfacing with C/C++. Additionally, the chapter discusses memory management, optimization, concurrency, parallel processing, and practical examples for tackling sophisticated programming challenges.

10.1 Introduction to Advanced Perl Programming

Advanced Perl programming involves exploring sophisticated features of the Perl language that enable developers to write more efficient, modular, and maintainable scripts. These features include references, complex data structures, advanced regular expressions, autoloading, closures, anonymous subroutines, evaluation, exception handling, interfacing with C/C++, memory management, optimization, concurrency, and parallel processing.

References are fundamental in advanced Perl, allowing the manipulation of complex data structures like arrays of arrays, hashes of hashes, and more. By utilizing references, programmers can create intricate, nested data formats enabling more efficient data management.

```
my @array = (1, 2, 3);
my $array_ref = \@array;
print $array_ref->[1]; # Outputs: 2
```

Complex data structures enable intricate data storage and retrieval. For example, using a hash of arrays allows grouping related data for more straightforward access and manipulation.

```
my %hash = (
  fruits => [ 'apple', 'banana', 'cherry' ],
  animals => [ 'dog', 'cat' ]
);
print $hash{fruits}[1]; # Outputs: banana
```

Advanced regular expressions further extend Perl's powerful text manipulation capabilities. Perl's regex engine provides an extensive set of features for matching patterns within strings, making it ideal for tasks like text parsing, validation, and substitution.

```
my $text = "The price is \$100.";
$text =~ s/\$(\d+)€/$1/;
print $text; # Outputs: The price is €100.
```

Autoloading in Perl enables on-demand loading of subroutines, reducing memory overhead and improving script performance. It is implemented using the 'AUTOLOAD' subroutine, which gets called when an undefined subroutine is invoked.

```
sub AUTOLOAD {
    our $AUTOLOAD;
    my ($sub) = $AUTOLOAD =~ /::(\w+)$/;
    print "Undefined subroutine & called: $sub\n";
}
undefined_subroutine(); # Outputs: Undefined subroutine & called:
      undefined_subroutine
```

Closures and anonymous subroutines allow the encapsulation of behavior within a block of code, facilitating the creation of flexible and reusable code segments. Closures can capture and retain access to variables from their enclosing scope.

```
sub make_counter {
    my $count = 0;
    return sub { return ++$count };
}

my $counter = make_counter();
print $counter->(); # Outputs: 1
print $counter->(); # Outputs: 2
```

Evaluating expressions and exception handling are crucial for robust Perl programming. The ‘eval‘ function allows dynamic execution of code contained in a string, and it can also be used for context-based error trapping.

```
eval {
    die "An error occurred";
};
if ($@) {
    print "Caught exception: $@";
}
```

Interfacing with C/C++ extends Perl's capabilities by allowing integration with existing libraries and applications written in these languages. Perl's XS (eXternal Subroutine) allows linking with C code directly for performance-critical tasks.

Memory management and optimization are vital for creating efficient Perl programs that do not waste system resources. By understanding Perl's internal memory allocation strategies and tools, developers can write scripts that handle large datasets effectively.

Concurrency and parallel processing enable Perl programs to perform multiple tasks simultaneously, greatly enhancing processing speed for computationally intensive applications. Modules such as ‘threads‘ and ‘Parallel::ForkManager‘ provide the necessary tools for implementing concurrent execution.

In advanced Perl programming, it is imperative to have hands-on experience with practical examples that showcase how these concepts are applied to solve real-world problems. By practicing and integrating these advanced features, developers can significantly improve the performance and maintainability of their Perl scripts.

10.2 References and Data Structures

In this section, we will explore Perl's references and complex data structures, which are essential for building sophisticated applications. This knowledge will extend the reader's capability in managing and manipulating more complicated datasets and structures than simple arrays and hashes.

References in Perl are akin to pointers in C/C++ but come with additional safety features. A reference is, essentially, a scalar data type that holds the memory location of another value, enabling the creation of nested data structures such as arrays of arrays, hashes of arrays, and more complex arrangements.

To create a reference to a variable, place a backslash (\) before the variable, and to dereference it, use the appropriate type symbol ($, @, %) followed by the reference, enclosed in curly braces. Consider the following examples:

```
# Creating references
my $scalar_ref = \$scalar_variable;
my $array_ref = \@array_variable;
my $hash_ref = \%hash_variable;

# Dereferencing
my $scalar_value = ${$scalar_ref};
my @array_values = @{$array_ref};
my %hash_values = %{$hash_ref};
```

Complex data structures often consist of nested references. Below is an example of creating and manipulating an array of arrays:

```
# Create an array of arrays
my @array_of_arrays = (
    [1, 2, 3],
    [4, 5, 6],
    [7, 8, 9],
);

# Access an element
print $array_of_arrays[1]->[2]; # Outputs 6

# Adding a new array reference
push @array_of_arrays, [10, 11, 12];

# Iterating over an array of arrays
foreach my $array_ref (@array_of_arrays) {
    foreach my $element (@{$array_ref}) {
        print "$element ";
    }
    print "\n";
}
```

In this example, creates a reference to each array, and the arrows (->) are used to dereference the array references within the outer array. This syntax highlights Perl's flexibility in creating and manipulating nested data structures.

Hashes of arrays are another common complex structure, often used to group related data:

```
# Create a hash of arrays
my %hash_of_arrays = (
    'first' => [1, 2, 3],
    'second' => [4, 5, 6],
    'third' => [7, 8, 9],
);
```

```
# Access an element
print $hash_of_arrays{'second'}->[1]; # Outputs 5

# Adding a new array reference
$hash_of_arrays{'fourth'} = [10, 11, 12];

# Iterating over a hash of arrays
foreach my $key (keys %hash_of_arrays) {
    print "$key: ";
    foreach my $element (@{$hash_of_arrays{$key}}) {
        print "$element ";
    }
    print "\n";
}
```

Here, we use the keys function to iterate over the hash, and ${hash_of_arrays{$key}} to access each array reference. This structure allows efficient grouping and retrieval of related sets of values.

References also enable the creation of more dynamic and flexible data structures like hashes of hashes:

```
# Create a hash of hashes
my %hash_of_hashes = (
    'alpha' => { 'A' => 1, 'B' => 2, 'C' => 3 },
    'beta' => { 'D' => 4, 'E' => 5, 'F' => 6 },
    'gamma' => { 'G' => 7, 'H' => 8, 'I' => 9 },
);

# Access an element
print $hash_of_hashes{'beta'}->{'E'}; # Outputs 5

# Adding a new hash reference
$hash_of_hashes{'delta'} = { 'J' => 10, 'K' => 11, 'L' => 12 };

# Iterating over a hash of hashes
foreach my $outer_key (keys %hash_of_hashes) {
    print "$outer_key:\n";
    foreach my $inner_key (keys %{$hash_of_hashes{$outer_key}}) {
        print " $inner_key => $hash_of_hashes{$outer_key}{$inner_key}\n";
    }
}
```

In this example, {} creates references to inner hashes, and nested loops allow for comprehensive traversal of the hash of hashes.

Beyond arrays and hashes, Perl supports more intricate data types such as objects. References become crucial when working with these advanced data types, facilitating the implementation of object-oriented programming principles in Perl.

To summarize the significance of references in Perl:

- References are essential for creating complex and hierarchical data structures.

- They enable efficient memory usage and manipulation of nested data.
- Understanding references supports advanced Perl programming techniques, including object-oriented programming and interfacing with external libraries.

In the following sections of this chapter, we will see more advanced usages and practical examples demonstrating the full potential of Perl's references and complex data structures in real-world programming scenarios.

10.3 Advanced Regular Expressions

In Perl, regular expressions provide a powerful tool for text processing and pattern matching. Leveraging advanced features of Perl's regular expressions can significantly enhance text manipulation capabilities, allowing the programmer to perform complex matching and substitution tasks efficiently.

To illustrate advanced regular expressions, consider the qr// operator, named patterns, the x modifier, assertions, and some nuances of capturing groups. Understanding these will enable more precise and readable regular expressions.

The qr// Operator

The qr// operator compiles a regular expression, returning a regex object that can be reused. This is valuable for complex regular expressions that appear multiple times in your code, thereby improving maintainability and performance.

```
my $regex = qr/^foo|bar$/;
if ($string =~ $regex) {
    print "Match found\n";
}
```

Named Patterns

Named patterns increase readability by allowing you to label subpatterns for later reference. This feature is particularly useful for intricate regular expressions.

```
my $pattern = qr/
    (?<year>\d{4})-
    (?<month>\d{2})-
    (?<day>\d{2})
```

```
/x;

if ('2023-10-15' =~ $pattern) {
    print "Year: $+{year}\n";
    print "Month: $+{month}\n";
    print "Day: $+{day}\n";
}
```

The /x Modifier

The /x modifier allows inclusion of whitespace and comments inside the regular expression for better readability, without those spaces affecting the pattern matching.

```
my $pattern = qr/
    \b # word boundary
    foo # 'foo'
    \d+ # one or more digits
/x;

if ($string =~ $pattern) {
    print "Complex pattern matched\n";
}
```

Assertions (Lookahead and Lookbehind)

Assertions, including lookahead and lookbehind assertions, enable checking for a criterion without including the checked characters in the match.

```
// Positive lookahead
my $pattern = qr/foo(?=\d)/; # 'foo' followed by a digit

// Negative lookahead
$pattern = qr/foo(?!\d)/; # 'foo' not followed by a digit

// Positive lookbehind
$pattern = qr/(?<=\d)foo/; # 'foo' preceded by a digit

// Negative lookbehind
$pattern = qr/(?<!\d)foo/; # 'foo' not preceded by a digit
```

Non-capturing Groups

Non-capturing groups, created with (?: ...), group the contained pattern as a single unit, which is useful when only grouping is needed, and you do not want to capture the match for back-references.

```
my $pattern = qr/(?:foo|bar)baz/; # Matches 'foobaz' or 'barbaz'
if ($string =~ $pattern) {
    print "Match found\n";
}
```

Backreferences

Backreferences hold the text matched by capturing groups, which you can reuse within the same or subsequent regex matches, enhancing the pattern's capability to adapt to dynamic content.

```
my $pattern = qr/(foo|bar)\1/; # Matches 'foofoo' or 'barbar'
if ($string =~ $pattern) {
    print "Duplicated pattern found\n";
}
```

Recursive Patterns

Recursive patterns enable the regex engine to handle nested structures, such as balanced parentheses, which are crucial for parsing strings where elements can be recursively embedded within each other.

```
my $pattern = qr/
    \( # Opening parenthesis
    (?: # Non-capturing group
        [^()]+ # Any number of non-parenthesis characters
        |
        (?R) # Recursive reference to the entire pattern
    )*
    \) # Closing parenthesis
/x;

if ($string =~ $pattern) {
    print "Balanced parentheses found\n";
}
```

Lastly, Perl's regular expressions support a variety of other advanced features such as code execution embedded within the regex itself, conditional expressions, and branch resets. Utilizing these advanced techniques judiciously can transform how patterns are parsed and text is manipulated, thus adding to both efficiency and functionality of your Perl scripts.

```
// Conditional expressions
my $pattern = qr/
    (?(DEFINE)
        (?<number>\d+)
    )
    (?(?{ $var > 10 })(?&number) | \w+)
/x;

if ($string =~ $pattern) {
    print "Conditional match found\n";
}
```

10.4 Autoload and Ties

In Perl, the concepts of AUTOLOAD and ties provide powerful mechanisms for handling method calls and variables in a flexible and dynamic manner. These features can simplify the management of object methods and facilitate the handling of complex data structures by mapping variable accesses to object method calls.

AUTOLOAD is a special function in Perl that acts as a catch-all for undefined subroutine calls. When a method that does not exist in the object is called, the AUTOLOAD method is invoked. This provides an opportunity to dynamically handle calls for missing methods.

```
package MyModule;
use strict;
use warnings;

our $AUTOLOAD;

sub new {
    my $class = shift;
    my $self = bless {}, $class;
    return $self;
}

sub AUTOLOAD {
    my ($self, @args) = @_;
    my $method = $AUTOLOAD;
    $method =~ s/.*:://; # remove package name from method name

    if ($method eq 'dynamic_method') {
        print "Dynamic method called with arguments: @args\n";
    } else {
        die "Undefined subroutine $method called\n";
    }
}

sub DESTROY {
    # Perl requires a DESTROY method in modules that use AUTOLOAD
    # to prevent AUTOLOAD from being called on object destruction.
}

1;
```

In this example, the AUTOLOAD method intercepts calls to undefined methods. The method name is extracted from $AUTOLOAD and processed. If the method is recognized as a valid dynamic method, it is handled appropriately. Otherwise, an error is raised.

The concept of tie in Perl allows variables to be tied to objects. This means that operations on the variable are delegated to methods on the tie object. It can be used for scalars, arrays, hashes, and filehandles.

```
package MyTie;
```

```
use strict;
use warnings;

sub TIESCALAR {
    my ($class, $value) = @_;
    return bless \$value, $class;
}

sub FETCH {
    my $self = shift;
    return $$self;
}

sub STORE {
    my ($self, $value) = @_;
    $$self = $value;
}

1;
```

```
use MyTie;
my $var;
tie $var, 'MyTie', 'initial value';

print "$var\n"; # prints 'initial value'
$var = 'new value';
print "$var\n"; # prints 'new value'
```

Here, a scalar variable $var is tied to an object of class MyTie. The TIESCALAR method initializes the object, and the FETCH and STORE methods manage access and modification of the tied variable. The tie function associates the variable with the object, enabling customized behavior.

Tying can be applied to other data types as well. For arrays, implement the methods TIEARRAY, FETCH, STORE, FETCHSIZE, STORESIZE, EXTEND, EXISTS, DELETE, CLEAR, and PUSH, POP, SHIFT, UNSHIFT, SPLICE.

```
package MyArray;
use strict;
use warnings;

sub TIEARRAY {
    my $class = shift;
    my @array = @_;
    return bless \@array, $class;
}

sub FETCH {
    my ($self, $index) = @_;
    return $self->[$index];
}

sub STORE {
    my ($self, $index, $value) = @_;
    $self->[$index] = $value;
```

```
}

# Other required methods would be implemented similarly...

1;
```

```
use MyArray;
my @array;
tie @array, 'MyArray', (1, 2, 3);

print $array[1]; # prints '2'
$array[1] = 4;
print $array[1]; # prints '4'
```

For hashes, implement the methods TIEHASH, FETCH, STORE, DELETE, CLEAR, EXISTS, FIRSTKEY, and NEXTKEY.

```
package MyHash;
use strict;
use warnings;

sub TIEHASH {
    my $class = shift;
    my %hash = @_;
    return bless \%hash, $class;
}

sub FETCH {
    my ($self, $key) = @_;
    return $self->{$key};
}

sub STORE {
    my ($self, $key, $value) = @_;
    $self->{$key} = $value;
}

# Other required methods would be implemented similarly...

1;
```

```
use MyHash;
my %hash;
tie %hash, 'MyHash', (key1 => 'value1', key2 => 'value2');

print $hash{key1}; # prints 'value1'
$hash{key1} = 'newvalue';
print $hash{key1}; # prints 'newvalue'
```

Lastly, tying filehandles involves implementing TIEHANDLE, PRINT, PRINTF, WRITE, READ, READLINE, GETC and other relevant methods. This can be advantageous for manipulating and extending the functionality of standard I/O operations in Perl.

By leveraging AUTOLOAD and tying mechanisms, advanced Perl programming allows developers to create extensible modules and manage complex interactions dynamically, ensuring robust and maintainable code.

10.5 Closures and Anonymous Subroutines

Closures and anonymous subroutines are critical concepts for those delving into advanced Perl programming. They provide the power and flexibility necessary for complex functional programming, modularity, and encapsulation.

An *anonymous subroutine* in Perl is simply a subroutine that is defined without a name. Instead of being bound to an identifier, the subroutine reference is returned by the sub keyword, which can subsequently be assigned to a scalar variable or directly invoked.

Consider this basic example of an anonymous subroutine:

```
my $anon_sub = sub {
    print "This is an anonymous subroutine.\n";
};

$anon_sub->();
```

Anonymous subroutines become particularly powerful when they are returned as values from other subroutines. This brings us to *closures*. A closure is a subroutine that captures and retains access to the lexical variables from its containing scope, even after that scope has exited.

For illustrative purposes, here is an example demonstrating a closure:

```
sub make_counter {
    my $count = 0;
    return sub {
        $count++;
        return $count;
    };
}

my $counter1 = make_counter();
print $counter1->(); # Outputs: 1
print $counter1->(); # Outputs: 2

my $counter2 = make_counter();
print $counter2->(); # Outputs: 1
print $counter2->(); # Outputs: 2
```

In the make_counter subroutine, when the anonymous subroutine (closure) is returned, it retains access to the lexical variable $count defined in make_counter. Each invocation of a closure increments its own $count independent of other closures created by make_counter.

This encapsulation makes closures useful for creating stateful iterators and encapsulated environments.

```
sub make_power {
    my $exponent = shift;
    return sub {
        my $base = shift;
        return $base ** $exponent;
    };
}

my $square = make_power(2);
print $square->(3); # Outputs: 9

my $cube = make_power(3);
print $cube->(3); # Outputs: 27
```

In this example, make_power generates and returns a closure capturing the lexical variable $exponent. The assigned variable $square holds a reference to an anonymous subroutine designed to square its argument, while $cube references a subroutine designed to cube its argument.

Closures can be layered to form more complex structures. This inherent flexibility makes them an invaluable tool in advanced Perl programming. They enable the creation of higher-order functions, which take functions as arguments and return functions as results.

Additionally, closures facilitate the implementation of currying, a technique by which a function with multiple arguments is decomposed into a series of functions with single arguments. Consider the following example:

```
sub curry {
    my ($func, @initial_args) = @_;
    return sub {
        my @rest_args = @_;
        return $func->(@initial_args, @rest_args);
    };
}

my $add = sub { $_[0] + $_[1] };
my $add_five = curry($add, 5);
print $add_five->(10); # Outputs: 15
```

Here, the curry subroutine returns a closure that partially applies the arguments to the input function $func. This technique is widely utilized in functional programming to create more modular and reusable code.

As always, careful memory management is crucial when working with closures. The captured lexical variables ensure their values persist, which may lead to unintentional memory retention if closures are not managed appropriately. Employing WeakRef (or similar strategies) can help mitigate potential memory leaks by weakening references to external variables, ensuring they can be garbage collected when no longer needed.

Closure capabilities extend beyond simple variable encapsulation. Combined with anonymous subroutines, they underpin many advanced programming techniques, facilitating lazy evaluation patterns, callbacks, event handling, and more. Mastery of these concepts in Perl provides the proficiency required to tackle complex scripting, ensuring flexible and performant code.

Meticulous application of closures and anonymous subroutines is essential. They are indispensable for areas requiring high customization and modularity, laying the foundation for sophisticated functional paradigms and patterns in Perl programming.

10.6 Evaluation and Exception Handling

In this section, we explore the use of eval for dynamic code evaluation and exception handling in Perl. Understanding these concepts enables programmers to execute Perl code contained in strings and manage errors gracefully, ensuring robustness and flexibility in their scripts.

The eval function in Perl comes in two flavors: string eval and block eval. Both forms are used to trap exceptions but differ in their evaluation context and behavior.

String Eval:

The string form of eval executes a string of Perl code in the current context. Its syntax is:

```
eval $string;
```

The return value of eval is the value of the last expression evaluated within the string, or undef if an error occurs. Errors are stored in the special variable $@.

For example:

```
my $code = 'print "Hello, World!\n";';
eval $code;
if ($@) {
    print "Error: $@\n";
}
```

In this example, the eval block evaluates the content of $code. If the evaluation fails, the error is captured in $@.

Block Eval:

The block form of eval is more commonly used for exception handling. Its syntax is:

```
eval {
    # code that might throw an exception
};
if ($@) {
    # handle the exception
}
```

For example:

```
eval {
    open my $fh, '<', 'nonexistent_file' or die "Cannot open file: $!";
};
if ($@) {
    print "Caught an exception: $@\n";
}
```

Here, the eval block attempts to open a non-existent file. If it fails, the die function throws an exception, caught by eval, and stored in $@.

Using die and croak:

The die function raises an exception, terminating the current sequence of statements unless trapped by eval. It prints a message to STDERR and exits the script if uncaught.

```
die "Fatal error: something went wrong.";
```

The croak function, from the Carp module, works similarly to die, but it reports the error from the caller's perspective, which is useful for debugging.

```
use Carp;

sub example_sub {
    croak "An error occurred in example_sub.";
}
```

Using try and catch with Try::Tiny:

The Try::Tiny CPAN module provides a more elegant and reliable way to handle exceptions, avoiding some pitfalls of the native eval.

First, install Try::Tiny:

```
cpanm Try::Tiny
```

Then use it as follows:

```
use Try::Tiny;

try {
    open my $fh, '<', 'nonexistent_file' or die "Cannot open file: $!";
}
catch {
    warn "Caught an error: $_";
};
```

In this code, the try block contains the code that might throw an exception. If an error occurs, the catch block captures it. The variable $_ contains the error message.

Propagating Errors with rethrow:

Sometimes, after catching an exception, you might want to propagate it upstream. Use the rethrow function from Try::Tiny.

```
use Try::Tiny;

try {
    try {
        open my $fh, '<', 'nonexistent_file' or die "Cannot open file: $!";
    } catch {
        warn "Caught an error: $_";
        die $_; # Re-throw the exception
    };
}
catch {
    warn "Re-caught an error: $_";
};
```

Using eval for Error Checking in Expressions:

Besides exception handling, eval {} can be beneficial for validating expressions that might fail under certain conditions.

For example:

```
my $result = eval { 1 / 0 };
if ($@) {
    print "Division by zero error: $@\n";
} else {
    print "Result is $result\n";
}
```

In this snippet, the division by zero triggers an exception caught by eval, and $@ captures the error message.

By mastering eval and exception handling, Perl programmers can effectively manage errors and ensure their scripts are more robust, preventing unexpected terminations. This capability is particularly essential when dealing with external inputs, file operations, or dynamic code execution.

10.7 Interfacing with C/C++

Interfacing Perl with C/C++ is a powerful technique that leverages the capabilities of lower-level programming languages while retaining the ease and flexibility of Perl scripting. This section covers the Perl XS (eXternal Subroutine) mechanism, which allows you to write Perl subroutines in C, and the 'Inline::C' module, providing a more straightforward method for integrating C code into Perl.

Perl XS Mechanism (eXternal Subroutine)

Perl XS is the primary way to write Perl subroutines in C. The process involves several steps, starting with creating an XS file, compiling it, and then linking it with Perl. Below is a step-by-step guide on how to create and use an XS file:

1. **Creating an XS File:**

An XS file typically has the '.xs' extension. It contains declarations of Perl functions mapped to C functions. Below is a simple example demonstrating how to create an XS file.

```
#include "EXTERN.h"
#include "perl.h"
#include "XSUB.h"

MODULE = MyModule
PACKAGE = MyModule

void
hello_world()
    CODE:
        printf("Hello, World from C! ");
```

2. **Creating a Perl Module File:**

Next, create a Perl module file (with a '.pm' extension) that will load the XS file. The module file manages the interaction between Perl and the C code.

```
package MyModule;

require Exporter;
require DynaLoader;
our @ISA = qw(Exporter DynaLoader);
our @EXPORT = qw(hello_world);

bootstrap MyModule;
```

```
1;
```

3. **Creating a 'Makefile.PL':**

The 'Makefile.PL' script uses 'ExtUtils::MakeMaker' to create the appropriate Makefile for building the XS module.

```
use ExtUtils::MakeMaker;

WriteMakefile(
    NAME => 'MyModule',
    VERSION_FROM => 'MyModule.pm',
    LIBS => [''],
    OBJECT => '$(O_FILES)',
    DEFINE => '',
    INC => '',
);
```

4. **Compiling and Building the Module:**

Run the following commands to compile and build your XS module:

```
perl Makefile.PL
make
make test
make install
```

5. **Using the Module:**

Once compiled and installed, you can use your module in Perl scripts.

```
use MyModule;

hello_world();
```

Using Inline::C Module

The 'Inline::C' module simplifies the process of mixing C code with Perl. It allows C code to be written directly inside the Perl script. Below is an example of how to use 'Inline::C'.

1. **Installing Inline::C:**

Install the 'Inline::C' module from CPAN if it is not already installed.

```
cpan Inline::C
```

2. **Writing Inline C Code:**

Include the C code directly within your Perl script using the 'Inline' keyword.

```
use Inline C => <<'END_OF_C_CODE';

#include <stdio.h>

void
```

```
hello_world() {
    printf("Hello, World from C using Inline::C!\n");
}

END_OF_C_CODE

hello_world();
```

Contextual Differences and Performance Considerations

When deciding between XS and 'Inline::C', consider the following:

- **XS Advantages:**

  - - More control over the integration process.
  - - Suitable for complex modules or performance-critical tasks where fine-tuning is essential.

- **Inline::C Advantages:**

  - - Simplifies the process, plugging C code directly into a Perl script.
  - - Excellent for smaller code segments or rapid prototyping.

Performance considerations include:

- **Function Call Overhead:** Calling C functions from Perl incurs overhead, though generally much less compared to pure Perl for computationally intensive tasks.

- **Memory Management:** Properly manage memory in C to avoid leaks. Use Perl's API for memory management when necessary.

Safety and Debugging

When interfacing with C, maintain diligence regarding safety and debugging:

- **Safety:**

  - - Properly handle pointers and memory allocation.
  - - Avoid buffer overflows and null pointer dereferences.

- **Debugging:**

  - - Use debugging tools like 'gdb' for C code.
  - - Perl debugger can help trace issues in the Perl layer.

- - Compile with debugging symbols enabled (e.g., 'gcc -g').

Interfacing Perl with C/C++ enhances the functionality of Perl scripts, providing the efficiency and computational power of compiled code. Understanding both XS and 'Inline::C' methodologies equips you with the flexibility to choose the appropriate tool for varying levels of complexity and project requirements.

10.8 Manipulating Complex Data Structures

In advanced Perl programming, manipulation of complex data structures is essential for efficiently managing and processing large volumes of data. This section explores the creation, manipulation, and traversal of multidimensional arrays and hashes, focusing on practical applications and best practices.

Multidimensional Arrays

A multidimensional array in Perl is essentially an array of arrays. This structure allows the representation of more complex data. To create a two-dimensional array, one initializes an array of array references. Here is an example code illustrating this concept:

```
# Initializing a 2D array
my @matrix = (
    [1, 2, 3],
    [4, 5, 6],
    [7, 8, 9],
);

# Accessing elements
my $element = $matrix[1][2]; # This retrieves the value 6

# Iterating through the 2D array
for my $row (@matrix) {
    for my $col (@$row) {
        print "$col ";
    }
    print "\n";
}
```

In this example, matrix is a two-dimensional array where each element is a reference to a one-dimensional array. Accessing an element within this structure involves specifying both row and column indices, as demonstrated by $matrix[1][2].

Hashes of Arrays

Another powerful data structure is a hash of arrays, allowing one to associate lists of values with specific keys. This is particularly useful for categorizing collections of data. The following example demonstrates initializing and operating on a hash of arrays:

```
# Initializing a hash of arrays
my %hash_of_arrays = (
    fruits => ['apple', 'banana', 'cherry'],
    animals => ['cat', 'dog', 'elephant'],
);

# Accessing elements from the hash of arrays
my $first_fruit = $hash_of_arrays{fruits}[0]; # This retrieves 'apple'

# Adding elements to an array in the hash
push @{$hash_of_arrays{fruits}}, 'date';

# Iterating through a hash of arrays
while (my ($category, $array_ref) = each %hash_of_arrays) {
    print "$category: ";
    for my $item (@$array_ref) {
        print "$item ";
    }
    print "\n";
}
```

Here, %hash_of_arrays holds references to arrays keyed by strings such as ${fruits} and ${animals}. One accesses elements using the key and array index, i.e., $hash_of_arrays{fruits}[0].

Arrays of Hashes

Perl's flexibility extends to arrays of hashes, which can be employed to manage lists of associative arrays. This structure is useful for handling records where each element is a named value. The following code snippet provides an example of initializing and traversing an array of hashes:

```
# Initializing an array of hashes
my @array_of_hashes = (
    { name => 'Alice', age => 30, job => 'Engineer' },
    { name => 'Bob', age => 25, job => 'Designer' },
    { name => 'Carol', age => 27, job => 'Manager' },
);

# Accessing elements in an array of hashes
my $first_person_name = $array_of_hashes[0]{name}; # This retrieves 'Alice'

# Iterating through an array of hashes
for my $record (@array_of_hashes) {
    print "Name: $record->{name}, Age: $record->{age}, Job: $record->{job}\n";
}
```

In this example, array_of_hashes is an array where each element is a reference to a hash. This allows straightforward access to individual records within the array.

Hashes of Hashes

A hash of hashes offers an even more sophisticated means of managing nested data. This structure is suitable for scenarios requiring multi-keyed access. Consider the following example to understand the initialization and interaction with a hash of hashes:

```
# Initializing a hash of hashes
my %hash_of_hashes = (
    'john' => { age => 28, city => 'New York' },
    'jane' => { age => 22, city => 'San Francisco' },
);

# Accessing elements in a hash of hashes
my $johns_age = $hash_of_hashes{john}{age}; # This retrieves 28

# Iterating through a hash of hashes
while (my ($person, $details) = each %hash_of_hashes) {
    print "$person: ";
    while (my ($key, $value) = each %$details) {
        print "$key = $value ";
    }
    print "\n";
}
```

Here, %hash_of_hashes holds hashes, each keyed by a string like ${john} and ${jane}. Accessing nested values involves specifying the outer and inner keys, as shown by $hash_of_hashes{john}{age}.

Understanding these complex data structures provides a foundation for effectively organizing and processing data in Perl. By mastering multidimensional arrays, hashes of arrays, arrays of hashes, and hashes of hashes, one can develop robust scripts that handle intricate data manipulation tasks with ease and efficiency.

This version resolves the issue with special characters in text mode and adheres to the formatting guidelines laid out for the content.

10.9 Advanced File and Data Handling

Advanced file and data handling in Perl involves a range of techniques for efficiently managing and processing data. This section builds upon the basic file operations discussed previously and introduces more sophisticated methods, such as file locking, non-blocking IO, directory handling, and the utilization of Perl's built-in modules for data manipulation.

File locking is crucial to prevent data corruption in environments where multiple processes might access or modify a file concurrently. Perl provides the flock function for this purpose. The flock function applies or removes an advisory lock on an open file. To use flock, the file must first be opened in the appropriate mode. The following example demonstrates how to lock a file for both reading and writing.

```
open(my $fh, '>>', 'example.txt') or die "Could not open file: $!";
flock($fh, 2) or die "Could not lock file: $!";
print $fh "New data\n";
flock($fh, 8) or die "Could not unlock file: $!";
close($fh);
```

The above code opens a file in append mode, locks it using flock($fh, 2) (where 2 represents an exclusive lock), writes data to the file, and then unlocks it using flock($fh, 8) (where 8 releases the lock).

Non-blocking IO allows a program to perform IO operations without freezing the entire process while waiting for data. This is particularly valuable in network programming and real-time data processing. Perl's select function can be used to achieve non-blocking behavior with filehandles.

```
use IO::Select;
my $select = IO::Select->new();
open(my $fh, '<', 'example.txt') or die "Could not open file: $!";
$select->add($fh);

if ($select->can_read(0)) {
    print <$fh>;
} else {
    print "No data available for reading\n";
}
close($fh);
```

In this example, IO::Select is used to see if the filehandle is ready for reading without blocking the program using can_read with a timeout of 0 seconds.

Directory handling is another essential aspect of advanced file management. Perl provides the opendir, readdir, and closedir functions for basic directory operations. For more advanced tasks, the File::Find module is effective in traversing directory trees. The following snippet shows how to read the contents of a directory.

```
opendir(my $dir, '.') or die "Cannot open directory: $!";
while (my $entry = readdir($dir)) {
    next if $entry =~ /^\./; # Skip hidden files and directories
    print "$entry\n";
}
closedir($dir);
```

In cases where it is necessary to recursively search through directories,

File::Find can be used:

```
use File::Find;
find(\&wanted, '/path/to/start/directory');

sub wanted {
    print "$File::Find::name\n" if -f;
}
```

The find function initiates the search starting from the specified directory and calls the wanted subroutine for each file or directory found. Inside wanted, $File::Find::name contains the complete pathname of the currently processed file.

Perl's built-in modules, such as File::Copy, File::Path, and File::Spec, offer comprehensive functionalities for file operations beyond basic reading and writing. For example, to copy and delete files and directories, the following can be used:

```
use File::Copy;
use File::Path 'rmtree';

copy("source.txt", "destination.txt") or die "Copy failed: $!";
rmtree(['directory_to_remove'], 1, 1);
```

The above code copies source.txt to destination.txt and removes an entire directory tree with rmtree.

When dealing with large datasets, efficient data manipulation is crucial. Modules like Tie::File allow you to treat files as arrays, enabling random access to file lines without loading the entire file into memory. Here is a simple example:

```
use Tie::File;

tie my @array, 'Tie::File', 'largefile.txt' or die "Tying failed: $!";
print $array[10]; # Access the 11th line directly
untie @array;
```

The Tie::File module ties an array to a file, allowing direct access to specific lines of a large file without reading it all at once.

In addition to the aforementioned techniques, Perl's capability to handle various file formats (such as JSON, XML, CSV) through dedicated modules (JSON, XML::Simple, Text::CSV) enriches its utility for diverse data handling tasks. Utilizing these formats often involves encoding and decoding structured data. For example, to handle JSON data, the JSON module can be used as follows:

```
use JSON;
```

```
my $json_text = '{ "name": "John", "age": 30 }';
my $perl_data = decode_json($json_text);
print $perl_data->{name}; # Outputs: John
```

John

Similarly, to generate JSON from a Perl data structure:

```
use JSON;

my $data = { name => "Jane", age => 25 };
my $json_text = encode_json($data);
print $json_text;
```

{"name":"Jane","age":25}

By leveraging these advanced file and data handling techniques, Perl scripts become more robust, reliable, and capable of managing complex data efficiently. The concepts discussed here should be combined with good programming practices to achieve optimal performance and maintainability.

10.10 Memory Management and Optimization

Memory management and optimization are critical components of advanced Perl programming, essential for creating efficient and robust scripts. Proper memory management ensures that your Perl programs use resources judiciously, avoiding leaks and excessive consumption. Optimization techniques, on the other hand, enhance the performance of your scripts, reducing execution time and resource usage.

Perl's memory management involves understanding how the language allocates, uses, and deallocates memory. By default, Perl handles memory allocation and garbage collection automatically. However, advanced programmers often need to intervene or monitor these processes to optimize the performance of their scripts.

Memory Allocation:

Perl allocates memory for variables dynamically, based on their usage. Scalar variables, arrays, and hashes require different amounts of memory depending on their contents and complexity. Understanding how these structures consume memory can help you write more efficient code. Here is an example of how memory is allocated for different data structures:

```
# Scalar variable
my $scalar = "Hello, Perl";

# Array
my @array = (1, 2, 3, 4, 5);

# Hash
my %hash = (apple => 'red', banana => 'yellow', grape => 'purple');
```

When large data structures are needed, such as arrays or hashes, consider the implications on memory usage.

Garbage Collection:

Perl's garbage collector automatically reclaims memory used by variables that are no longer in scope. The reference count mechanism tracks how many references exist for a given variable, and when this count drops to zero, the memory is freed.

Circular references can cause memory leaks because the reference count never drops to zero. To mitigate this, use weak references from the Scalar::Util module when creating circular structures. Here's an example demonstrating circular references and weak references:

```
use Scalar::Util 'weaken';

# Circular reference
my $a = {};
my $b = { reference => $a };
$a->{reference} = $b;

# To break circular reference
weaken($a->{reference});
```

Memory Optimization Techniques:

- **Preallocation:** Preallocating memory for arrays and hashes can reduce the overhead of dynamic resizing.

```
# Preallocate array with 100 elements
my @large_array;
$#large_array = 99;

# Preallocate hash with specified size
my %large_hash;
keys %large_hash = 100;
```

- **In-place Modification:** Modifying data in place rather than creating copies helps save memory.

```
# Inefficient - creates new list
my @new_array = map { $_ * 2 } @large_array;
```

```
# Efficient - modifies array in place
foreach my $element (@large_array) {
  $element *= 2;
}
```

- **Using Efficient Data Structures:** Selecting appropriate data structures for your needs can improve memory usage and performance. Consider arrays for ordered data and hashes for fast lookups.

Memory Profiling and Analysis:

Profiling tools such as Devel::Peek, Devel::Size, and Devel::NYTProf can help identify memory usage patterns and bottlenecks in your code.

```
use Devel::Size qw(size total_size);

my $var_size = size(\$scalar);
my $total_size = total_size(\@array);
print "Size of scalar: $var_size bytes\n";
print "Total size of array: $total_size bytes\n";
```

Devel::NYTProf offers comprehensive profiling for both memory and performance, providing detailed reports and visual charts.

Lazy Evaluation:

Lazy evaluation defers the computation of expressions until their results are needed, which can save memory by avoiding unnecessary calculations. In Perl, you can implement lazy evaluation using subroutines and closures.

```
# Define a lazy iterator
sub lazy_iterator {
  my $start = shift;
  return sub {
    return $start++;
  };
}

my $iter = lazy_iterator(10);
print $iter->(); # Prints 10
print $iter->(); # Prints 11
```

These memory management and optimization techniques are essential for writing high-performance Perl applications and scripts. A thorough understanding of how Perl handles memory allocation and garbage collection, coupled with effective optimization strategies, can greatly enhance the efficiency of your programs. Make use of profiling tools to gain insights into your application's memory usage, and adopt best practices to keep your codebase robust and performant.

10.11 Concurrency and Parallel Processing

Concurrency and parallel processing are critical concepts in advanced Perl programming, pivotal for optimizing the performance of your scripts, especially when dealing with I/O-bound or CPU-bound tasks. Concurrency involves multiple tasks making progress over the same period, while parallel processing involves executing multiple tasks simultaneously. This section delves extensively into Perl's capabilities in handling these paradigms using threads, forks, and more.

Perl Threads

Perl supports threads through the 'threads' module, enabling the creation of parallel flows of execution within a single process. Initializing and managing threads can help in leveraging multi-core processor architectures efficiently. Below is an example illustrating the basic usage of threads:

```
use threads;

# Thread routine
sub thread_function {
    my $thread_id = threads->self->tid;
    print "Thread $thread_id is running...\n";
    sleep(1);
}

# Creating threads
my @threads;
for (1..5) {
    push @threads, threads->create(\&thread_function);
}

# Joining threads
foreach my $thread (@threads) {
    $thread->join();
}
```

The above script creates five threads, each executing the thread_function. The threads->create function initiates a new thread, while thread->join ensures that the main program waits for each thread to complete.

Shared Variables in Threads

When working with threads, sharing variables safely across concurrent threads is often necessary. Perl provides the 'threads::shared' module to facilitate this. Here's a modified version of the previous example that demonstrates shared variable usage:

```
use threads;
use threads::shared;

my $counter :shared = 0;

# Thread routine
sub thread_function {
    lock($counter);
    $counter++;
    my $thread_id = threads->self->tid;
    print "Thread $thread_id incremented counter to $counter\n";
    sleep(1);
}

# Creating threads
my @threads;
for (1..5) {
    push @threads, threads->create(\&thread_function);
}

# Joining threads
foreach my $thread (@threads) {
    $thread->join();
}
```

In this script, the $:shared attribute allows the $counter variable to be shared across all threads. The lock function ensures that only one thread increments the counter at a time, maintaining data integrity.

Forking for Parallel Execution

Perl's fork function can be leveraged for parallel execution by creating child processes. Each child process runs independently of the parent, with its own memory space. Below is an example illustrating the usage of fork:

```
use strict;
use warnings;

$SIG{CHLD} = 'IGNORE'; # To prevent zombie processes

for (1..5) {
    my $pid = fork();
    if ($pid) {
        print "Parent process, created child $pid\n";
    } elsif ($pid == 0) {
        print "Child process $$ is running...\n";
        sleep(1);
        exit(0); # Terminate the child process
    } else {
        die "Fork failed: $!\n";
    }
}
```

In this script, fork creates five child processes. Each child prints a message and terminates after one second. The $SIG{CHLD} = 'IGNORE' assignment prevents zombie processes by automatically reaping child processes as they terminate.

Parallel::ForkManager

For more sophisticated parallel processing, the Parallel::ForkManager module provides a high-level interface to manage multiple child processes efficiently. Here's an example:

```
use Parallel::ForkManager;

my $max_processes = 5;
my $pm = Parallel::ForkManager->new($max_processes);

for my $data (1..10) {
    $pm->start and next; # Forks and returns from the child process
    print "Processing $data in process $$\n";
    sleep(1);
    $pm->finish; # Terminates the child process
}

$pm->wait_all_children; # Wait for all child processes to finish
```

This script processes ten data items using up to five parallel child processes. The start method forks a new process, and finish terminates it. The wait_all_children method waits for all child processes to complete.

Asynchronous I/O with AnyEvent

AnyEvent is a popular module for handling asynchronous I/O in Perl. It allows the creation of non-blocking event-driven programs. Below is a simple example:

```
use AnyEvent;

my $cv = AnyEvent->condvar;

my $w = AnyEvent->timer(
    after => 1,
    interval => 1,
    cb => sub {
        print "Tick...\n";
    },
);

$cv->recv; # Enter the event loop
```

In this example, the AnyEvent->timer creates a repeating timer that prints "Tick..." every second. The $cv->recv enters the event loop, allowing the timer callback to execute.

This section has explored various techniques for achieving concurrency and parallel processing in Perl, illustrating critical methods and modules through practical examples. Understanding and utilizing these techniques can significantly enhance the performance and responsiveness of your Perl applications.

10.12 Practical Examples of Advanced Perl Programming

In this section, we will explore several practical examples that illustrate the advanced concepts discussed in the earlier parts of this chapter. These examples are designed to consolidate your understanding of Perl's advanced features and demonstrate their utility in solving complex programming tasks.

Example 1: Parsing and Transforming XML Data

Suppose you are given an XML file and need to extract specific information while transforming the structure for another application. Perl with its modules like XML::LibXML can effectively handle this task.

First, ensure you have the required module:

```
use XML::LibXML;
```

Consider the following XML data:

```
<catalog>
  <book>
    <title>Learning Perl</title>
    <author>T.Christiansen</author>
    <price>25.00</price>
  </book>
  <book>
    <title>Programming Perl</title>
    <author>L.Wall</author>
    <price>45.00</price>
  </book>
</catalog>
```

To parse this XML and transform it into a hash, use:

```
use strict;
use warnings;
use XML::LibXML;

my $xml = 'path/to/xml/file.xml';
my $dom = XML::LibXML->load_xml(location => $xml);

my %books;

foreach my $book ($dom->findnodes('/catalog/book')) {
    my $title = $book->findvalue('title');
    my $author = $book->findvalue('author');
```

```
    my $price = $book->findvalue('price');
    $books{$title} = {
        author => $author,
        price => $price,
    };
}

print "Parsed and transformed XML data:\n";
use Data::Dumper;
print Dumper(\%books);
```

Output:

```
$VAR1 = {
    'Learning Perl' => {
        'author' => 'T.Christiansen',
        'price' => '25.00',
    },
    'Programming Perl' => {
        'author' => 'L.Wall',
        'price' => '45.00',
    },
};
```

This example demonstrates how to parse an XML document and store the extracted data into a more manipulable Perl hash.

Example 2: Implementing a Simple Web Server with Concurrency

Using Perl's threading capabilities, we implement a simple multi-threaded web server. Ensure you have the Thread::Queue module:

```
use IO::Socket::INET;
use threads;
use Thread::Queue;
```

Server code:

```
use strict;
use warnings;
use IO::Socket::INET;
use threads;
use Thread::Queue;

my $queue = Thread::Queue->new();

sub handle_client {
    my $client_socket = shift;
    while (<$client_socket>) {
        print $client_socket "HTTP/1.1 200 OK\n";
        print $client_socket "Content-Type: text/plain\n\n";
        print $client_socket "Hello from Perl server!\n";
        last if /\r\n$/;
    }
    close($client_socket);
}

my $server = IO::Socket::INET->new(
```

```
    LocalPort => 8080,
    Type => SOCK_STREAM,
    Reuse => 1,
    Listen => 10
) or die "Cannot create socket: $!\n";

print "Server listening on port 8080...\n";

while (my $client_socket = $server->accept()) {
    $queue->enqueue($client_socket);
    threads->create(sub {
        while (my $socket = $queue->dequeue_nb()) {
            handle_client($socket);
        }
    })->detach();
}
```

This example sets up a web server that listens on port 8080 and handles multiple client requests concurrently using threads.

Example 3: Using Regular Expressions for Log File Analysis

Analyzing log files often involves extracting information based on patterns. Here's a script using advanced regular expressions to parse Apache log files.

Sample log line:

```
127.0.0.1 - frank [10/Oct/2000:13:55:36 -0700]
"GET /apache_pb.gif HTTP/1.0" 200 2326
```

Code to extract details:

```
use strict;
use warnings;

my $log_line = '127.0.0.1 - frank [10/Oct/2000:13:55:36 -0700] '
            . '"GET /apache_pb.gif HTTP/1.0" 200 2326';

if ($log_line =~ /^(\d+\.\d+\.\d+\.\d+) - (\S+) \[(.*?)\]
                  "(\S+) (\S+).*?" (\d+) (\d+)$/x) {
    my ($ip, $user, $datetime, $method, $resource, $status, $bytes)
        = ($1, $2, $3, $4, $5, $6, $7);
    print "IP Address: $ip\n";
    print "User: $user\n";
    print "Datetime: $datetime\n";
    print "Method: $method\n";
    print "Resource: $resource\n";
    print "Status: $status\n";
    print "Bytes: $bytes\n";
}
```

Output:

```
IP Address: 127.0.0.1
User: frank
Datetime: 10/Oct/2000:13:55:36 -0700
Method: GET
Resource: /apache_pb.gif
Status: 200
Bytes: 2326
```

This example demonstrates the utility of regular expressions in extracting meaningful information from log files for further analysis.

Example 4: Creating and Using Perl Closures for State Management

Closures in Perl can maintain state between calls. This feature is particularly useful for creating objects with private attributes.

Closure to create a counter:

```
use strict;
use warnings;

sub create_counter {
    my $count = 0;
    return sub {
        $count += 1;
        return $count;
    };
}

my $counter = create_counter();

print $counter->() . "\n"; # Output: 1
print $counter->() . "\n"; # Output: 2
print $counter->() . "\n"; # Output: 3
```

In this example, the counter keeps track of the state between different invocations while avoiding global variables.

These practical examples illustrate how advanced Perl programming concepts can be used to solve sophisticated problems efficiently. Each example builds upon the foundational knowledge introduced earlier, demonstrating real-world applications of advanced Perl features.

Made in the USA
Monee, IL
13 September 2026

62981855R00167